THE HIDDEN TRUTH

an autobiography by

Maurice R Hamlin

Published in 2014 by FeedARead.com Publishing

A CIP catalogue record for this title is available from the British Library.

To Jaye:

At the age of thirty-six it was pure chance that I met you and we married within just weeks. You gave up your own promising career to back me in all my ventures, regardless of success or failure. Now, after more than fifty-three years of marriage, you are still my main supporter, my very best friend, my one love. You are also the best editor anyone could hope for - I could have achieved nothing without you.

Acknowledgments:

To my son Steven, who as a young teenager, specialised in learning the complications of computer software development and assisted me greatly over the initial years of trial and error until perfection.

My thanks to my good friend Dave Lever who, whilst keeping my computer alive, also helped me to solve the problems of self-publishing. I also owe a lot to his wife Jaz and our good friends Janet and Keith Worthington who all took turns in caring for our dog, Tango, on the many occasions when we needed a break.

To David and Gillian Cowlishaw who were my initial proof readers and to Peter and Maureen Howells who carried out the final checks and gave me such great encouragement.

My thanks also to our dear friends Jesus and Chelo Fuetes who were the first to greet us in Spain. They are no longer neighbours but family. Their help and kindness has made our retirement to Spain a total success.

20% of all Author Royalties are to be donated to The RAF Benevolent Fund.

In memory of my brother Cyril (Phil)
killed in action whilst flying over the
Pacific Ocean on 21st April 1945

CONTENTS

PART 1 – Unamenable to Discipline

PART 2 – CON-sultancy

PART 3 – Journey into the Third Age

PART 1

Unamenable to Discipline

Chapter 1 – Childhood before TV

I was born in February 1925 amid the great depression which covered the land after the First World War. The country suffered  from high unemployment and an escalating cost of living. Infant mortality was high due to poverty and poor health care. Home ownership, cars and foreign travel were only for the rich, in fact, few people had seen an aeroplane let alone flown in one. Houses and roadways were lit by gaslight. Television had not yet been invented and radio sets offering limited news and music were expensive and reception was usually by earphones via a crystal set.

A person was considered to be well off if he could afford a taxi fare. Most of the transport was horse driven and private cars were few and unreliable. Telephones were rare and usually installed in businesses or very large houses but this was the year when the first red public telephone boxes were introduced into our lives.

The moon was solely for love songs and romance, yet it was an era of immense technical and social change. My life was fairly typical of many boys of the time, brought up by loving and perhaps over indulgent parents in an honest and hard working family.

I recall that our main indoor entertainment was from 'His Master's Voice', a wind-up gramophone which gave our lives a  background of my sister's popular dance music, also records of day like 'Climbing up the Golden Stairs' and Dad's preference for light classics such as 'In a Monastery Garden', a refrain I can still bring to mind. I  think our first radio set arrived when we lived in a terraced house lit by gaslight and with a coal fireplace in the living room. We were considered to be quite well off because we had an indoor toilet; only the well to do had proper bathrooms. There were no talking pictures until about 1929 and then only fairly primitive black and white films until 1936.

In the Thirties a man's average wage was less than £4 a week for a six day, forty-eight hour week but my Dad had a day off on Sunday and a half day off on Wednesday. Many people were forced to work much longer hours and frequently in poor and dangerous conditions. The unreachable dream was to earn as much as a £1000 a year and to own a car.

I remember great excitement in about 1936 when, opposite our home, some new semi detached houses were being built at the price of £395 each. When the workmen finished work for the day, my best friend Tim Bush and I used the site for climbing and playing games and afterwards telling Mum about the fully fitted kitchens, internal toilets and bathrooms. Most people thought the houses were very expensive but today those same properties have been modernised and sell for £300,000.

In some ways we children, despite the lack of antibiotics, were often far healthier than many children of today. There were no easy fast foods outlets, except the chippie, so you ate what your Mum cooked. We were always out playing on the recreation ground or in the street. There was none of the present day mollycoddling restrictions where the State forbids all manner of fun that might cause a fall, a bump on the head, etc. Many an independent spirit is stifled today.

My home was a modest and happy place but well cared for. As boys my brother Cyril (nicknamed Phil) and I had a love hate relationship; we were always scrapping. He was the brainy one and I was probably more irresponsible, always playing games and pranks and getting into minor scrapes. I wasn't really interested in my studies, except for history, geography and arithmetic. Swimming was my sport but I was useless at football and cricket. On the only try out I had for the school football team, I kicked the ball into my own goal, after which time I was only allowed to be a right back - right back behind the goal.

I enjoyed school but with Tim I would sometimes play hooky and spend the day exploring the fields, climbing hills, cycling (we both had second hand bikes), scrumping apples or exploring the new building estates the Government were building to help

unemployment. I remember one particular day when I was about seven years old, I played truant because my brother had dared me to run away from home; he even gave me tuck and cash from his money box and told me to take the green 'bus which travelled from Eastbourne and over the Southdown Hills towards Brighton where we had many relatives. About two hours after starting out, I reached the village of Alfriston over the top of the South Downs, and then I became scared. I got off the bus and started making my way

back home. In the meantime, when my Mother realised that I had not returned home for lunch, she asked my brother where I was. He told her that I had stolen his tuck and his money and run away. Understandably she was distraught and contacted the school, then the Police. When I finally arrived home after being found by a policeman at a 'bus stop, my Mum believed only my dear big brother's story and would not listen to my explanation.

For the only time in my life, she bent me over a chair and gave me a hard strapping. She would never, during her long life, ever believe that her dear good boy Cyril could have lied. Yet, just a week after this incident, this same ghastly brother, when we were playing together in Princes Park met his best friend and I, acting my usual self, for some reason so aggravated his friend that he thumped me and knocked me down. Big brother Cyril then chased his mate for over a mile to catch up with him and gave him a real drubbing saying that no one but he could hit his baby brother. Happily, as we grew older we became very close friends.

My Dad was an upholsterer and French polisher by trade, a foreman for Bindon's Furnishing Company in Eastbourne. His skills in the restoration of antique and high-class furniture made him be in great demand by local wealthy clients, however, because of the depression he also took on an evening job as a telephone operator at the GPO where he quickly became a supervisor. He worked a normal eight hour day and then another three or more hours from 8.00 p.m. for the GPO. He was such a very conscientious man, caring and providing for his family. Unfortunately, it was only after I had grown up that I appreciated just how hard he had worked for us.

Mum was an attractive, most loving and energetic lady, brought up with strict Victorian manners and the belief that you must treat your neighbour as you would wish to be treated. Her family had been farmers and wealthy landowners but she had, unusually for the time, a very open mind to the emerging new beliefs of equality and advancing technology. She was a pioneer of DIY and one of my first memories was hearing a very loud bang and seeing my Mother float across the kitchen ceiling. She had been knocking down a gas fired stone washing tub to modernise the kitchen but when she disconnected the gas pipes from the mains supply, a spark from her hammer had caused a small explosion. She said afterwards "It was a wonderful feeling of floating through the air." Fortunately she landed softly with only a few bruises but minus eyebrows and eyelashes.

My sister Gladys was fourteen years older than me. She was a hairdresser, always keeping up with the latest fashions and often trying out new cutting exercises on my hair. On one occasion when I was about eleven, she slipped and cut my ear and she gave me half a crown to keep quiet - not bad for a snip. At 25 she married Bill, a quite good amateur boxer but he left her with baby Elaine and

emigrated to Australia. In later life Gladys met a new partner, Pat, who was an engineer. They became antique car enthusiasts taking part in the London to Brighton and other car rallies, frequently winning 'best exhibit' awards.

Another memory, one that made a strong impression and taught me the importance of good speech happened at the age of six or seven. As usual, I was playing in the street with my friend Tim when a huge, very expensive open touring car stopped nearby. It was the first quality car we had seen and it was driven by a well dressed man, a real toff, as we said in those days, and he had a film-starish lady passenger. He called over to me in what we thought of as a 'la-de-da' voice and asked for directions. Being totally over awed and lost for words I replied "Eh, yer what?" He snapped back "Don't say 'what' to me boy, where are your manners?" Tim and I laughed at him and ran off but somehow that man's correction stuck in my mind and I believe it had a major influence on my manner of speech and my attitude to life. I have always remembered him with gratitude.

Dad was always taking the family on excursions to Air Shows, Exhibitions, etc. and I remember him taking us to see Sir Alan Cobham's Flying Circus when it was held at Wick's Field in Findon, West Sussex. We were allowed to sit in an aircraft cockpit and this was my first introduction to the thrill of flying.

I also learned that in September 1919 a Belgian banker named Lowenstein, on his first flight in an open cockpit, insisted that he must open his umbrella to protect himself from the wind and rain. His pilot, Commander Biard, flying the submarine route between

Southampton and Le Havre, considered this to be a very dangerous act, which would upset the aircraft so he turned round, hit his passenger with his fist and knocked him unconscious. The passenger succumbed quietly and the flight landed safely.

Another passenger describing his flight to Paris in the 1920s said "They put you in a box, shut the lid, splash you all over with oil, you are sick, then you are in Paris."

Each year Dad took us to the Ideal Home Exhibition at Earls Court in London which Mum particularly enjoyed as it always included the latest inventions, even newly built houses in which were exhibited every modern labour saving device, furniture fashions, etc. He also took us twice to the Bourneville chocolate factory (my favourite) where the girls made a great fuss of us. We left, feeling sickly but happy.

My parents always ensured that each year we had one good holiday away from home, one of our favourite places being Stoke Poges near Tunbridge Wells where we climbed rocks, flew kites and home made aeroplanes. Brighton was another favourite holiday place where we spent several weeks of our summer school holidays each year with our Aunt Annie. She was a large, very jolly but strong lady. One day a tramp knocked on the kitchen door and asked if he could have some fresh water in his old kettle but, as she took hold of it, he tried to push her aside to get into the house. What a mistake! She took hold of the man, lifted him off his feet and threw him down the steps into the rear garden. When she started walking towards him, he ran off as though the devil himself was after him.

I was forever impressed by Aunt Annie, a really lovely lady. There was another story my Mother told about Aunt Annie when, as a young girl, she lived on the farm. Annie loved helping with the animals but there was a particular donkey that was always very awkward and would not move unless she showed him the business end of the pitchfork. One day friends were laughing at her inability to make him move so, as usual, she picked up the pitchfork but this time the donkey didn't shy away but charged straight at her and killed himself. Her father was angry and punished Annie by making her dig the animal's grave.

During these holidays I spent many happy hours on Brighton Pier and underneath the sea front promenade where the fair stalls and wide boys operated. In those days children and old people were pretty safe, even looked after by the local rough boys. It was a very different and much simpler world; people cared for the young and respected the old and when a policeman caught a youngster up to mischief, he gave him a clip on the ear. Police were respected and the punishment accepted as normal.

Brighton was the birthplace of my parents and one of my favourite towns; it held so much of interest, particularly the back streets crammed with dozens of curio and antique shops. I also enjoyed visits to the Royal Pavilion, which was originally the site of a farmhouse before it was converted by architect Henry Holland into a

neoclassical villa and then finally bought in 1815 to be transformed by John Nash into its current style of a Regency Indian Palace for King George IV. William IV. Queen Victoria also used it. Today it is an enchanting place, rather like a mythical world of a bygone culture. Brighton was of particular interest to my Mum because her father and ancestors had owned much of the farmland around the Brighton racecourse.

The Brighton Bell paddle steamer was our favourite mode of travel from Eastbourne to Brighton or Hastings and sometimes we would just go for a day trip. There were few of the current day safety restrictions and it was tremendously interesting exploring below decks, particularly above the engine room where my

brother and I could stand over the giant pistons driving the paddle wheels, or up in the bows where we were close to the parting of the waves. There was always an adventure waiting for us and the crew were very friendly.

Mum always took us to church on a Sunday, much of which sounded like mumbo jumbo to us because in those days a lot of the service was in Latin which was probably to overawe the poorly educated congregation and remind them of their place in society. Cyril and I found it intimidating and extremely boring.

Tim and I were soul mates, always involved in each other's childish adventures. One day Tim fell off his bicycle just as a car came by. The vehicle had driven right over him before it could stop. We all screamed, and then realised that Timmy had emerged from beneath the car laughing in terror but exclaiming, "It never touched me." Luckily cars of those days had very high suspension.

When we were about nine years old, we were fooling about on top of a big slide in the playground. I went down headfirst and Tim came close behind and rolled over the top of me. One of his boots collided with my head, banging my face down and the impact broke two of my front teeth. It was painful but we treated it as a laugh. Some three years later we were out pole-vaulting over rivers on nearby farmland but when we reached the last one, it was about ten feet across so we decided to take a running jump at it. Unfortunately as I started forward, Tim brought his pole back and I ran straight onto it and the pole made contact with the same teeth he had broken earlier. I was not a pretty sight.

On another Saturday morning our County Schools Physical Training Officer, Captain Stainsfield, had assembled about two hundred senior schoolgirls to rehearse gymnastics for a special demonstration at the large Whitley Road Recreation Park. Tim and I were quite fascinated by all these well-grown girls showing off their uniform expertise, particularly as they were doing so in their official blue school bloomers. The Captain was standing in front of the girls controlling the sets of movement but, whilst he was demonstrating, Tim and I stood behind his back performing all sorts of lunatic antics. Suddenly the girls stopped exercising and started giggling and falling about. The Captain turned round, exploded when he saw us, lost his temper, left the girls and chased us through the streets. Fortunately he didn't catch us but recognised me and knew which school I attended. I can only add that the next morning the Head Master made it very difficult for me to sit down. Tim got off as he went to a different school and wasn't identified.

Dad and Mum bought our first wireless in 1936 and my Dad took a great interest in the news programmes. Cyril and I heard a lot about Mosley's fascists and when the Spanish Civil War started in July, we heard all about the Royalists, Republicans and Communists fighting against the Fascists who were supported by Hitler. My Dad was very 'anti-Hitler' and his ravings, especially when he sent ten JU 52 troop carriers to airlift Franco's Spanish Legion troops from Morocco to Spain. Hitler then gave further support to the war by sending in the Kondor Legion of supposed volunteers, which was actually a major force of fighter-bomber aircraft and aircrews. This gave Germany a three-year combat training ground to build up its Luftwaffe into a war experienced, highly trained tactical force before the start of the European War. Italy did likewise. Many volunteer brigades opposed to fascism were formed by British, French, American, Canadians, etc. to support the Spanish Republican Government whilst Germany and Italy gave major support to General Franco, the "would-be" Spanish Dictator.

In this same year Sir Oswald Mosley, leader of the British Union of Fascists, married British heiress Diana Mitford (a rabid Nazi) in Germany at the home of Joseph Goebbels, a "violent anti-Semite" who eventually became the German Minister of Propaganda. Adolf Hitler was the guest of honour.

The UK Government appeared to largely ignore the obvious signs of Germany's military intentions until September 1938 when Germany invaded the Sudetenland of Czechoslovakia causing great concern to Britain, France and Italy. A conference was held in Munich to solve the land dispute which ended with what was called the Munich Agreement but which in effect gave in to all of Germany's demands. British Prime Minister Neville Chamberlain returned to England waving a piece of paper, which he stated would give us "Peace in our Time."

I only remember that there was much 'hoo ha' with many Members of Parliament and prominent people declaring that it was pure capitulation and appeasement to German aggression. The Czechoslovakian Government, which was not present at the Conference, was forced to hand over Sudetenland to Germany.

However, not long afterwards the British Government was forced to mobilise the Royal Navy when Germany announced it was building massive fortifications in the Rhineland. Hitler, on coming to power as Chancellor of Germany in January 1933, had been building a massive army under the guise of the Hitler Youth Movement. He was forming a secret navy with huge flotillas of submarines and heavy warships. Also setting up airfields for training glider pilots and secretly, aircrews to form the Kondor Legion fighter and bomber units.

As boys of eleven we had no thoughts of war and, if we did, it was believed to be all glamour and adventure. Tim and I had just acquired our own canoe from our friendly neighbourhood policeman who lived next door to me. It was about fourteen feet long and three feet wide, had oars and sails, and could hold up to six of us in a slightly sinking condition. We used it for fishing and sailing along the foreshore. We weren't allowed to keep it on the beach and used to wheel it home on a trolley every day and were allowed to take it into the driveway at the back of the policeman's house so that we could lift the boat over the wall and into our enclosed back garden.

On one occasion we saw that a massive three-foot wide beach ball had floated hundreds of yards out to sea. A man rushed up to us and asked us to go out and rescue the ball but when we agreed, he so badly handled our canvas boat over the rocky shore in an effort to launch us quickly that, unbeknown to us, he ripped a large slit in the hull. By the time we had got out to sea and retrieved his ball, we had to bail furiously to save the canoe from sinking which it finally did as we beached in the shallows. Even though the man saw the damage he had caused, he gave us only a sixpence and walked off with his expensive ball intact but without saying he was sorry.

Chapter 2 Bombed Out and Strafed (Angels 1 & 2)

August 1939 a worried British Government declared a mandatory night time blackout for all of Britain; you could be fined if you showed any house lights and car headlights also had to be shielded. Plans were put in place for the likely evacuation of all non-essential civilians living in London and other towns likely to suffer from heavy bombing. Many members of both the British Government and the general public, including my Dad, greatly underestimated Germany's hidden strength, however, what Neville Chamberlain had done at Munich should have been honoured for one essential reason - it ensured Britain had time to greatly increase the production of Hurricanes and Spitfires and to recruit and train new aircrew to ensure the RAF became a meaningful offensive force.

On the 1st September 1939 Germany invaded Poland and Czechoslovakia and launched the first aerial Blitzkrieg to wipe out resistance; Britain and France gave Germany an ultimatum saying that unless they removed all of its troops from those countries, the allies would declare war. Germany ignored this and the Luftwaffe quickly gained superiority over the Polish and Czech air forces so on the 3rd, Britain and France, followed by South Africa and the Commonwealth, declared war on Germany. Then, almost unnoticed by the British public, Russia jumped on the bandwagon and on the 7th launched Red Army attacks on Poland from the East.

The public was stunned by an attack on HMS Royal Oak on the 7th October. It had been considered to be secure in the Naval Base at Scapa Flow but U-Boat U47 torpedoed it with a great loss of life.

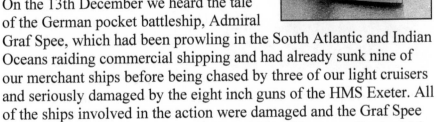

On the 13th December we heard the tale of the German pocket battleship, Admiral Graf Spee, which had been prowling in the South Atlantic and Indian Oceans raiding commercial shipping and had already sunk nine of our merchant ships before being chased by three of our light cruisers and seriously damaged by the eight inch guns of the HMS Exeter. All of the ships involved in the action were damaged and the Graf Spee took refuge in the neutral port of Montevideo, Uruguay. On the 15th

Captain Hans Langsdorff, Captain of the Graf Spee, attended the burial of his ship's dead in a Montevideo cemetery; at the grave side ceremony he used the Naval salute whilst those around him used the Nazi salute.

Two days later with his ship more badly damaged than our navy realised, Captain Langsdorff believed that the Royal Navy had had time to bring up heavy battleships to swamp him with massive broadsides. To save unnecessary slaughter of his crew, and with little to gain, he sailed  the German warship just outside the harbour where it was scuttled. Three days later he shot himself. Captain Hans Langsdorff was greatly praised by the crews of the ships he had sunk because he had always adhered strictly to the rules of mercantile warfare and saved the lives of all the crew members of the sunken ships. In fact, not a life was lost in those sinkings. He was obviously not a Nazi.

Eastbourne received thousands of London's evacuee children and hospital patients as refugees during 1940. The Government considered my hometown to be safe from air attack, however, the blackout of all lights was strongly enforced and we children were told to either shield our bicycle lights or not go out.

On the 20th March the SS Barnhill, a five thousand ton merchant ship, was attacked and bombed in the Channel and could be seen  blazing fiercely off Beachy Head. An attempt was made to save the ship from sinking but it was badly holed and it was finally beached at Pevensey Bay but Captain O'Neil and his six crewmen were saved. I remember this particularly well as the ship carried a mixed cargo of tinned groceries and fruit, large cheeses, roller skates, typewriters and all manner of general goods. Tim, Cyril and I together with hundreds of other people went to gather whatever we could salvage. I recall Tim and I rolling a large cheese home; it was great fun until Customs and Excise placed the wreck under guard. Seventy years after the event, the ship's forlorn rusted skeleton can still be seen at low tide.

In April that year German forces invaded Denmark and Norway. The French Army collapsed and the British Army was forced to retreat towards the Channel ports of Dunkirk and St. Valery. Prior to the war, France had relied on a strategy of defensive fortifications built along the whole of the French/German border. It was called The Maginot Line and ignored the fact that France would be totally undefended if their army was circumvented by German forces attacking through Belgium and other weaker neighbouring countries. When this became fact in May/June, the weakness of the French Government and the inability of the French Army to hold the German advance (despite the gallantry of many particular army corps) made the Allied Forces' position indefensible.

On the 10th April 1940 Winston Churchill became Prime Minister of Britain and gave his famous speech:

We shall fight on the beaches,
We shall fight on the landing grounds,
We shall fight in the fields and in the streets,
We shall fight in the hills and
We shall never surrender.

The British Expeditionary Force (BEF) was forced to retreat towards the ports of Calais and Dunkirk on the 26th May. Mr Churchill and his Amy Commander in Chief realized that the whole central core and brain of the British Army was stranded in France and that Dunkirk and St Valery were the only possible sites for rescue. Without the BEF we stood little chance of defending Britain's shores against an invasion. Some units were ordered to fight a fierce rear-guard action whilst a massive rescue effort was launched to retrieve the major portion of our most experienced fighting troops.

21

During the Dunkirk Evacuation only seven thousand men were evacuated on the first day but by the ninth day a total of 338,226 soldiers - 198,229 British and 139,997 French - were rescued by the hastily assembled fleet of eight hundred and sixty boats. Many of the troops were able to embark from the harbour's protective mole onto the forty-two British destroyers and other large ships which kept up a shuttle service across the Channel whilst others had to join the long lines of soldiers wading out from the beaches towards the small rescue boats. Many waited for hours to board, shoulder deep in water and periodically strafed by enemy fighter-bombers. It took tremendous courage to wait there, hour after hour, in the forlorn hope of survival. The now famous 'Little Ships of Dunkirk', a flotilla of some seven hundred merchant ships, fishing boats, pleasure boats, paddle steamers and RNLI lifeboats, carried thousands back to England. It was heralded as a miracle of deliverance.

Eastbourne's lifeboat, the Jane Holland, returned safely from her first trip but on a later journey was severely damaged and abandoned. Later, perforated with bullet holes, she was washed up on the beach, however, she was repaired and lived to serve another day.

A special thought should be given to the rear-guard troops who fought so hard to keep the Germans at bay whilst the main Army escaped; their only future was death, injury or almost certain capture and imprisonment for the duration of the war.

Britain was suffering its greatest military defeat of modern times but Hitler's muddled decision, against the advice of his generals, to hold back the final advance of his overwhelming Panzer tank units, allowed the evacuation to succeed.

The German Army's advanced troops were now only sixty miles from my home in Eastbourne and for days we could hear the massive explosions of shells and bombing from France. At night the noise continued and the whole sky was alight with brilliant flashes. To boys of fourteen it was dramatic. But for those watching who had loved ones serving in France, not knowing if they were safe or mixed up in the worst of the fighting, it must have been a terrifying sight. It was impossible to imagine the carnage and devastation being wrought on our troops and the French town's people.

Tim and I were fascinated by the sounds and site of our Hurricanes and Spitfires flying overhead to fight the German Air Force. It made such an impression on me that it changed my attitude to learning. I realised that if I wanted to join the RAF and fly, I  had to pass the aircrew entrance examination, and so I paid a little more attention to school.

On the 17th June 1940 France asked Germany for an armistice. Marshall Petain formed the Vichy Government and willingly collaborated with the occupying German forces. By this time, all British forces had been withdrawn from France and both the German Air Force (Luftwaffe) and the RAF had lost many aircraft and their trained crews. Several weeks passed whilst the Luftwaffe replaced its losses and took over airfields in the countries they had captured. The lull in the fighting as the German forces consolidated their position was vital to the British Armed Forces as it allowed them to prepare for the next phase. By the beginning of July the RAF had rebuilt its strength up to 640 fighters but this was against the Luftwaffe's 2,600 bombers and fighters. The stage was set. In the skies above South East England the fate of Britain was about to be decided.

The Prime Minister, Winston Churchill, explained it and said, "What General Weygand called the Battle of France is over, the Battle of Britain is about to begin."

The war now interrupted canoeing adventures for me and Tim as the promenade and beaches of Eastbourne were declared off-limits with barbed wire and in some areas mines were planted on the beaches. There was also a curfew restricting visitors' access to within twenty miles of large stretches of the southern coastline.

On Sunday the 7th July as I was getting ready to go out to meet my friends, I heard the sound of an aircraft overhead and then the note changed to a scream as it dived. We all scrambled into the metal Morrison Shelter in our living room. There were a few terrifying moments as we heard the exploding bombs getting closer and closer until there was one final massive explosion which rocked the house filling it with glass, dust and debris. Then all went quiet. It had happened so fast, we just cowered there in the shelter until we heard a shout through the gloom - the voice of an Air Raid Warden yelling "Anybody alive in there?" Birchfields, our local grocery and sub post

office, just fifty yards away on the opposite side of the road had received a direct hit killing those inside. It had been a sneak raid carried out by a Dornier. Two people were killed and seventeen injured. Nine houses were destroyed and many, including ours, rendered uninhabitable. My family emerged, dusty, covered in rubble, but unharmed. This was the first visit of my Guardian Angel.

We were evacuated to an emergency centre and then to the home of some very good friends of my parents, the Vernon family, who invited us to live with them in Tideswell Road.

This particular bombing was the start of Eastbourne's wartime ordeal. The town had one hundred and twelve bombing raids, with about seven hundred bombs exploding on impact and another ninety, which exploded later. Others needed deactivation by the Army Bomb Disposal boys (the real heroes) whilst some weren't discovered until after the War. The town also suffered no less than four thousand thermite incendiary bombs, which caused fires and were dealt with by Air Raid Wardens and residents. If these bombs landed in the streets they were not so dangerous so we kids would go out and cover them with a bucket of sand. In addition to this, the town was also tormented by countless attacks from fighter aircraft strafing the streets with machine gun and cannon fire.

During the next three years the town was struck by hundreds of explosions from the Doodle Bug V1 unmanned flying bombs, followed by the massive V2 stratosphere rockets. There were over eleven hundred casualties and one hundred and seventy four people were killed. Five hundred houses were totally destroyed and another thousand very badly damaged. See also ISBN Y 871896.00.1

In the springtime I had bronchitis, which made it impossible for me to take my final school examinations, however, the thought of staying on at school to swot and take the exams again with the possibility of continuing onto higher education did not appeal to me. My brother was already attending the Grammar School but I decided I would rather try for a job; earning money seemed more attractive to me than school and my Dad had said he could get me an interview for a job with the GPO (General Post Office).

On the 31st July, Eastbourne was shelled by a U-Boat. This gave everyone a warning that we had more than the Luftwaffe to worry about and reminded us to give a prayer for our seamen who faced this threat every day they spent at sea. The U Boat caused some damage in Wish Road but it was thought that its real purpose was  to photograph possible invasion obstacles and likely landing sites.

By the 13th August the Battle of Britain was at its most fierce. Eastbourne was considered to be a likely landing point for the expected German invasion and all children were evacuated.

Names and directions to Eastbourne were removed from all signposts as a deterrent to enemy agents or parachutists. The town itself and Beachy Head became major gathering points for the Luftwaffe passing over on their daily raids on the RAF fighter airfields in the Southern Counties and also for the bombers to reach

London at night whilst they were endeavouring to accomplish Air Marshal Herman Goring's promise to Hitler that he would wipe out the RAF and provide clear skies for his invasion of England.

We were fourteen years old and it was very exciting to see the Hurricanes and Spitfires roaring overhead to intercept the vastly superior numbers of German aircraft. To us, watching aerial dog fights above, hearing the sounds of constant machine gun fire and thud of our anti aircraft guns didn't bring home the true seriousness of the situation even when we saw a fighter or a bomber smoking or on fire, crashing into the sea or the fields. To us, as children, we didn't realise that people were actually dying. On one particular occasion when Tim and I were out on our bicycles on the road to Hampden Park, we saw a Spitfire crash land in a field close by and were the first to reach the aeroplane. The Free French pilot had made a 'wheels up' landing and had slithered to a stop without too much damage. He was uninjured and had apparently run out of fuel during the fighting. I remember he said "Hello" to us in English with a funny accent.

The seriousness of the situation became more visible towards the end of the Battle of Britain when both sides were recouping their resources and the Luftwaffe appeared to be using Eastbourne as a target for training their new pilots as sneak raiders. We were continually being attacked and the constant chatter of machine gun fire and the showers of broken pieces of exploded anti aircraft shells landing on our roofs and in the streets was my first real awareness of what being at war really meant. We all became uptight every time we heard the sound of aircraft engines.

My brother and I became members of the Air Defence Cadet Corps (ADCC) set up by Air Commodore Chamiers to train young men who had an interest in aviation and we paid three pence per week towards uniform costs, etc. We received general rifle training, attended lectures on service life and learned something of wireless communications and the Morse code. We had the occasional trip to a local RAF airfield but were unable to have flights as we were so close to live action. It was the ADCC that convinced us that the RAF was the right choice for us and we knew we would volunteer as soon as we were old enough.

In August, a strafing attack brought personal tragedy to my friend Tim when his cousin Frank Edwards was killed in an air raid whilst working for the Council at Hampden Park. One of the raiding fighter-bombers was strafing all in sight so Frank and his friends took cover underneath their council vehicle. They were all killed when the petrol tank was hit and exploded.

When I was fourteen I started my first job at Eastbourne's General Post Office. I was a Telegraph Boy, the nickname for which was 'Murger'. I found that cycling all over the region, particularly in the open countryside away from the constant air attacks, gave me the feeling of not having a care in the world. It was most enjoyable. The war seemed far away but suddenly we started getting more and more telegrams from the War Ministry telling people that their loved ones had been killed, lost or believed to be prisoners of war; some wives and mothers broke down in front of us and others would just thank us with a frightened smile. It became worse, very much worse, so that people were afraid at the very sight of our uniform.

On the 10th August the Home Office ordered all non-essential families to be evacuated from Eastbourne. We were exempt due to Dad's work at the GPO telephone exchange but for those people who were forced to leave Eastbourne, the Government offered free rail travel warrants to any unrestricted part of the country. This resulted in a reduction of the local population from sixty thousand to just thirteen thousand.

On September 17th 1940, Hitler's "Operation Sealion" plan for the invasion of Britain was cancelled. He felt it was vital to win the air battle before risking his invasion barges and that only by destroying the RAF would the Luftwaffe be able to protect the invasion force from the Royal Navy. Hitler is said to have raged at Field Marshall Goring for the Luftwaffe's inability to beat the RAF and achieve command of the skies.

On the 28th we were bombed out again. Our temporary home was straddled by eight bombs dropped between Cavendish Bridge and our new home in Tideswell Road. The house was made uninhabitable and we were once again evacuated to temporary accommodation. Second visit of my Guardian Angel.

In October we moved into our new home at 7 Crunden Road, which was in the older part of the town. It was a semi-detached house with a big garden. It had apple trees, gooseberry bushes

The scene at the junction of Cavendish Place and Tideswell Road on September 28.

and a large vegetable patch which was an absolute boon with all the new rationing restrictions. The house was on a high hill leading up to the South Downs, which gave us some protection from the fighter-bomber raids.

November brought freezing cold and snowy weather. At work I was ordered to deliver a telegram to an address in Alfriston, a village over and beyond the top of Beachy Head. As I began to dress in my cold weather gear, I found that one of my fellow Murgers (a senior and a bully) had hidden my cycling gloves. I was unable to find them and being a bit of a wimp and anti any type of bullying, I refused to go out delivering telegrams until my gloves were returned to me. The Telegraph Control Supervisor ordered me to go out but I refused to go without my gloves. Next, the Chief Inspector of Postmen was called and ordered me to go out but I still refused to go without my gloves. It was then that the matter became serious and I was sent before the Head Post Master of Eastbourne District. (I imagined it must be the same as standing before a magistrate.) He was cross and said, "Don't be stupid boy, wasting my time. Off you go or you will be suspended." Again I refused to go out into the snow without my gloves. He became angry and took away my uniform hat and bicycle and sent me home to await a decision on my future. My Dad was a bit upset because he'd got me the position but accepted that I didn't have the right attitude for a career in the Post Office.

December came and I was offered my second job as a trainee salesman with the Eastbourne branch of the '50 Shilling Tailors', a fast growing group who were the first to offer the ordinary man in the street an affordable range of tailor made business and leisure suits at a fixed cost of just fifty shillings. It was my introduction into dealing with the general public, talking to them and trying to accept the attitude that the customer was always right. I enjoyed it and progressed with enthusiasm.

On the wireless, Hitler's propaganda announcer, English traitor William Joyce (laughingly known as Lord Haw-Haw) justified the raids on Eastbourne by reporting them as attacks on the Pevensey Bay Harbour installations. This was a reference to the 1940 wreck of the SS Barnhill beached in the Bay. We treated Lord Haw Haw as a joke but remembered that listening to the BBC News in occupied countries was punishable by death.

All through the year we suffered constant attacks by the Luftwaffe causing a great amount of damage and loss of life. It became almost standard practice to dive for cover as soon as the scream of a diving plane was heard - sometimes getting up rather sheepishly when you saw it was a Spit or Hurricane doing a victory roll to show us they had shot down one of our raiders.

The Japanese attacked Pearl Harbour on the 7th December 1941 and President Roosevelt declared war on both Japan and Germany; Roosevelt had always been a good friend to England.

On the 16 February 1942 my brother Cyril joined the RAF Volunteer Reserve as an Aircrew Cadet. He was just seventeen years old and very enthusiastic about his initial training and his introduction to flying. In June when he came home on leave he told us that he had been selected for training as a Radar Navigator for Bomber Command and was to be sent to Canada later in the year under the British/Canadian Commonwealth Air Training Plan.

On the evening before he left we had a great time together at the Winter Garden Ballroom but he was so disgusted with my poor efforts at dancing that on the way home, on a hill and in the moonlight at one o'clock in the morning, he gave me a really good lesson on how to do the quarter turn in a quick step. It was a memorable end to the evening and the beginning of my enthusiasm for dancing which became my most pleasurable pastime.

I had just turned sixteen when I was head hunted. I believe it must have been the smart new suit my dear Aunt Gladys had insisted I needed to improve my appearance. I was approached by a senior manager of the local Bobby's Department Store who offered me a job with more pay as a salesman in the Fabrics Department. I took the job and came into contact with their wealthier customers making me more conscious than ever of my appearance and attitude to people.

Throughout 1942 Eastbourne was attacked almost every week by bombers or strafed with machine gun fire. Otherwise life continued fairly normally. I think that unless you lived in London, one of the targeted cities, or in the South Coast towns, people had little idea of how great the strain was. One day my Manager told me Bobby's had

found that due to the constant bombings and damage in the town centre, travel restrictions, fear of invasion, the curfew and the reducing number of holiday visitors, fewer staff were required, however, they offered me an alternative position at their store in Bournemouth with removal costs included if I was willing to go. I agreed immediately so in December I moved to Bournemouth. It was an adventure and a good way to fill in my time whilst waiting to join up. I lodged with a delightful elderly couple, Mr and Mrs Rogers of Rosemary Avenue and their son of twenty-four who was disabled and had a mental age of about six years but was an extremely nice and well brought up young man. I had a very pleasant six months with the family.

Bournemouth was still very much a holiday resort, virtually untouched by the war. I spent a lot of time with my new girl friend Joyce, dancing, swimming and horse riding. I had also transferred to the local Air Training Corps (ATC) unit who arranged several instructional visits to nearby RAF stations.

In January 1943 my brother received orders to go to Canada. He had enjoyed his initial aircrew training and was being sent there to continue flying and navigational training. He had managed to get some embarkation leave and before going home to see Mum and Dad, he spent a weekend with me in Bournemouth and we had a very good time going out dancing. This was my last memory of a great friend and brother.

Whilst I was in Bournemouth I got engaged to Joyce Bucket who worked at Bobby's as a window dresser. She was an attractive girl and extremely artistic. I recall her mother insisting that their surname should be pronounced 'Bouquet'. They were a lovely family who made my months in Bournemouth a memorable episode. The engagement was broken later on in the war but we still kept in touch and she is to this day a very good friend of my wife.

The 4th February was my seventeenth birthday and I sent in my application to join the RAFVR as a volunteer Wireless Operator/Air Gunner; I was accepted and told to wait for joining instructions. I have to admit that my first year in the RAF was almost a holiday with far less hazard and stress than living in Eastbourne, and we were very well fed.

On the 23rd May I was at home in Eastbourne visiting my parents and getting ready to join the RAF the next week when Joyce 'phoned from Bournemouth to say that they had just had a heavy air attack and Bobby's had taken a direct hit. The bomb had dropped right down the lift shaft and totally destroyed the air raid shelter in the basement. It was fortunate for Bobby's employees that the attack occurred on a Sunday but sadly many of the hotels were hit where the Canadian servicemen were billeted and there were many casualties. It appeared that I had joined up at the right time.

31

Chapter 3 - A Teenager at War   (Angel 3)

I was just seventeen years old when I joined up as a VR (Volunteer Reserve) Aircrew Cadet and reported to RAF Cardington Recruitment Centre on 28th May 1943 for kitting out and initial square bashing. Cardington had been used in the 1914/18 war to build airships for the Royal Navy and had also been the home for the construction of the R101 launched by Imperial Airways in 1929 as the British passenger competitor to the German Zeppelin and Hindenburg line of airships. Tragically the R101 crashed in France on its maiden overseas voyage killing all forty eight people on board

which was an even worse disaster than Hitler's famed Hindenburg which crashed at New Jersey, USA in 1937 killing thirty five people. This last disaster virtually destroyed all ideas of large passenger airship production in England.

The fact that RAF life would be very different from any previous civilian experience was brought home quite forcefully on my very first day. As my draft of new recruits was marched off by a Sergeant, we heard loud howls and cries coming from a detention building and

when we enquired what was going on, we were told that on the previous night the Military Police had caught some deserters who were being cleaned up by scrubbing them with bristle brushes and cold water. A warning to new conscripts who weren't happy at being called up for the duration of the war.

In July I heard from my brother to say that he was stationed at a Royal Canadian Air Force base near Calgary in Alberta where he had met a new girlfriend, Bernice, whose father was a senior director of the Canadian Pacific Railway. He said she was a very good skier and he was taking lessons when they took trips to Banff, one of the best ski resorts in the country. He mentioned they were all very well fed and he was working hard on his advanced flying training course; he also said that the local people were extremely friendly to RAF trainee aircrew and he was constantly being invited out to parties, etc. He ended his letter by saying he had been to the Calgary Stampede which was a fantastic Wild West Rodeo and was really enjoying life.

That September I was posted to the RAF Signals Air Training School at Blackpool. It was like peacetime. Full of holidaymakers and with hardly any air raid warnings. I was billeted with several friends at a house in Albert Road and all cadets were supposed to obey a curfew and return to their billets by 10.00 p.m. each night. We were given radio and general physical training during the day but were free most evenings and weekends except for guard duty.

The Blackpool Winter Gardens gave a great welcome to the Armed Forces. For only nine old pence servicemen could attend a film at the Winter Gardens on a Saturday afternoon, go to a tea dance and return again to the ballroom in the evening for the main dance. A great time was had by all.

Most of the Blackpool landladies were great. Mine was an exception - a massive Lancashire woman with an unfriendly disposition. One night when we returned only a few minutes after the 10.00 o'clock curfew, we found she had locked us out. We kept banging on the door until she opened it, screaming abuse. Then her husband, the tiniest cockney, kept jumping up and trying to hit me so I picked him up and shook him. He was startled, but it changed his attitude to us and afterwards we got on well.

In January 1944, I was posted to RAF Compton Bassett. It was an Advanced Wireless Operator Training School but the course included firearms and ground combat training. It was the first time I had come face to face with the fact that war was no adventure. We were detailed to attend the Assault and Defence Training Grounds for advanced live rifle firing exercises and grenade training. Most of us found no difficulty with the firing range. Grenades were different.

We practiced how to hold them, remove the safety pin, throw and duck after throwing them. We were then shown how to prime, safely insert the detonator and locking key and then screw on the base plate; the training went well without problems.

For the live grenade throwing exercises we were assembled into squads of six. Each team filed into the safety of a chest high forward trench and again each man practiced throwing a live grenade but with the safety pin still in place. We were told to "Prepare, retain pin, throw and duck immediately and stay down counting up to five until we heard the explosion." All went well.

We were then ordered to pay particular attention, as the next throw would be live. The order was given "Pick up your grenade, pin out, arm back, throw, DUCK." There were six explosions. We all stood up except the friend beside me. He had frozen when he threw his grenade and didn't duck; the grenade base plate had come back and struck him in the head, killing him instantly. Much of the glamour disappeared and a very quiet Squad marched back to barracks. For the third time my Guardian Angel was with me.

In March, whilst waiting for my Air Gunnery Course, I was posted to RAF South Cerney near Cirencester. Most of my time was spent carrying out airborne flight testing of radio systems of repaired aircraft and acting as safety pilot during inflight testing after engine and radio maintenance.

I got on well with our senior Test Pilot who gave me my first unofficial flying lessons in Anson and Oxford twin-engine aircraft. His actual job was to give the engines and airframes a thorough

check before sending the aircraft back into an operational unit. So we practiced emergency single engine landings in the local farmers' fields which had been set aside for that purpose. It was excellent experience and great fun.

It was here that I also started a short boxing career. Tommy Thompson, the Station Warrant Officer, was a boxing enthusiast and in charge of the Station Boxing Team. Any airman who volunteered to be a member of the team was excused guard duties and to me it seemed worth joining, however, it was a short lived career. My first real fight was against a lad who later became the RAF Training Command Amateur Champion and in the third round he knocked me out of the ring and through the swing doors of the gymnasium. I saw stars, and that told me boxing was not for me. That was my last fight. I decided to become what I consider to be a practicing coward and live to fight another day. W/O Thompson was very good and never did put me back on the list for Guard detail.

6th June, D-Day. It was from South Cerney on a cloudy day that I watched our airborne troops take off from all the surrounding airfields. Hour after hour the sky was filled with thousands of Dakotas towing large Horsa Glider troop carriers on the way to invade France. This went on for some days. Sadly but inevitably many hundreds of badly injured casualties,  many horrifyingly burned by German oil bombs, were flown back to our airfield and transferred by ambulance to local UK and US hospitals.

Bomber aircrews had a life expectancy of about 60% but when they returned it was to the best possible food, a warm and somewhat safer bed whereas the Army could be crawling in mud, ice or broiling desert sand with no way home at the end of a day. No easy choice.

A V1 Flying Bomb was shot down behind Astaire Avenue on July 4, 1944 and caused tremendous blast damage to houses which subsequently had to be demolished.

Between June 1944 and March 1945, London was again subjected to major attacks. This time it was from the V1 flying bomb, the first cruise missile, and later the V2 rocket which was the first ballistic missile. These weapons killed 8,938 Londoners, seriously injured twenty five thousand people and destroyed tens of thousands of houses and other buildings. At home, Eastbourne was still under attack, Doodle Bugs doing great damage.

It's sad to say that, in my experience, the feeling between white and black American troops was not good. It was particularly noticeable when we were trying to get a lift from a US Army Driver. The black drivers would always offer a lift to UK servicemen but would very often pass white US personnel saying things like "Let the bastard walk." This was also borne out by our own RAF Jamaican personnel who had travelled via the USA to join up in either Canada or the UK. They told us that when they travelled on white only trams or busses with members of their white unit, intolerant white Americans often abused them.

During September I once again watched as our Horsa Gliders were towed off to drop Paratroops of the 1st British Airborne Division one hundred miles behind enemy lines. It was known as Operation Market Garden and the goal was to secure two bridges across the river at Arnhem in Holland, the objective being to allow the Allied army to advance rapidly Northwards to cross the river and then turn right into the lowlands of Germany thereby skirting around the German Siegfried

defence line in an attempt to end the war by Christmas of 1944.

Unfortunately this dramatic plan failed. The intelligence planners appeared to have miscalculated the strength and preparedness of the German forces under General Field Marshall Model; he had been able to reinforce the bridge

defences by calling in S.S. armoured divisions which, undetected by our own Intelligence Services, had been resting and re-equipping close by. We were also badly hampered by the atrocious weather and blocked roads so that General Horrocks armoured brigade of tanks was unable to bring relief as planned. There followed ten days of bitter fighting until the survivors were ordered to attempt to escape across the River Rhine. In all, over twelve hundred British soldiers were killed and nearly three thousand wounded and/or taken prisoner. Also, three thousand four hundred German troops were killed or wounded in the battle.

I had good news early in October; an old school chum, Bernard Watkins who lived behind us in Mona Road, had been amongst the troops dropped at Arnhem and had escaped by swimming across the River Rhine. He was back home on leave. A very good show.

On the evening of 14th December 1944, Major Glen Miller gave a concert to the patients at the American Hospital in Cirencester, Gloucestershire and the next morning I saw him take off in an RAF Lysander aircraft from the Airfield at South Cerney. We understood he was crossing to France to make final arrangements for his orchestra to entertain the troops but alas, the aircraft didn't arrive there. We heard later that after leaving our airfield, he had diverted to the USAF Base at Twinwood in Bedfordshire. One can only assume he hopped from the RAF Airfield by Lysander to the U.S Air Base and then transferred onto a USAAF single engine Norseman UC-64. There are numerous theories about what happened once he was on his way across the Channel; some believe he had been shot down by a German fighter, some that his aircraft was struck by bombs from a high flying US or RAF aeroplane which had aborted a bombing raid and had jettisoned their bombs before returning to base. Others were sure that the pilot had lost his way due to poor visibility (the weather was extremely poor) and that he crashed into the sea due to lack of fuel, engine trouble, etc. and some said that he escaped but was wounded and died. It is doubtful we will ever know the truth.

That December I was amongst sixty Aircrew Trainee WOP/AGs who were grounded and formed into Ground Mobile Signals Units to offer close liaison with our front line invasion forces. We all had a shock when we were informed that we needed toughening up to Army standard with the ability to independently support our Unit in the field.

For this purpose we were posted to Newlands Corner, a high and bleak wooded hill outside Guildford. This was a memorable event as that year the UK was in the grip of the worst winter in Guildford's recorded history and our camp was sited on the highest spot, covered in snow and ice; even the smallest twigs on trees and bushes were bowed down supporting ice collars three times their own size. were ordered to establish our tents on top of the hill and dig latrines, despite the fact that there was an established but abandoned wooden army camp on the site which included all mod-cons.

Our training included unarmed combat and carrying out escape and evasion exercises with an Army Unit acting most realistically as German assault troops. We hadn't been prepared to play soldiers and crawl all over frozen ground and bracken but the time element allowed for training us up to Army standard was only six weeks which was a bit of a joke. We had no hot water and lived on field kitchen food, however, we made the best of it and got stuck in but retained the odd RAF humorous side-track.

One particularly cold night, several of us on guard duty decided to get the old coke boiler in the army bathhouse working and then took turns to have a hot bath. Unfortunately when my turn came, I found our Duty Officer was a little sharper than I thought and he was not well pleased when he stumbled upon me in the bath, although I did have my rifle beside me. We all ended up on jankers (extra duties). Despite the grumbles, we became extremely fit with not a cold between us. The germs simply couldn't stand the freezing cold

39

temperatures.

On the odd free day we visited the Guildford Services Club where they treated us very well, gave us a good feed, extra chocolate and friendly female company.

In line with the Unit's independence capability we were then sent to the RAF Vehicle Driving School at Chigwell for introduction to our Mobile Signals Unit vehicles and told that we had seven days in which to learn to drive and to handle the radio equipment prior to embarkation. I was in one of three similar Units who had trained together and none of us knew how to drive and our heavy vehicles had no smooth modern gear changing; it was the double-declutching which gave us a problem. We were told that we would have to negotiate poorly maintained, high mountain passes. The course was quite hectic but enjoyable with a few minor knocks and crashes. I remember my second day on the road when I was having trouble double de-clutching and changing gear whilst approaching a roundabout. I didn't see the horse drawn coal cart in front of me slow down and I gave it a nudge causing the poor old horse to stumble and the driver, who sat up on a high pedestal seat holding the reins, fall off his perch. Fortunately neither rider nor horse were injured.

We were then sent to Edinburgh and lodged at RAF Turnhouse whilst waiting to embark on ship at Leith for Norway. At our earliest opportunity we went into Edinburgh to explore and were amazed at the quality of Scottish hospitality. On our first stroll along Princess Street we were stopped by many a charming young women (all nice young ladies) asking if we would like to go to this or that club for refreshments or a dance. They were connected to one of the 'Support our Troops' organisations. It was a very refreshing experience and my only adverse memory of our stay was breakfast porridge made with salt and water. No wonder Rob Roy was a rebel! To this day I have a very soft spot for our Scottish friends.

Regrettably, each of the three Units went to a different invasion area. The first Unit's landing craft hit a mine as it approached the French coast and sank without touching the shore and with much loss of life. The second Unit was caught in the Ardennes when Field Marshall Von Runstead launched a counter offensive, which became known as the Battle of the Bulge. The Unit was overrun and all personnel were shot against their vehicles.

This German push into the Ardennes was a last attempt to split the

American/British offensive and was possibly the last major threat to the success of the invasion. It was fought in the most bitter, freezing cold weather. One hundred thousand Germans were killed, wounded or captured. The British casualties were two hundred killed and fourteen hundred injured or captured. The American casualties were nineteen thousand killed, forty thousand injured and twenty-three and a half thousand captured. Each

side had eight hundred tanks destroyed and the Germans lost about one thousand aircraft.

We heard of the Malmedy Massacre, which was one of the worst atrocities committed against American troops during the course of the War in Europe when the Germans murdered eighty-six American soldiers who were held as prisoners.

My Unit had been held back from the initial invasion so once again I was lucky. We finally got embarkation orders in December for Norway when the war was almost over and it was a much softer posting than we expected. We crossed the North Sea in four large LSTs (Landing ShipTank) the weather was foul and developed into a full-blown gale.

Fortunately I am a good sailor so was unaffected but many of my Unit, and even some of the sailors, were seasick which was made worse by watching the other LSTs in the convoy. We could see them rolling over so

far that their flat, rusty, weed encrusted keels were exposed whilst others were being tipped over the other way. Many couldn't face going to the galley for food and if they wanted their daily cigarette and chocolate ration, they had to go down into the hold. Many felt unable to do this and gave their chocolate ration to anyone who would venture down into the bowels of the craft to collect their cigarettes. I didn't smoke but was a chocoholic so I went down several times and got their rations for them and ended up with a considerable store of chocolate goodies which made me very popular when meeting the local Norwegian girls. Looking back, I now realise how very unsportsmanlike I was.

We landed in Kristiansand in Southern Norway as part of the RAF 2nd TAF where Royal Norwegian Air Force Troops of the 132N Wing had taken over an ex German Luftwaffe fighter and bomber base at Kjevik, about sixteen miles inland from the town of Christiansand. My Mobile Unit was given the German Officers'

brothel as accommodation, the previous inmates having been removed. It took ages to clear away the stench of perfume and for some time we received the odd funny look from the local population.

Norway had been occupied by the Germans for five years and the Norwegians were portrayed as being treated far less harshly than other occupied countries. They were, in fact, a showcase for Nazi cooperation but even so, a great many of the population suffered very badly. Hitler's solution to the Jews and all non-conformists is well documented and Germany has quite rightly made it a criminal offense to state that the holocaust didn't happen.
See - www.ushmm.org/wlc/en/article.php?ModuleId
    I did not see any of the actual concentration camps myself but within days of their liberation the newspapers printed pictures; the technology of the day was too basic to have faked those dreadful sights as some weirdo fascists suggested. I met and spoke with many people who had liberated the camps, although liberation was too late for the hundreds of thousands of piled up corpses that were found.

My limited experience of Gestapo brutality was in the forced labour camp at Kjevik on the Luftwaffe airfield we had liberated; it housed a variety of non-British allied prisoners who had been forced to carry out repairs to installations and bomb damage. The prisoners' accommodation was appalling, housing twelve men to each eight by eight foot wooden hut, which contained twelve bunks in three tiers. There was no heating and the hut was without a door so it was fully open to the harsh Norwegian elements. Food was a form of gruel prepared in a massive cauldron and prisoners were allowed only one bowl each day. The site was a multiplicity of these open huts connected by earthen paths. All the way along these paths were small wooden crosses, each depicting where a prisoner had been shot and buried. The crosses were used as a warning to other inmates to either conform or be shot.

Most of the men we found were Russian Cossacks and so grateful to us that they stood up and saluted every British serviceman who passed them, of whatever rank. Regretfully, I understand that they were repatriated to Russia even though the British Government knew they would most likely to be shot by the Stalinist Regime.

As an invasion force, I believe we were fortunate that the German Army was at the end of both its strength and morale as they gave little fight. One night we had a scare when we were all ordered to "Stand to" and all personnel were issued with Sten machine guns and ordered to take up defensive positions. Our C.O. had been alerted that a German SS Armoured Unit was in the surrounding mountains and they were expected to take a last chance to break through and retake the Airfield.
We spent a long dark night imagining every sound and shadow to be the enemy preparing to attack. Luckily the Germans had no idea how weak we were or how useless we would have been against trained assault troops with tanks. Personally I only fired the Sten gun once, and that was at a snake in the woods. My Angel must have been watching because the S.S. retreated and then surrendered. The only casualties suffered by our Unit during the invasion were from poor driving: our one-week course in the UK had not prepared us for the atrocious mountain conditions. Some chaps unfortunately drove off one of the many cliffhanger roads encircling the fjords.

To say we were lucky in Norway was an understatement. The accommodation and food was usually good and the local population greeted us with friendliness, and once the threat of further German resistance had faded we were involved in much of the local entertainment. I personally found the young ladies very attractive but one day when I was travelling across the Fjord with my current Norwegian girl friend, Margerita Guianwold, she was suddenly accosted by another lovely girl (a previous acquaintance) who shouted "You have stolen my man" and leaped at Margerita with much hair pulling, screaming and rolling about on the deck. It took several passengers to part them whilst I, being rather naïve, just stood by, totally flabbergasted. I was relieved when the journey ended but some chaps from my Unit had been on the ferry and my macho reputation was considerably enhanced when they recounted the highlights of the ferry crossing.

One day I was invited to meet Margarita's parents at their villa style home. Her father was a town politician and was giving a reception for many of the senior officers of our invasion force. Dressed in my basic airman's uniform I felt rather out of place, however, I was the guest of the youngest daughter and the most glamorous of the ladies present. My C.O. was also a guest and was a bit put out when he was asked by the host to give me a lift back to the RAF Base but he concurred with good grace - a very decent chap.

Our next move was to Oslo. We loaded the vehicles onto a train and travelled in style. Well perhaps not quite in style, it was really a goods train with a carriage for a few civilians and us. It took two days without heat to travel over the snowy mountains with the odd stop at isolated villages where the locals greeted us joyfully. The other travellers shared their pasties with us whilst we provided everyone with hot tea made in large half-gallon cans from the steam pipe underneath the engine.

The 21st April was one of the saddest days of my life. My brother, Sergeant Navigator Cyril (Phil) Hamlin was reported missing. His aircraft had been seen to take a sudden dive and crash into the Pacific; aircraft and crew were never found and they were reported missing. It as not until after the war that we were advised that Cyril had been killed whilst in action.

The photograph is of Phil with his fiancée Bernice who lived in Calgary. Her father was a director of the Canadian Pacific Railway. I feel we owe much to the Canadian families who made all our sons and my brother's last two years so pleasurable.

Below is a photograph showing the memorial commemorating all those who served and died in the service of their country whilst training in Canada, or from the

American Air Force training bases who had no known graves. I am told it is built on a beautiful site at the meeting of the Ottawa and Rideau Rivers facing the Gatineau Hills and the Ridraux Falls.

My war ended when we reached Oslo on the 7th May 1945; the German Reich had surrendered unconditionally. VE Day (Victory in Europe) celebrations were held in Oslo's main square where most of the Capital's population waited for the Norwegian King Haakon VII to appear. He was particularly well respected by his people for the way he had stood up to the Germans during the Nazi occupation and although his appearance was delayed that evening, everyone stayed in high spirits.

One very merry British Tank Regiment Staff Sergeant treated us to a spectacular riding display. He had climbed up a lamppost and was waving a flag when a mounted Norwegian Policeman remonstrated on his unseemly behaviour. The Soldier leaped from the lamppost and onto the horse's back behind the rider. We were then treated to a ten-minute display of horsey antics whilst the Policeman tried in vain to unseat the Soldier and the horse charged up and down the huge concourse beflagged for the VE celebrations. The crowds cheered.

During the celebrations, I was enjoying an evening with friends when some American MPs entered the restaurant and approached four black soldiers who were sitting down quietly, causing no trouble. They were not asked to leave by the White Tops but dragged out of the place and chased down the road whilst being beaten with long wooden batons. We found it hard to understand the American idea of equality.

Peace brought a wonderful, almost unreal, feeling to us all. So many people had gone through combat or the repression of German occupation, the blitz, flying doodle bugs, V bombs, etc. that it took some time before we lost the automatic reaction to duck or dive for cover every time we heard an aircraft diving, flying low or even a car backfire. People who reacted to these noises would get up with an embarrassed expression or weak grin on their faces. Streetlights were switched on. Shops were brightly lit and cars used their headlights. It felt like a brand new world. To those poor prisoners released from the hellholes of the German concentration camps, it really was a new world. Sadly, many were never able to fully recover from the nightmare of their incarceration.

My Unit was next sent to Trondheim where I had another embarrassing moment. I was in the Docks area at night, although I can't remember why I was there, and bumped into another nice family who had just disembarked from a ship and were returning to their home after having been forced by the Gestapo to live elsewhere for the last five years. They were struggling with a mass of luggage so I helped them and then arranged to meet the daughter, Guilda, some days later and invited her to dine with me. Imagine my embarrassment when, after the meal, the waiter insisted on taking her ration coupons. Unfortunately I had not realised that it was only if you were an unaccompanied off duty servicemen that you were allowed to eat in restaurants without ration cards. Two days later we moved, so I didn't have chance to make amends.

Working in conjunction with Airborne Units of Bomber Command, we moved from Trondheim to Tromso in the Arctic Circle where we spent several months tracking the position of the North Star, the object being to assist future navigational positioning.

When the UK General Election was held on the 5th July, most of us assumed the result would be a foregone conclusion and were shocked when the Conservatives lost. It was a poor reward for the man who, I believe, had saved the whole world from Nazi domination but not being particularly politically conscious at that time; I gave it no further thought.

VJ Day on 15th August marked the end of the War with Japan. They surrendered after atom bombs had been dropped on Hiroshima and

Nagasaki which forced them to accept unconditional surrender and end the war. I can neither accept nor forget Japan's bestial treatment of both civilians and service personnel after the fall of Singapore. I heard many personal experiences from repatriated victims I met after their return to England.

The use of the atom bomb brought home to me the fact that, after

this, the world would never feel totally safe again because man now had the technology to destroy not just himself but the whole world. However, anybody who considers the Allies were wrong to end the war with the atom bomb should access

http://www.ww2pacific.com/atrocity.html

In Singapore, hospitals had been ransacked, patients bayoneted, nurses raped and tortured and in some areas nurses and hospital staff had been driven into the sea and then machine gunned down. Treatment of prisoners of war was inhumane yet few of the high command that sanctioned these atrocities paid the full price. Much later I was to meet a seventeen-year-old repatriated girl internee of the Japanese who had been raped and so ill-treated that it took years for her to overcome her terror of anyone in a uniform.

The city of Tromso is the great ice town of the Arctic and frequently called the 'Paris of the North'. When we were there, the place had been run down during the occupation and was then hosting many camps of German POWs. Covered in snow, the landscape was dramatic and although the fjords and mountains were perhaps not as majestic as those of Oslo and Southern Norway, they were still an imposing sight. In the summer when the weather was good, we shared the joy of a friendly, liberated people but it was always very cold. The autumn was full of colour with fruit, berries and mushrooms. It was, however, difficult to become accustomed to the midnight sun in the summer and the long winter with constant darkness. It made me understand why there has always been such a high rate of suicide in the Northern wastes of Norway.

We were stationed on what had been the Luftwaffe's main Northern Waterborne Operational Base for float planes because, so far north, there was no airfield for land-based aircraft. In addition, Skattøra had served as Germany's most Northern Weather Station but after the war it became one of the two major centres for Air Traffic Control in Norway, covering the airspace from Iceland, Jan  Mayan Island and Spitsbergen up to the Soviet border. The harbour held the capsized wreck of the mighty warship Tirpitz that RAF Squadrons 9 and 617 had successfully attacked and sunk on the 12th November 1944.

The Aurora Borealis is Tromso's most amazing attraction and I found the extraordinary phenomena of the 'Northern Lights' simply awe inspiring. It is visible by night from October to April and it is nature's own strobe lighting show caused by solar winds meeting atmospheric gases around the magnetic North Pole which creates the formation of the breath-taking movement of lights, constantly gyrating and turning every colour of the spectrum.

We finally completed our Star Gazing assignment and were shipped back to Leith in Scotland in September 1945 where my Unit was ordered to prepare for another overseas posting, this time to Italy, which sounded interesting but if I wanted to go with them I had to sign on for extended service as I was due for demobilisation within six months. I declined and was posted to RAF Blackbrook near St. Helens, Lancashire and trained as a wireless telegraphist.

This was a Bomber Command Underground Signal Centre built in the depths of a coal mine but it was also a working mine. I felt no envy for the Bevin Boys who had missed military service during the War by being forced to work as miners. One visit down the mine was more than enough to horrify me.

Off duty we had a great time, dancing in St Helens with occasional visits to Liverpool. When RAF Blackbrook started to wind down prior to being mothballed I was asked what I would like to do to fill in the few months left to complete my service and I opted to go to RAF Padgate as a driver taking convoys of troops to the docks for embarkation, mainly for the Far Eastern theatre.

On one particular trip I was driving my transport loaded with thirty WAAFs, all in a merry mood, on their way to Liverpool and embarkation. They were waving and gesticulating at everyone they passed when along came a gallant young Pilot Officer driving a nice shiny open top MG sports car; he began to get really impatient waiting behind the convoy whilst taking considerable cheek from the girls. When we stopped at the traffic lights, the hooting of his horn only caused more laughter and comments from my passengers. He revved up his engine for a racing style take off to impress them when the lights changed to green but, as I started off, I immediately had to slam on my brakes because the lead vehicle had stalled in front of me. Unfortunately the MG couldn't stop because the driver had accelerated so hard. His bonnet ended up right underneath the rear of my lorry. I didn't feel the bump but as I started off again most of the front end of his car tore away leaving a buckled radiator steaming in the middle of the road. I only stopped again because I heard the girls screaming and laughing so loud. The poor chap was not just horrified but felt a total fool. The girls were yelling and wolf whistling and then our Military Police escort arrived and read him the Law confirming it was a criminal offence to break into a military convoy. The girls thought it was very funny but I couldn't help feeling sorry for him and wondered what story he would tell his girlfriend or family.

1947 Space travel: will we or will we not conquer space travel:

Amazingly, in 1947, the question of whether or not we would conquer space was one of the most animated discussions taking place in newspapers, on radio, by politicians, by scientists and surprisingly, many senior RAF officers. They extolled the impracticability of space travel or a flight to the moon and many were convinced that man would be unable to withstand either the massive acceleration required to leave Earth's gravity or the continuous weightlessness. To my untutored mind, the ever increasing speed of jet aircraft exceeding the sound barrier, the G forces sustained by pilots of fighter aircraft and the experience we had had of the German V2 Rocket bombs which virtually entered space each time they were fired, made me positive it would happen.

At this time, well-experienced pilots were reporting sightings of UFOs whilst Governments hid any knowledge they had of them for fear of causing panic. Today the question is still open. Is there another life force in the universe?

When the time came for my departure from the RAF, I realised how very fortunate I'd been because I had not met with any really dangerous or dramatic experiences. I was one of the very lucky ones. So many others had had a terrible and disastrous war.

IN RETROSPECT:
It is my personal opinion that Britain and World Democracy survived due only to the tenacity and courage of three people and their supporters who gave Britain the moral strength and technical ability to survive Dunkirk, win the Battle of Britain and forestall the Germans' attempt at invasion. They also built the country into a place for the United Allies to launch D/Day and achieve the overthrow of fascism.

Sir Winston Churchill has never been given the world recognition he deserved. Yes, he made mistakes (which world leader has not) but it was his foresight prior to the War and his resolve and leadership as Prime Minister in 1940 that kept Britain fighting. Large numbers of politicians from all sides of the "pre-war" British Government were for appeasement and bowing down to Germany, as were the Americans at that stage. After Dunkirk, although much of our Army was saved by the magnificent efforts of the Navy and the mass of small ship volunteers, they were exhausted and were left with little equipment with which to fight. I think it is true to say that if Hitler hadn't been frightened of launching an invasion with our Navy and Air force still intact, we would have suffered a total defeat.

It is true that without the eventual massive support of America, we couldn't have finally defeated the Germans. It is also a true fact that without Churchill's resolve, the ingenuity of Sydney Camm's Hurricane and Reginald Mitchell's Spitfire, which allowed the RAF to win the Battle of Britain, we would have had no chance of retaining our freedom. Regrettably Reginald Mitchell died of cancer of the colon on the 11th June 1936 at the age of forty-two without realising how great was his contribution to Britain's survival. His memory has still not been honoured properly.

It was Britain and its Empire that saved the world from Nazism by its stand in 1940/41.

Chapter 4 – Demobbed and Married - What a Disaster!

I was demobilised in August 1947 and heard many ex-servicemen decrying the civilian clothes issued at the demob centres. I can only say that I must have been lucky because the business suit and raincoat I received fitted well and looked quite reasonable whilst the shoes were good, smart leather brogues. With no idea what I wanted to do with the rest of my life, I returned to live with my parents in Eastbourne. The RAF had taught me self assurance but I literally found I had no ambition other than to enjoy myself and try to make some money, yet I had no thoughts or plans as to how this could be achieved.

I took a number of jobs in Eastbourne, first as a clerk with the NHS at their new offices built on a bombsite in Meads then as an invoice clerk at the Grove Road offices of the Electricity Board. All were pleasant jobs but boring with few prospects, especially for a person with my lack of interest in accounting and office administration. In retrospect I believe much of my time was spent watching the clock and wondering whom I'd take to the dance at the weekend.

My childhood friend, Timmy Bush, and his family appeared to have been swallowed up by the war. I could find no trace of them in 1945 and to this day have been unable to do so; there is no mention of them in the town archives, electoral role, etc. If he or anyone who has ever heard of him reads this book, I would be eternally grateful for news.

In September 1948 I married Iris Holland, an Eastbourne beauty, a good dancer and from a very nice family. Bernard Compton, my closest friend, was best man at the wedding and his wife Peggy, was one of the bridesmaids. It was a very nice affair but even so, the honeymoon in Bournemouth was a total disaster; we cut it short and returned home.

Like so many ex-servicemen after the war, it was the idea of being married and having a family that attracted us and not the commitment; we were both far too young and immature in many ways.

On the 26th June 1949 my daughter Susan was born. She was adorable and it was for her sake that Iris and I tried to make the marriage work but sadly we were totally incompatible.

Bernard and I enjoyed spending much of our spare time together but we were always looking for ways to augment our income. He was an electrical engineer and I was an invoice clerk and both considered ourselves lucky when we were offered extra work as ice cream salesmen by Benton's of Eastbourne.

Initially we shared an ice cream tricycle using it on alternate evenings and travelling as far as the villages of Pevensey Bay, Stone Cross, Polegate and back via Willingdon - about a fifteen mile trip. It was hard work after a normal eight-hour day but great fun.

The following year sugar supplies were more plentiful for ice cream manufacture so we were given the use of a proper ice cream van, which allowed us to attend all the local and distant village fetes. We offered sweet luxury and each evening we would find queues of children and parents waiting to hear our Pied Piper bell ringing. It was good fun to see so many smiling faces but also very financially rewarding.

The Conservatives came to power in 1953 but it was another two years before food rationing began to ease. Sweets were the first to be freed in February (my birthday) and then sugar in September but it was not until 4th July 1954 that all the restrictions ended with meat and bacon the last to go.

That September I had been ill yet again with stomach ulcers and was spending a short holiday at my Aunt Annie's house in Brighton. My father came over from Eastbourne to spend a day with me and together we took a walk to visit his sister Rosa and brother Burt (a widower) who shared a house in the higher part of the town. I was very fond of them; for years when I was a boy my Aunt Rosa had cut out and saved the stories of Rupert Bear from the newspaper so that I could read them when I went to stay with her during school summer holidays.

Dad and I had a happy day but I think the heavy walking up the hills rather tired him out. He was in a very cheerful mood when I saw him off on the train but next morning the 12th September, my sister Gladys telephoned to say that Dad had died peacefully in his sleep during the night. A very sad end to my holiday but it left me with an enduring joyful memory.

By February my marriage had become intolerable and the trauma caused me to be frequently off work with my stomach problem so I came to the conclusion that with a disaster of a marriage and poor business prospects in civilian life, I should apply to re-join the RAF and attempt to continue a flying career.

Initially the Air Ministry rejected my application because at twenty-seven I was considered to be too old for the training programme. I immediately requested an interview and an age waiver on account of my past experience as a fully trained wireless operator who had passed the aircrew entrance examination in 1943 as a WOP/AG and had been waiting for final flying training in 1944 when I'd been transferred to an invasion force Mobile Signals Unit.

I waited anxiously for a response and when it did arrive I was in hospital as an inpatient undertaking an eight-week treatment for duodenal ulcers. I was drip fed eight pints of milk a day via a tube but I was also allowed unrestricted ice cream and milk chocolate - not a bad diet for a chocoholic - and it appeared to be working although I think probably the separation from my wife and the attendant trauma was the main benefactor.

The RAF invited me to attend a medical and an interview in London the following week. I applied to the Hospital for a day out to visit my solicitor in London for urgent business reasons; they agreed to release me for one single day provided that I returned within twenty-four hours.

I went to London with some trepidation about the medical but as I looked fit and there were no records of my hospitalisation and no operating scars, I passed the interview and medical with flying colours. I was asked how quickly I could join and start training so I asked for three months to clear business matters. They agreed, and I returned to hospital for a further month to finish the treatment, give notice to the Electricity Board and set matters right at home. My wife agreed that she would join me once I had completed my flying training, established myself on a Squadron and had obtained married quarters.

Chapter 5 - Crash after Crash after Crash (Angels 4,5 & 6)

I re-joined the Royal Air Force on the 29th April 1952 and once again reported to the RAF Cardington Recruitment centre where I had first joined in 1943.

From there I was posted to No.1 Air Signallers/Air Electronic School at Swanton Morley but found settling in was not as easy as I had thought it would be. It was largely my own fault as I am a doer, not an academic, so paid less attention to my written studies than I should have done, however, I was brought up rather sharply when I failed badly on my final passing out examination in aircraft electronics. I was called in front of the Confirmation Board and told that this failure was a matter for which I could be discharged. I talked myself into a re-sit, which was to take place the following morning with the other half of the course who had not previously taken the examination.

I knew it was make or break time, so I spent the entire night memorising the total electrical circuit of the Lancaster bomber. This proved to be somewhat uncomfortable as the only place where electric light was allowed throughout the night was in the toilets. Not a seat I would recommend but the electrical circuit was pressed well and truly upon my mind.

The next morning I re-sat the examination and scored 98%, however, this was not acceptable to one particular senior Member of the Board who insisted that I must have cheated; so I sat in front of them and from memory drew the total schematic diagram of the aircraft's wiring circuit and proved that with the schematic memorized, it was possible to answer any question. One examiner was still not pleased - he had obviously suffered a bad night but not as uncomfortable as mine.

The remainder of the Board Members accepted that I knew the subject thoroughly so I was confirmed Sergeant Air Signaller and received my Aircrew Brevet.

My personal life was still a disaster. Although my wife had agreed that once I had completed my flying training and could obtain married quarters, we would try to make the marriage work but this did not happen. She had no interest in moving away from our home in Eastbourne; to be honest it was for the best. I applied for a divorce and started custody proceedings.

My next posting was to RAF Leconfield where I found a crowd of like-minded chaps, one of whom was a real prankster. We were stationed close to the town of Beverley where I enjoyed myself and met a nice girl called Ann, a good dancer and the daughter of the local Police Chief Constable.

All went well until the Squadron's practical joker excelled himself when, one Saturday evening, a crowd of us went to the local dance at the Beverley Town Hall. We were having a great time dancing until the evening was interrupted by a senior Police Officer who climbed onto the stage and made the following announcement "Due to a bomb threat at the RAF Leconfield Base, all Air Force personnel stationed there are to leave immediately and assemble in the street below. Any person disagreeing with this order should look out of the window facing towards the front of the building to see what awaits you." We looked out and saw that the main road was lined with armed soldiers. Bren gun carriers were patrolling the road and there were also vehicles waiting to take us back to the Base.

We had apparently upset the Army, the Police and our Station Commanding Officer. It appeared that our prankster had built a cardboard bomb, smuggled it into the rear of the RAF Station's Telephone Exchange and then, after we had arrived at the dance, telephoned the Base and in a broad Irish accent told them that they had thirty minutes to evacuate the Base because there was a bomb in the Telephone Exchange. The threat was taken very seriously as there had been a general IRA alarm earlier that day.

The Army's Bomb Squad had been alerted, the Communications Centre had been evacuated and both the Army and Police had been placed on alert.

Unfortunately, this was also the night of the local Police Federation Annual Ball when all of the Constabulary senior officers were in attendance. All were recalled to duty - which totally ruined the evening for both them and their guests.

When the Bomb Squad arrived and searched the Exchange they found our prankster's toy bomb and this, understandably, caused a great deal of anger. They were able to trace that the alleged IRA warning had been made from a call box in the Town Hall where a dance was in progress and rightly assumed that an RAF person must be responsible

We were held in isolation for some thirty hours and continuously interrogated to obtain a confession. None of us had known that our prankster was the culprit and we all kept quiet but when we were asked to swear on the bible that we had not been involved, our wayward friend was either too religious or too honest to let us purge ourselves and admitted that he was the culprit. He was arrested and everyone else was released. Considering the enormous cost to the Army and the total collapse of the Police Ball, I should imagine that he was dismissed from the Service and served some sort of sentence. We never heard of him again.

A year passed before my next posting to RAF St Mawgan 2360 Conversion Unit which was a Maritime Reconnaissance Training School where I flew in Lancaster bombers and occasionally took part in Air Sea Rescue searches. This was a really enjoyable time.

Farms surrounded the Station and I was soon on friendly terms with the local people and enjoyed helping at haymaking time. Being a non-drinker from choice (I just don't like the taste of the stuff) my only worry was flying stone cold sober with crews who had been out the previous night on a heavy Scrumpy cider bender.

I remember on one trip over the North Sea we intercepted a May Day call between a destroyer and a large freight ship which was in danger of capsizing. Weather conditions were very bad and the sea so rough that the destroyer was having trouble locating the freighter. Luckily I was able to identify it by Radar and guide the two ships to an intercept. The Captain of the freighter called us and expressed his gratitude at finally seeing the destroyer's approach and I heard later that it reached shelter safely with the Navy standing by.

In August I was posted again, this time to RAF Kinloss, 236 Operational Conversion Unit; a lucky break as this was for training on the new American Lockheed P2V4, re-named the Neptune. They were submarine chasers and housed two very powerful Pratt and Whitney engines which were capable of long distance, eighteen-hour endurance flights searching over the Atlantic. The aircraft also had sophisticated radar and anti submarine sonar detection equipment on which I specialised. Kinloss was an excellent place to be; close to Lossiemouth and Fort William where I met a very nice Scottish girl and learnt about Burns night and first footing. When I completed the course, I was promoted to Flight Sergeant and posted to 36 Squadron flying Neptunes from RAF Topcliffe.

On arrival at the Base I saw a strange sight - a Sergeant Air Signaller who had one arm in a sling was being marched under close arrest by two Flight Sergeants and I was given the following amazing story.

The news headlines read: "FATAL ACCIDENT REPORT ON THE RAF'S FIRST NEPTUNE TO CRASH.
The aircraft WX542 was on a return flight to RAF Topcliffe and was commencing its initial approach. It had its wheels lowered for landing when witnesses said "It appeared to stall, strike a raised mound of ground which damaged its undercarriage, then it tried to continue but crashed and burst into flames."

AIRMAN SURVIVES 2000ft FALL WITHOUT A PARACHUTE:
Sergeant Lucas was the sole survivor of the Neptune WX542 previously reported as having crashed with no survivors. He had apparently abandoned the aircraft at a height of two thousand feet without a parachute and landed through trees and bushes onto a steep slope. He suffered a broken arm, concussion, cuts and bruises and had been found unconscious at the bottom of a steeply wooded hill. When he was taken to hospital he could tell them nothing. He had no memory of his last flight, where he was, what he had been doing or how he came to be where he was found. As there was no sign of a parachute, this injured man was not initially connected to the aircraft accident. It was only two days later when his identity and injuries were reported to his Squadron that it was realized he had been a member of the ill-fated Neptune crash. He never recovered his memory of why he abandoned his aircraft and after discharge from hospital, he was held in close arrest whilst waiting Court Martial.
It was a total mystery how anyone could manage to abandon this

type of aircraft without other members of the crew realising what had happened and reporting it to the pilot. The aircraft's Captain had been in direct VHF communication with Air Traffic Control for some time prior to and up to the actual time of the crash but had not commented on any problem. Subsequent rigorous technical crash site checks and enquiries could produce no explanation or theory why or how Sgt Lucas had abandoned the aircraft. The Court Martial was discontinued and the charges were dropped.

How can you sentence a man for being alive?

36 Squadron was often employed on reconnaissance flights during the Cold War period, exercising with NATO Naval Forces searching for non-friendly iron curtain submarines. Once we discovered a submarine we would shadow it with under water airborne sonar detection devices, frequently for hundreds of miles from the North Sea through the English Channel and round to the Mediterranean. Anti-submarine detection by sonar was a particular art and the aim was to force the submerged vessel to surface so that we could take photographs of it which would give intelligence on the type of sub it was and possibly reveals modifications, etc. They hated being photographed.

Submarines would either try to escape detection by lying silent or find a surface vessel and hide underneath it, trusting that their own propeller noises would be lost within the other vessel's louder thrashing sounds. The ability to appreciate the variance in propeller sounds was something I excelled at and enjoyed.

Another function of the Squadron was to deliver mail to the isolated weather ships stationed in the depths of the oceans. We would attach the mail to a flotation chamber and send it down by parachute; the ship would then have to launch a boat to recover it. Seeing the way their small boats were launched and bobbed about in the waves to retrieve the mail package confirmed my preference to be an airman.

Occasionally we had the opportunity to assist with long range search and rescue mayday calls, a task everyone took most conscientiously.

There were times when those eighteen hour trips were scheduled to take off at midday with the flight briefing held at 10.00 a.m. after which we could be told that for tactical reasons the take off time had been delayed by two, four or even six hours. This meant that although we had been briefed in the morning, the flight didn't actually take off until perhaps six hours later. There were enough crew members on aboard to allow for some rest periods but the day could become a thirty-hour stretch. After landing my legs would feel somewhat shaky. Very different from flying under Civil Airways regulations.

In February 1954 the Squadron was due for detachment to RAF Luqa in Malta and was to fly out in formation for a six-week stay. On the evening scheduled for leaving, we all assembled in the Crew Room ready to take off at ten-minute intervals. Our aircraft was the last in line and at 1-00 am, our  scheduled departure time, we saw Lucas, somewhat the worse for wear, asleep in a corner. We reasoned that because of the long wait for take off, he had somehow missed boarding his own aircraft so we bundled him into ours to save him from a very severe reprimand. Six hours later, just as we were circling Malta and about to land, he woke up and was suddenly quite graphic saying that he had only been down to the Crew Room to see us off but had fallen asleep because he'd had a few too many drinks. He had to spend six weeks in Malta acting as every Crew's spare job man. Alas for Lucky Lucas!

At that time it was the rainy season in Malta and the Sergeants' Mess was being rebuilt so we were housed in temporary accommodation which was surrounded by eight-foot deep development holes. It was pouring cats and dogs but our Lucas was not a man to be dismayed by either his predicament or bad weather - he borrowed enough money for a good night out in Valletta and off he went.

That night I went to bed early but during the night I kept waking up and thinking I heard mews or moans like a cat crying at the door: Twice I got up and opened the door but could see nothing through the heavy downpour.

The next morning the weather had cleared and on the way to breakfast I once again heard moaning. I looked around and found Lucas, up to his knees in water, sitting in one of the eight-foot holes. As usual, with his luck, he had lost his way home in the dark, slipped and dropped into one of the holes and had been stuck in the water for hours. I felt sure it was only the quantity of local hooch he had consumed the night before that saved him from pneumonia.

We had a further two weeks enjoying the attractions of the island before we returned to England.

One particularly turbulent night we left Topcliffe for a ten-hour trip patrolling the seas above Iceland. At the end of the sortie we turned for Base, the wind force increased, throwing us about and causing deep air pockets. As we lined up for touchdown on the Topcliffe approach, a massive side wind struck us. We felt the aircraft drop and heard a bang. We had struck the field's lead-in lights. The Skipper, Geoff Finding, instantly feathered the damaged engine, thrust full power onto the other; recovered control and we went round again for a rather hairy single engine landing.

As soon as we cleared the runway, a voice check was made of all ten crew members. Only Lucas failed to answer. I went back to check him at his radar position and found he was sitting, frozen to his seat, with a five foot section of a starboard propeller blade projecting through the side of the aircraft having missed his face by about six inches. To say there was an odour in the air was putting it mildly. Soon after this my friend Lucas was posted and we lost touch. I often wonder if he continued to suffer unlucky situations with such lucky solutions. This was my Angel's 4th visit.

On another occasion whilst we were on a reconnaissance sortie in beautiful weather near Jan Mayen Island some four hundred miles above Iceland, we noticed a slight whiff of burning. An immediate search found nothing amiss on the flight deck but the Flight Engineer detected the source - the aircraft's radar system had caught fire and this was situated in a large well underneath the body of the aircraft. Due to the possibility of explosion, there was no accessible runway for landing in Iceland and we couldn't land at a civilian airport. We closed all air access to the radar well, shut down all non-essential power sources and flew back fifteen hundred miles to Base with what was affectively a smouldering bomb. As we approached Topcliffe we were advised to land as softly as possible, taxi well away from the buildings and, as they expected the undercarriage to collapse, to vacate the aircraft from the side emergency exit widows. Needless to say, it didn't cave in and the trip ended happily. This was my Angel's 5th visit.

A new friend, Seth Crabtree, was another lucky chap who survived two air crashes within three months of each other. He was an Air Signaller and had been flying in a Hastings aircraft in India but on his last operation his aircraft had been forced to ditch in the Indian Ocean. Together with other members of his Crew, he floated for two days in a life raft before being spotted by a rescue 'plane  and then picked up by a merchant ship. After recuperation he was transferred back to England on sick leave and finally posted to join our Crew with 36 Squadron.

Seth was still with us when on the 13th January 1956 we were once again sent on detachment to RAF Luqa in Malta which we all thoroughly enjoyed. The local people were always friendly but it was important to remember that they were also very strong Catholics and girls from good families were carefully chaperoned. The only time the girls had a little freedom was when they went out on a group swimming party but, if you wanted to kiss one, you had to tip a lilo onto its side and hide behind it because wherever the girls went, they were usually watched through binoculars.

One time when we were returning to Luqa Airfield to land after a long navigational exercise, our Skipper, Flt.Lt. Geoff Finding called out "Three greens" which showed that the under carriage was down and locked but, as the aircraft's wheels touched the runway, we felt a lurch and a thump as the port undercarriage wheel retracted. There was only time for Geoff to shout "Brace, Brace" as the aircraft rolled, crunched and cartwheeled for several hundred yards down the runway. Immediately we came to a stop, the shout was "Abandon, abandon and run" because we all fully expecting the aircraft to explode. The amazing thing was that by the time we were clear, Seth was about fifty yards ahead of us and still running. It's surprising what a previous rehearsal will do for your reactions.

Luckily we were on dry land this time but the aircraft was declared to be a total write off. Just how lucky we had been was only brought home to us when we returned to the aircraft after the danger of explosion had passed. The fuel tank of one of the smashed engines was leaking gasoline down onto the ground and to within two feet of the flames given off by an oil-fuelled lead-in flare. We had been a mere fraction away from a very big bang. Later inspection confirmed our landing gear contained a faulty solenoid in the left safety light so that it showed green when it should have shown red.

This was my Angel's 6th visit.

Well into her seventies Mum was still living in Eastbourne and insisting on her independence but her hearing and eyesight were poor. She was a gentle lady, always showing concern for others. One day as she walked down to the shopping parade, she saw a man writhing in agony on the pavement whilst passers by completely ignored his plight. She walked over to him, touched him gently with her walking stick (disguised as an umbrella) and said "Don't worry my good man, I will fetch assistance." The man looked up at her and replied "I don't know what the 'ell you're on about lady, I'm trying to turn this ruddy stop cock off." She laughed all the way home.

Chapter 6 – The Bermuda Incident

The 10th June 1956 was a great day. We were told that 36 Squadron was to take part in Operation Hour Glass, a large scale NATO exercise to be held in the Western Atlantic where we would be co-operating with the Royal Navy, the Netherlands Royal Navy, the United States Navy and the Royal Canadian Navy on anti-submarine work and convoy escort duties. After leaving Topcliffe we made an overnight stop at a Portuguese Air Force Base in the Azores but due to unforeseen circumstances we arrived very late that evening, however, they had laid on a sumptuous meal for us. I was starving and took a good slice from a superb sirloin steak but to my horror found it was infused with strong garlic, which I couldn't stand. The chef had gone home so I had to do without the main course but their hospitality couldn't be faulted.

We were up early the next morning for our two thousand mile flight to the USAF Base at Kindley Field, Bermuda and it must be noted that the previous night's enthusiastic Portuguese hospitality ensured there were many bleary eyes among the pilots and some rather wobbly take offs.

We settled down for the long, somewhat boring flight over endless water; the pilots of each aircraft were able to take turns and as we were flying as a Squadron in loose formation, each Crew's Navigator could compare position with the Leader. Each crew included five Signaller/Radar Operators for communications but as I was the Squadron's only non drinking member (I'd had a good night's sleep) I did much of the communication for us all - advising Kindley Field of the flight's position and anticipated arrival times, etc. We arrived at the USAF Base on Friday afternoon in Squadron order as forecast and were made extremely welcome by members of the USAF and the Royal Navy. We had a magnificent time, both operationally and socially.

Fortunately for me, my old girl friend Anne, whose father was the Chief Constable of Beverley, had a sister Julia who was working as a teacher in Bermuda and they had asked me if I would be kind enough to call on her. Lucky me! I found Julia - twenty six, attractive, intelligent, friendly, unattached, and she had entre into many Government functions and local society families to which she immediately introduced me and which in turn lead to many superb parties.

On our arrival Pat O'Malley and I decided that we needed to find someone to improve the appearance of our new RAF issue khaki drill uniforms and were told that the only decent tailor's shop was situated in the British Army Barracks near the town of Hamilton. So, dressed in civvies and with our uniforms draped over our arms and my red haired friend sporting a large handlebar moustache, we went to find the shop. It was a Saturday and the Barracks were deserted except for a squad of Army defaulters who were being marched around and who had obviously been given extra square-bashing as a punishment. They were being disciplined by a very smart but obviously newly commissioned Second Lieutenant.

As he marched past I asked "Excuse me Old Chap, can you advise me where I can find the tailor's shop?" He looked a little flustered, ordered his squad to halt, about turn, and then marched them up to me, halted them, came to an elegant attention, saluted me and stood respectfully whilst giving me instructions. I thanked him and he saluted me again, took one step backwards, about turned, ordered his squad to about turn and then marched them away. Class superiority must have been so ingrained in him that he considered anyone speaking to him in a normal friendly manner must be his superior.

Hamilton is an elegant city of Old World charm and even today, I understand, its large British community retains its unique character expressing an almost extinct way of life. Its colonial architecture can still be admired in the buildings of the Cathedral and Sessions House.

As mentioned earlier, I was introduced to many wealthy Bermudian families who were a pleasure to be with, however, Andy the twenty eight year old son of one family whilst friendly, gave me the impression that he was a rather useless bum  who spent his whole life travelling throughout the world as an amateur painter, selling little, giving little.

His family lived in a palatial villa on the harbour side of Hamilton with a yacht tied up alongside their personal jetty.

One day whilst visiting this family with my friend Julia, an attractive barque sailed in and anchored about a mile out in the bay. I'd never seen a ship like this before and was enraptured by its elegance and grace so I decided to swim out to it and have a closer look.

It was crewed mainly by college students who had signed on as crew to gain experience during their vacation. I swam to the ship and the owners invited me on board, showed me around and we enjoyed a cool drink together before I dived back into the sea to return to the Island.

By this time the sky had clouded over and the sea had become quite choppy with the tide turning against me. I was a strong swimmer so there was no problem until I met the son, Andy, struggling towards me on a lilo. The family had thought I was in trouble because they could no longer see me due to the rising sea swell and the change in the weather. Andy, who hated the water and couldn't swim, had overcome his fear so that he could help me. When we met in the sea, he was totally exhausted so I put him onto the lilo and pushed him the half mile back to shore by which time I was worn out but most impressed by this young man; Andy was not just a soft amateur artist but a chap with real guts. On shore, a doctor was waiting for us. What a wonderful family!

Julia and I spent many friendly off duty hours with our Royal Navy friends, a really great crowd but all good things must come to an end. The night before the Squadron was due to depart for Canada, Julia's friends invited us to a farewell party held in their Mess on board ship. There were about twelve in our party including the aforementioned Second Lieutenant of our uniform tailoring episode. One of the junior naval officers said to me "Maurice, it's been good to have you here but we know very little about you. What are you and what do you do on the Squadron?" I replied, "I'm a signaller covering radar and communications but my specialty is in undersea submarine detection with sonar". He then asked, "Yes, we know that but what is your rank?" I replied, "I'm a Flight Sergeant." He was horrified, and then said to me "You are non commissioned. Do you realise how privileged you are and what benefits you are getting being able to mix with your betters?"

I burst out laughing and, to give them credit, his senior colleagues told him to "Shut up, he's our friend" in no uncertain terms and our very pleasant evening continued although the young Army Second Lieutenant did look rather sick remembering how he had treated me with such respect at our first meeting.

The party was a great send off and at a later date I was able to assure the Chief Constable how well his daughter had integrated into the high society of Bermuda.

Fortunately for me, discipline amongst aircrew was due more to trust and mutual respect than rank. When I first joined the RAF, the pilot of an aircraft was the captain regardless of rank and I have often flown with a crew, which included officers of quite senior ranks, however, if the pilot was a senior NCO, he was the Captain, and gave the orders and took the decisions. Sadly this has changed.

On the 27th June we somewhat reluctantly left our American friends and took off for the fifteen hundred mile trip to Nova Scotia to join our Canadian Air Force counterparts at the RCAF Base at Greenwood where senior military staff from both sides of the Atlantic were to meet for discussions on the different tactics within their own operational theatres whilst our Squadron carried out various exercises with the Canadian Navy.

We had a good flight to Canada, flying over the length of the USA and taking photographs of many interesting sights. One particular USAF Base had such massive runways it was capable of accommodating three Super Strategic Bombers in line abreast for take-off. We also passed over the Everglades of Nova Scotia, a wonderful but frightening wilderness area where it would be truly unhealthy to suffer a forced landing.

As the Squadron landed at the RCAF Greenwood Base, my aircraft was ordered to a specific parking slot. A stretch limousine drew up alongside the aircraft and our Squadron C.O. contacted me over the intercom and said that a Mr Tom Calhoun, Head of the Nova Scotia Light and Power Company, had requested that I be released from duty so I could stay with his family. It appeared Mr Calhoun was a very important man and had known my brother. I had written to him to say that I hoped I would be able to meet him to thank him for the kindness he had shown to Phil during the war but I didn't expect a holiday. The C.O. said that as a goodwill gesture and a matter of diplomacy, I should stay with Mr Calhoun for the length of our stay. I was more than happy to comply and only had to telephone the base each day to enquire when I had to return to the Squadron.

Tom and his wife turned out to be a lovely couple. Their home was in the town of Kentville but they took me to their impressive summer log cabin where we spent our time canoeing, fishing and shooting. They warned me not to let my hands trail over the side of the canoe as there was an abundance of poisonous water snakes. They also took me to visit various local tourist sites – one was the relic of an old fort used in the 1700-1800s for refuge from the Mikmaq Indians. We drove to Halifax, a thriving city a hundred miles across the other side of the Peninsular to meet more of the Calhoun Clan.

Apparently Tom and his wife always lived in the cabin during the hot summer and he conducted all essential business over the telephone, visiting his office only when his secretary called to say his signature was required. Tom's main disappointment in life was that his only son had left university to get married just six months before taking his finals for a forestry degree. He had given up the prospect of a degree because the university didn't accept married students.

Tom's son, Bob, then bought a large house, a massive concrete mixer vehicle and started his own business, all on the never-never. But how different is that from getting a Bank loan to start a business?

When I was there, he had been operating for a year and was doing well but working a sixteen-hour day, however, Bob was a chip off the old block; his father was a self made man who started as an electrical engineer and had reached the peak of his profession. Before I left, Tom very kindly suggested that when I finished my contract with the RAF I should immigrate to Canada when he would find me a position.

I was finally ordered to leave this wonderful family who had treated me so well and return to the Squadron where we all enjoyed a wild last night party at Greenwood RCAF base. The whole trip had been an incredible experience and we parted leaving behind many new friends.

36 Squadron's detachment ended on 6th July when we took off for the four hundred and fifty mile flight to our overnight stop in Newfoundland which was rather desolate with a somewhat violent, windy and rain swept landscape but the people there were friendly and helpful. The next morning, with a maximum fuel load for our

long two thousand and one hundred and fifty mile trip back home, our take off was again rather hairy but this time caused by the heavy driving rain, strong side winds and very poor visibility that worsened all the way across the Atlantic.

As we approached Ireland, we had to advise both the Shannon Air Traffic Control and our Base of our Irish landfall and estimated time of arrival but none of our aircraft could achieve contact. I persevered but with little success until we were about a hundred miles off the Irish coast. The weather was still atrocious and affecting all Squadron aircraft when I managed to raise contact with an American Air Force Strata Cruiser. He called me asking if I was Air Force 553 and I replied, "No, this is Royal Air Force 553 and I'm having trouble raising Shannon." He came back and offered to relay our arrival times to Shannon Air Traffic Control so they could be passed on to RAF Topcliffe. I gratefully accepted the offer, advised the Squadron that I was now in contact and acting as a call centre. After all the details had been passed to Base, we had a friendly exchange and I asked our American friend where he was. He told me that he was in a USAAF Strata Cruiser flying over Miami on course back to his base in the States. Amazing! He was more than four thousand miles away yet able to enjoy excellent worldwide communications. I thanked him and we all landed safely.

Destroyer/Neptune co-operation: As I had excelled in the use of anti submarine sonar detection and identification of submarine propeller sounds hiding under merchant ships, our CO volunteered me to join a destroyer for a two day exercise to compare techniques. When I joined the ship I was invited into the Petty Officers' Mess where lunch was being served just as we got under way. These hospitable chaps offered me sippers of rum. I explained that I didn't drink but took a small sip to be polite. It was my downfall. The rum didn't taste like alcohol. It was so smooth, without any bite, really delightful.

I cannot remember the next thirty hours; I was out cold, unrevivable. They told me I had enjoyed a very hot curry (my most disliked dish) before passing out. I woke up the next day, as we were re-entering port. For the first time in my life I had not been my usual sober self. Neither the ship's Captain nor my Squadron CO were too impressed with my performance.

Chapter 7 – Manslaughter at London Airport

I was posted back to Bomber Command HQ Signals Unit at High Wycombe where the V Bomber Force was being developed as one of the main arms of British defence strategy. The British manufacturers had produced three different types of aircraft.

The Valiant B1, which first flew in 1951 and entered service in June 1954 at RAF Gaydon with 232 Operational Conversion Unit followed by the Avro Vulcan and the HP Victor in 1952. Later in 1956 RAF Marham and RAF Honington were prepared to accommodate V-Force operations and five more Valiant Squadrons were formed. These aircraft, combined with the introduction of in-

flight refuelling (by using a modified Valiant bomber carrying a refuelling pack in its bomb bay so that it acted like an airborne tanker) gave our V bombers tremendous endurance and brought almost any belligerent target within range thereby making our V Force a major deterrent against war.

I found my work at Bomber Command very rewarding and I also enjoyed the social delights of the surrounding area. I was fortunate to find one of my closest friends, Sgt. Paddy Moore, had been transferred to serve in my team. Paddy, his wife Lorna and their two small children had settled in private accommodation in the local village where we made good friends with members of the

Cricket Club. Although I didn't play, the Club had a very active social life which included frequent dance nights, and as many of the husbands didn't dance, I was never without good partners.

Following the successful deployment of the V Force, the Air Ministry decided to impress the world with a dramatic exhibition of the Vulcan's capabilities. Air Vice Marshall Broadhurst, Commander in Chief of RAF Bomber Command, took a Vulcan XA897 and a full crew on a round the world tour. The last leg was to be a dramatic non-stop flight from Australia to London which was only made possible by the use of air refuelling. This was a momentous task, with its final landing to be at London Heathrow Civil Airport where the crew were to attend a grand reception and receive the well-deserved approbation of a large assembly of aviation media experts and distinguished guests.

On the 1st of October 1956, the morning of the Vulcan's return flight, the weather at Heathrow was atrocious with extremely poor visibility. Unfortunately, at that time, the RAF Vulcan B1 XA897 was not equipped to use the Civil Instrument Landing Systems installed at London airport. Additionally, the official pilot, Squadron Leader Howard, had no experience of carrying out a GCA (ground control approach) landing in a Vulcan.

The Air Ministry considered that with zero visibility at ground level at London Airport, a ground control approach (GCA) was not possible and I was told to have a "Class A" Diversion transmitted to the aircraft which ordered Sqd Ldr Howard (the official pilot) to divert to a named alternative airfield. The signal was sent, received and acknowledged by the Vulcan's Air Electronics Officer.

It should be noted that due to the appalling weather three Russian TU-104 jets bringing the Bolshoi Ballet group to London had already been forced to divert 70 miles away from London and land at the U.S. Air Force base at Manston.

By mid morning, about forty minutes before the Vulcan's estimated time of arrival, we had still not received notification from the aircraft that it intended to divert. The weather at London Airport was still considered to be impossible for landing and was worsening.

Again I was ordered to send a "Class A" Diversion Order to the aircraft and yet again, it was transmitted, received and acknowledged.

Note: An RAF pilot cannot refuse a "Class A" Diversion Order. It is mandatory. Failure to divert was a Court Martial offence.

Just minutes, ten at the most before the attempted landing, the Air Ministry Operations Centre were extremely worried they had not received notification of the aircraft's intention to divert and the name of the intended diversion airfield.

I was once again ordered to re-transmit the "Class A" Diversion order. As before, the order was transmitted and again the aircraft's Electronic Officer, Sqdn/Ldr Gamble, acknowledged receipt of the order.

What must have been Sqdn/Ldr Gamble's thoughts when AVM Broadhurst again refused to accept this direct order from Bomber Command HQ.

Radar showed that it was obvious that all of the diversion commands were being ignored by both pilots.

Without proper guidance from the pilot, the aircraft struck the ground about two thousand feet short of the runway. The pilot attempted to apply power and go round once more but the damage sustained on the initial impact was too great. As the aircraft rose into the air again, the Pilots Howard and Broadhurst ejected from the aircraft and landed safely. The pilotless aircraft then fell sideways and dived into the ground, breaking up in a fireball. There were no survivors.

When my fellow flyers and I heard that the Vulcan had crashed, killing the four rear crew members whilst the pilots ejected, we were horrified. Most of us loudly condemned Broadhurst for his total lack of thought for his crew, however, we were immediately ordered that the incident was not to be discussed with anyone outside the Bomber Command Headquarters Operations Room.

I was so incensed that I telephoned a newspaper with the facts but an Editor, asking for confirmation of the story, called back to HQ Bomber Command. Consequently the Commanding Officer threatened me with a Court Martial for contacting the newspaper and immediately a 'D' Notice was issued to all media which prevented any reporting of the true facts for fifty years.

Together with some of my colleagues, I later saw a film of the crash which showed the aircraft was still trying to climb away from the runway when the pilots left the aircraft - without ejection seats, the rear crew had no chance of survival.

NEWS HEADLINE ON 1st October 1956 read: "Vulcan V Bomber Crashes at London Airport "

Air Vice Marshal Broadhurst, Commander in Chief of Bomber Command was one of the Second World War's celebrated airmen but his refusal to divert was criminal. Even more so was his claim that it was solely Sqd Ldr Howard's decision to attempt a landing. (What junior officer would ignore three direct orders to divert?). AVM Broadhurst killed his crew by glory seeking and should have been Court Martialled but instead he and his official pilot were promoted.

Sqd Ldr Edward Eames, Sqd Ldr Stroud, Sqd Ldr Albert Gamble and Mr Frederick Bassett of A.V. Roe & Co. having no ejection seats, were given no chance to escape and were killed.

The Air Traffic Controller was partly blamed for this disaster and his reputation ruined over an action which should not have taken place and over which he had no control. His life was damaged to satisfy the ego of one man. His family should be compensated.

The families of the crew should be told the truth.

Class A Diversion Orders: I and any sane RAF aircrew member will confirm that no aircraft captain would hazard his crew, aircraft and his career by disobeying just one "Class A" Diversion Order.

Despite my protests, my statement was not recorded and the true facts were not allowed to be included in the Crash Enquiry Report. It appears obvious that Sqd Ldr Howard was either overruled or coerced into ignoring all three Diversion Orders by AVM Broadhurst who was determined to receive the plaudits of the prestigious gathering of dignitaries and media pundits waiting his return at the London Airport reception.

Did they face a Court Martial? No. The Air Vice Marshall was appointed to NATO and the Squadron Leader was promoted to Wing Commander.

The Air Ministry should be made to acknowledge the following true facts and the records of these Flyers and the Air Traffic Controller put right.

Fact 1. Three "Class A" Diversion Orders were sent, received and acknowledged by the Crew.

Fact 2. Mr Birch, the Secretary of State for Air, did not mention the Diversion Orders in the report made to the House of Commons on the 20th August and they were not mentioned when Mr Birch was asked the direct question "Should the aircraft not have been diverted?"

Fact 3. The Diversion Orders were also not mentioned when Mr C I Orr-Ewing M.P raised the question in the House asking about the "Advisability of diverting military aircraft flying in such poor weather conditions." He also asked, "Should it not have been diverted?"

Fact 4. Totally ignored was the fact that Squadron Leader Howard had never practised a full Ground Controlled Approach (GCA) in a Vulcan or practiced landing approaches using the Instrument Landing System (ILS) in a Vulcan or any similar type of aircraft.

I draw your attention to the following statement, which has since been released on the Internet.

I strongly believe if Captain Hunt had known that the Pilot of the Vulcan had received three "Class A" Diversion Orders, which had been acknowledged and ignored, he would have had no option but to declare both Pilots totally responsible for the disaster and the Air Traffic Controller devoid of all responsibility.

What is even more amazing is the fact that Broadhurst wrote a letter to the Board of Enquiry accusing Howard of full responsibility.

If his letter was to be believed, Sqd Ldr Howard was fully responsible for four deaths and the loss of the aircraft by disobeying three direct orders to divert. Why then did Broadhurst use his influence to get Howard promoted?

Few aircrew members serving at the time ever believed Broadhurst's excuses and afterwards when he was present at RAF receptions he was frequently shunned and even booed by serving aircrew personnel.

The above facts can be corroborated by the Radio Operator who sent the diversion messages who, after retiring from the RAF, enjoyed a long and well-respected career in civil aviation.

Chapter 8 -Tragedy at the Mull of Kintyre (Angel 7)

Following my confrontation with Bomber Command over the Vulcan crash, I was immediately ordered to report back to RAF Topcliffe and to re-join 36 Squadron and my crew. We were told to prepare for a six-week detachment to HMS Sea Eagle in Londonderry, Ireland where we were to take part in a NATO anti-submarine exercise.

We all looked forward to this return visit to the Navy barracks where there was friendly rivalry between the two services. On the 5th October the Squadron, under the command of Sqd Ldr P.R.Godby took off in the early morning and landed at Ballykelly from where we were transported to the Navy Base accommodation 'Sea Eagle'.

On the third day of our visit, after some rather boring lectures, we lads decided to take part in two of the Navy's unusual customs.

1. HMS Sea Eagle was a Navy Shore Base without a spot of water in sight - not so much as a moat, however, before you could cross the road, enter or leave the barracks, you had to wait for the Ferry or the Liberty boat which was actually authorisation to cross the road. This was too much for us, so after returning from a late night out, twelve of us stepped into a fantasized boat, cast off and all facing backwards and waving our arms as though we were pulling oars, rowed across the road shouting "Ahoy shipmates, can we come aboard?" and then we all saluted the flag as we marched past the gates. We achieved confusion from the Guard Duty Platoon because the ferry hadn't been authorised.

2. The Naval Officers had adopted a particular dress fashion - when off duty in mufti they had taken to wearing flat caps and the armed Entrance Guard Detail was expected to recognize this affectation by offering anyone so dressed a 'Present Arms' salute. Excellent custom we agreed, so we senior RAF NCOs bought flat caps which resulted in no one knowing who to salute. Stupid, but it gave us some amusement.

On the 10th October we attended a detailed inter-service briefing explaining how the joint Navy/RAF anti submarine operation was to be controlled and how the RAF anti submarine detection exercise was to be conducted.

An Admiral was in overall command and addressed a briefing of all the NATO services involved. He made a special point to all the

RAF Squadron Air Crews about aircraft safety. He said that despite the bad weather, blanketing fog and heavy rain clouds which were giving very poor visibility, he knew that the air crews wanted to detect and catch the submarines, however, he continued, despite the fact that the subs have anti aircraft radar detection equipment, "All RAF Aircrew are to use their hazard radar detection intermittently as a safety measure, even within inshore waters."

He went on to say that it was essential to do this to avoid the danger posed by the notorious high mountainous crags of the Mull of Kintyre.

At the end of the briefing our Squadron Commanding Officer, Sqd Ldr Godby, ordered all Aircrew to remain seated. When only Aircrew remained he countermanded the Admiral's direct order stating, "Aircrew are not to use radar within the inshore waters." and stressed, "We are going to catch the submarines napping and teach the bloody Navy a lesson."

I was the senior Air Signaller of Flt.Lt. Finding's crew. Late in the evening of 10th October all the crew, including myself, went out to the Neptune MR1 (WX545) preparing for take off. As I entered the aircraft, I collapsed (apparently with flu) and was carried out and taken by ambulance to the Base Hospital.

'C Charlie' took off without me.

The following morning I was woken in hospital and told that my aircraft had crashed on the Mull of Kintyre and that all of my friends were dead. This crash was caused solely due to our C.O. countermanding the Admiral's order.

I was angry. Horrified to lose my crew due to one man's crass stupidity so as soon as I was discharged from the hospital, I confronted Sqd Ldr Godby and told him that he was a bloody murderer. I was once again threatened with a Court Martial and told to be silent and to leave matters to the Court of Enquiry.

As before, I telephoned a newspaper but once again, a 'D' Notice had been placed on all statements to the press. I was ignored.

The following week I was one of the pallbearers at the funeral service of my Crew held at Topcliffe Village Church. In memory of my Crew:

Flt Lt Geoffrey Finding, Captain
FO James Alexander Campbell, Co Pilot
FO Gilbert Rishton, Navigator
Sgt Cyril Armstrong, Flight Engineer
Flt Sgt Raymond Fox, Radio Operator
Flt Sgt Ronald Mark Noble, Air Signaller
Sgt Eric Honey, Air Signaller
Sgt Bernard Edward Lynn, Air Signaller
Sgt Roy Vincent Smith, Air Signaller.

Here follows the official Court of Enquiry crash report on Neptune MR1 (WX545) Code 'C' from 36 Squadron. See the typed version below.

The above report reads –

"Whilst carrying out an anti-submarine exercise the A/C flew into high ground and disintegrated killing all the crew. The aircraft caught fire on impact.

The court considers that responsibility for the accident must rest with the captain in that he ignored the safety of the aircraft by not taking reasonable precautions in the vicinity of high ground. The navigator may have made an error in his working or failed to have warned his captain in the immediate vicinity. Further more the Radar operator presumably did not report land contacts ahead, but then the Radar may have been switched off or at standby. The C in C is of the opinion that no court or authority can categorically state that the fatal accident was caused by pilot error.

Fire C-N- IFR-
The CinC considered that the positioning of the APS should be left to the pilot and that a fixed ruling in this respect should not be laid down. The court agreed that the J.A.S.S should advise Joint Unit courses that for Inshore waters activity the use of Radar is to be unrestricted when other means of accurate position fixing (visual or Electronics) are not available."

One can only understand the Court's decision when one appreciates that the truth was hidden from them - I was silent under threat of Court Martial.

However, my statement, relating to the orders given by the Admiral in charge of the exercise (which were overridden by Sqdn Ldr Godby) together with the following written statement by Sgt Jeff Jenks proves that the above Court of Enquiry report should be corrected and the true reason for the crash placed at the door of Sqdn. Ldr.Godby.

The survival of his aircraft was due solely to this Junior Radar Operator who became so stressed when the aircraft was lost in cloud that he disobeyed Sqd Ldr Godby's order - he used his radar and saw the aircraft was flying straight at the mountain and shouted a warning.

By taking violent action, his aircraft Captain only narrowly avoided crashing into the mountain.

Flt Lt Finding was not advised by radio of this near accident report because radio silence had been ordered. The enquiry was a white wash of the true events.

Statement by Sgt Jeff Jenks.

"I was a junior signaller on the Neptune which was the first to take off on the night of October 10th. Weather conditions were very poor, and as I understand it the exercise was devised by a scientist who was working with Coastal Command. The object of the exercise was to take off with radar switched on, and gain height until we detected a submarine which was lying submerged in the lee of the Mull, and then, after making a note of its position we were to switch off the radar, and maintain Radar/ radio silence throughout the experiment.

The aim was to see how near we could get to an attacking position, using instruments only, before the submarine detected our presence.

When we were in the vicinity of the submarine I had an awful premonition and surreptitiously switched on the radar and saw a large land mass ahead of us. I shouted to our pilot and he hauled back on the controls, taking evasive action, to such an extent that he lost the power of one engine. I switched off the radar again and we headed back to base observing the order to maintain radio silence. We landed and WX545 took off to repeat our exercise without having had any information passed to them about our near miss. I was only a junior signaller and didn't feel that I could have any say in the events.

To any interested party: -

I am willing to repeat under oath that Sqd Ldr Godby countermanded the Admiral's direct order and that he told all Air Crews they were to ignore the order. He stated categorically that we were not to use radar when over inshore waters.

Signed - Maurice R, Hamlin,
Ex RAF Flt Sgt Signaller 1943 to 1964

Over the years I have made many attempts to bring the truth to the media. Perhaps now that the 'D' Notice is over fifty years old and has expired and the facts are widely exposed, someone will make the truth known.

NATIONAL PRESS EDITORIAL COMMENT
"For many years the coastline of Kintyre and in particular the area around the Mull, has been known to pilots as a dangerous area to fly at low level because of the freak weather conditions that frequently affect the coastline. The first recorded military air accident on the Mull was in 1941 when an Armstrong Whitworth Whitley from No.502 Squadron crashed on the west slope of Beinn na Lice, no more than one tenth of a kilometre from the site of the Neptune crash. Since then there have been nineteen recorded air accidents in the vicinity of the Mull and over a hundred and twenty lives have been lost in this remote corner of Scotland making it one of the most notorious areas in the whole of the UK for air accidents."

Lt Geoffrey Finding and his crew died solely because they strictly followed the unlawful orders insisted upon by Sqd Ldr Godby, their Commanding Officer.

RAF HISTORICAL RECORDS
versus
THE HIDDEN TRUTH

Should history hide the truth of those responsible for the avoidable death of 13 RAF Aircrew?

Here follows the conclusion of my 60 year fight to obtain justice for those aircrew killed when Vulcan B1 XA897 crashed at London Airport on 1st October 1956 and Neptune C Charlie crashed on the Mull of Kintyre just ten days later.

Both of these accidents were caused by glory seeking officers acting unlawfully.

I claim that the truth is being covered up and recorded incorrectly by the RAF's Historical Records Unit. The fact that 'D' Notices were placed on both incidents cannot be ignored, despite there being no threat to National security. Also, why the 'gagging order' and threat of Court Martial against me for contacting the media?

Early in 2016 Mr Sebastian Cox, Director of the RAF Historical Records Unit of the Ministry of Defence, wrote to me objecting strongly to the way my autobiography -The Hidden Truth - explains the true cause of these accidents.

Remember, this was peacetime and both of the accidents were caused by senior RAF officers who showed total disregard for the safety of their aircrews.

The Director claims that his interpretation of the two official accident reports are historically correct and that no blame can be placed against anyone involved.

I emphatically disagree. I know the true facts. I was there.

The Vulcan Crash

Mr Cox rests his conclusions on the following statements:-

1. AVM Broadhurst stated that the decision to land at London Airport was the sole responsibility of Sqdn Ldr Howard who was the official pilot.

2. He said they had received approval by voice radio from the Group Captain i/c Bomber Command HQ Operations to make one try at a landing at London Airport.

3. Finally, he states that regardless of all other considerations, the pilot, as captain of an aircraft, always has the final authority as to where it will land.

Here are the true facts regarding responsibility for the crash -

1. The Court of Enquiry was not told that the Vulcan aircraft captain had been ordered three times to divert and that Sqdn Ldr Gamble, the aircraft's communications officer, had acknowledged receipt of the orders but both pilots refused to take action.

2. At the Court of Enquiry, a Member asked why the pilot was not advised to divert due to the terrible weather conditions. The question was ignored.

3. The Court was told that the pilots had not been trained to land a Vulcan using GCA. They were also told that Sqdn/Ldr Howard had set a break off glide-path height of 300 feet, but on approach went above the glide path by 80 feet and then over corrected and dropped 100 feet too low, believing he was still on the correct glide path. He then went even lower for the attempted landing and crashed.

Yet the Court still placed blame towards the ground controller.

4. Members of the Enquiry also asked whether or not the decision to land was coerced by AVM Broadhurst's wish to attend the massive media reception waiting to celebrate his arrival after the first ever Non-stop flight from Australia. No response was given.

5. Finally, Mr Cox ignores the fact that it was the Grp/Captain of HQBC who ordered me to send the diversion orders. (There is no question that any earlier voice communication made by Broadhurst could have overruled these direct orders.) All the diversion orders had been acknowledged by Sqdn/Ldr Gamble. The last one just before the crash.

Mr Cox (a civilian who was born the year the aircraft crashed) declares that I, one of the last persons directly in communication with the aircraft just minutes prior to the crash, am not eligible as a witness. Why? I may be 91years of age but my memory is clear and I am willing to take any manner of medical examination.

Neptune C Charlie Crash

Mr Cox disagrees with my explanation of the true facts leading up to the cause of the crash of Neptune C Charlie.

He admits that whilst I was the senior signaller of the crew of C Charlie and recorded all of the NATO Admiral in Command's orders stating that aircrew must use radar during the Squadron's in-shore attacks because of the atrocious weather. Also that I recorded the controversial orders given by the C.O. of 36 Squadron when he countermanded the Admiral's orders and said that "we must not use radar". I claim this amended order caused C Charlie to crash.
Mr Cox states "This is not evidence"

I was on board C Charlie until minutes before take-off on the night of 9th October but collapsed and was taken to hospital by ambulance. Mr Cox states that as I did not fly with the crashed aircraft, I could not be considered as a witness.
Likewise, he claims that Sgt Jeff Jenks (Radar Operator on the previous Neptune to fly that night, who gave a written statement describing how his unauthorised use of Radar on the earlier flight saved his aircraft and crew from crashing) could not be used as a witness of the true facts relating to the Admiral's orders being over-ridden by a junior officer.

After the crash, the official Court of Enquiry made the decision that the cause of the crash of C Charlie was "due to Pilot, Navigator or Radar operator error in NOT using Radar during in the in-shore water attack approach".

I'm convinced that Flt/Lt Finding followed his C.O's last illegal order too closely.
I would emphasise that Flt/Lt Finding was one of the best pilots I flew with and he saved our crew on several hazardous occasions.

Correction to cause of crash

I am now pleased to state that the C in C of Coastal Command, when shown the Court of Enquiry's decision against C Charlie's crew, emphatically disagreed with the Court's findings that the crew were responsible, and has changed the decision of the Court to **"Cause of crash, unknown"**.

Conclusion.

As you will read, no one will put the blame where it truly belongs - on the officer who countermanded the Admiral's orders.

Maurice R Hamlin. Ex Flt/Sgt - !943/64. I will not change history nor deny the true facts written in The Hidden Truth.

If any reader wishes to contact me I shall be pleased to respond.
Email – hamlinmaurice@gmail.com

Chapter 9 – Vulcans Can't Fly with Empty Tanks
(Angel 8)

1957, and I was once again posted to HQ Bomber Command Signals Unit at High Wycombe but first I travelled to Eastbourne to collect my daughter and take her for a two week holiday to stay with my friends Paddy and Lorna Moore. We had a great time together and Susan asked if she could live with me. Sadly I had to say it wasn't possible at that moment but she could come to me as soon as the Court allowed it.

Upon my return to Bomber Command HQ I was elected Sergeants' Mess Entertainments Manager for the period leading up to Christmas. It was a job I thoroughly enjoyed and some two months before Christmas I began planning the raffle, selling tickets and approaching local businesses for prizes. We sold almost two thousand tickets and accumulated and bought over one hundred very good prizes.

My friends and I had been offering invitations to the Christmas Ball to every attractive female we met and on Christmas Eve free busses were provided to accommodate the many guests from Princess Risborough, High Wycombe and the local villages. Everyone agreed it was a great success.

In July I went to Eastbourne to surprise my daughter on her eighth birthday but on arrival I found turmoil. My wife was in bed saying she was very ill and Betty and Everard, good neighbours, were looking after Susan. My wife then said she had changed her mind and didn't want a divorce. I wasn't too kind and said that there was no chance and walked away but at that moment, there was a knock on the front door. It was a policeman who said it had been reported that someone at this address had taken an overdose of drugs. It later transpired that my wife had actually made the call herself as a safety measure.

I had almost convinced the Policeman that my wife had not actually taken an overdose and that she was just being over dramatic when there was the sound of a heavy thud from upstairs. We rushed up to her room and found she had thrown herself out of the bed and was lying on the floor. I was not sympathetic and just lifted her up and put her back into the bed. The Policeman said it was more than his job was worth to leave her and he sent for an ambulance. She was taken off to hospital and the Policeman asked if I would report to Inspector Pugh at the Central Police Station.

I went to the next-door neighbours and asked Betty if she would get Susan ready for me whilst I visited the Police. The Inspector, who knew my family, told me that my wife was being retained in hospital and asked if I would remain in Eastbourne whilst matters were settled. Tongue in cheek I assured him that I would do so, however, I planned a hasty retreat. I returned to Betty and told her that I couldn't leave my eight year old daughter in the middle of so much stress and that I was taking Susan with me for good and would keep her informed. I packed Susan's clothes and we left by train having first telephoned and advised my wife's sister what had happened; Vera was a very understanding lady and agreed that my action was for the best. We travelled by train to High Wycombe and then to my friends, Paddy and Lorna, who immediately said I could leave Susan with them until I got settled. I then reapplied for divorce and custody.

One evening in July I went to a dance in High Wycombe and returned to the Base after midnight. Purely by chance I called into the HQ Signals Centre for a cup of tea and to see how communications were going but I had only been there a few minutes when one of the Radio Operators called me over and said, "I have a Vulcan bomber calling for help in CW (Morse code). The pilot says he's at thirty thousand feet, has lost VHF communications and that his navigational instruments are dead. He's lost and his fuel gauges are showing empty "Can we help?"

I immediately told the operator to advise the pilot to start descending to twenty thousand feet and await instructions. I 'phoned Air Traffic Control at RAF Wittering, told them about the problem and said I was giving the pilot orders to descend and was now going to tell him to make ninety degree turns to starboard to allow the radar to identify him. Air Traffic radar identified him and with me acting as an in-between Air Traffic Controller, we enabled the Pilot to control his decent and direction and finally, when he advised, "in sight of airfield" I passed him instructions for a safe emergency landing.

This was accomplished within a very short time and we were all delighted when we heard he was safely on the ground.

Before leaving to go to bed I received a telephone call from the

'V' Bomber's Pilot saying how thankful his crew were that I had been on duty as they had landed with only fumes in the tank. Next, just as I was going out of the door, the telephone rang again. It was RAF Wittering's Station Wing Commander in Charge of Flying calling to say what wonderful initiative I had shown and thanking me heartily. I went off to bed smiling.

The next morning when I went on duty, I was told to report to the Senior Operations Officer HQBC. He accused me of acting irresponsibly the night before and without authority and warned me that my actions would be considered for a Court Martial. I was amazed. I told him heatedly that because I was aircrew, I had the immediate knowledge that had been necessary at the time. I also stated that if I had taken the time to find the Night Duty Officer (who was probably a wingless wonder) and would most likely have needed to refer to someone else for instructions and then follow the normal laid down procedure, the aircraft would have crashed. I asked what he would have preferred to happen? I told him quite forcefully that his interpretation of the incident was totally opposite to that of the pilot of the aircraft and the Wing Commander in Charge of Flying at Wittering and added that he could do what he liked but I would not take it quietly. I think in my anger I was perhaps somewhat blunt. Nothing more was said but at a later date when I was put forward for promotion, the Selection Board's response was "This man's records show he is unamenable to discipline."

On the 1st April I was posted to RAF Shawbury. Due to the shortage of pilots I served as a safety pilot on Vampire jet aircraft whilst we

were acting as targets in Landing Approach Procedures for trainee Air Traffic Controllers. This posting turned out to be the happiest time of my service career and gave me a great deal of small plane piloting experience which was very different from flying a Neptune.

The village of Shawbury is near the fine medieval market town of Shrewsbury in the County of Shropshire. Charles Darwin was born and educated there and it is famous for having six hundred listed buildings including the Castle which houses a regimental museum. It is also the site of the world famous Shrewsbury Abbey, the suggested home of the  twelfth century fictional Welsh Benedictine monk detective, Brother Cadfael, who is one of my favourite reads and was the Sherlock Holmes of the period. It's an interesting and relaxing place to visit with the River Severn looping around the town centre, offering pleasant riverside walks.

Taking care of Susan was my first priority and my most immediate problem was to find a suitable home for her whilst I tried to obtain a house of my own so that my Mother could come and live with us. Fortunately I found temporary accommodation for Susan with a nice couple and their young son in Shawbury village. They owned the local sweet shop and cafeteria and treated her very well.

By this time, I had been given full custody of my daughter but had agreed that she should go on visiting holidays to see her Mother in Eastbourne provided she stayed with, and under the control of, her Aunt Vera (her mother's very caring and able older sister). This worked out well and I believe she was a happy child.

Life within a Squadron is rather like a close knit family and morale, to a great degree, depends on its Commanding Officer as proven by our C.O., Squadron Leader Munday, an extremely professional and understanding man. He and his wife had heard of my family problem, talked it over and said they would be pleased to take Susan to live with them as part of their family until my own married quarters were allocated. Susan was with them for many months and I cannot speak too highly of how well they looked after her.

In March 1960 I was at last allocated married quarters and my Mother moved from Eastbourne to help to take care of Susan. Life was good but my duties meant I couldn't always be on hand for Sue, however, Mum was always there and although she was seventy-five years old, she was very active and Susan was delighted as Mum was a favourite of hers.

I learned to cook and often exchanged the crew's flying rations for eggs, butter and flour and made apple or lemon meringue pies, bread pudding, etc. for the Squadron tuck box. I remember baking apple pies one weekend when I was Duty Station NCO and the fire alarm sounded. I dashed off to see the cause of the alarm and found there was no major problem, however, I created a bit of a laugh by arriving with white flour finger marks on my hat.

I bought an Alsatian puppy called Tanya to take care of Sue and the dog became the Squadron mascot. It was my first experience of dog training and although Tanya was exceedingly friendly, she was highly protective of both Susan and the car. I didn't appreciate quite how well I had trained this dog or how strong were her inbred instincts until one day when I was in the Squadron Crew Room waiting for my next flight when a friend called "Crazy Horse" (he was another second pilot but was also an honorary Sioux Indian Chief) was chasing Tanya round the Crew Room's table tennis table chanting "Guard dog. She's a pussy cat!" Without thinking I snapped, "Seize him" and the dog instantly turned and leaped at Crazy Horse, pushed him to the floor and stood on his chest growling. What a shock! I hastily said, "Good girl Tanya, leave." She then licked Crazy Horse's face but after that he was always respectful of the dog and I was always more careful of my instructions.

Another of my oldest and best friends, Sergeant Collin Carpenter and his wife Micheline joined me at Shawbury. Collin was serving on the Meteor jets but this was very dangerous for him because he was so tall that no matter how he sat in the aircraft cockpit, his head was always pressed hard at an odd angle against the canopy. Every trip caused him great discomfort and any hard landing could have caused him a major injury. The Medical Officer got involved and Collin was transferred over to the Vampire Squadron.

Susan was taking a short horse-riding holiday with the family of one of her school friends. Bob Owen and his wife lived in a country village near Whitchurch and as the weather was so perfect Mother and I had been invited over to spend the Saturday with them. Bob was a police dog handler, quite distinguished, as he had been instrumental, with the help of his Doberman, in capturing a murderer known as the Mad Poet.

On the drive there, my Mother and Tanya the Alsatian sat in the back of the Bedford conversion. The area was new to me and I drove on a long, straight, upward sloping road closely lined with bushes and tall trees. All was well until there was a flash of colour in front of me and the car twisted, skidded and rolled over.

When I came to, the van was upside down facing back the way we had come from and with the engine still running. I quickly turned it off, crawled out and searched for Mum. I found that she had had a very lucky escape as she had been sandwiched safely between the dual mattresses of my Bedford's bed conversion and had only a tiny bruise on her nose caused by a flying object. Although she was quite old, she was amazingly calm. The dog had disappeared.
This was my Angel's 8th visit.

The accident happened because at the top of the long, slight hill there was a cross roads of which I was unaware. The flash of colour I had seen was another car and I had hit the back end of it as it passed. The car suffered considerable damage and the passengers were injured. Ambulances arrived on the scene very quickly and my Mother and all of the car passengers were taken to hospital. Mother was hospitalized for three days, as the doctor was worried about her having delayed shock.

I walked back past the cross roads to look at the approach road

94

and found that due to the bushes, high trees and the contours of the land, it was impossible to see that there was a main road ahead. I crossed over to the hedge on the left and uncovered a signpost completely hidden by overgrown bushes. I found Tanya and then collapsed with fractured ribs. Subsequently I was charged with dangerous driving but it was two days before I could return to the scene of the accident with my camera where I discovered that bushes had been cut back but even so, it was still difficult to see the signpost clearly.

A month later when the prosecution came to Court, I explained the problem but a Police Inspector produced photographs showing the sign post to be at least a yard clear of all obstruction. I protested and showed my photographs, which were dated and showed the post was obstructed, however, the Inspector insisted I had been responsible for dangerous driving.

A Constable who had been on duty at the time was called and he restored my faith in the average copper because, even under strong pressure from his Inspector, he reiterated that if the sign was obscured, the road layout gave no indication that cross roads were ahead. The Magistrate asked if I would accept his judgment. I agreed, and was found guilty of driving without due care and attention but there was no fine. The Inspector was not happy.

The next day I once again went out to see the crash site and found that, as well as cutting back the bushes, the Council had actually moved the sign post several feet towards the road. The Police photographs had shown this rearranged scene with the signpost glaringly visible.

On the 27th July 1960, after years of trying and three High Court cases, I obtained my divorce and was granted full custody of Susan.

I won't say that I had denied myself female company whilst waiting but the one person who stands out most was Joyce of Princes Risborough, a great dancer, tall, intelligent and attractive girl from a friendly family. Joyce and I had seriously considered a future together but the Church put a stop to any serious intentions. She had been over indoctrinated and it had been drummed into her that once someone had been married by the Church, there was no way that person could ever be recognised as being truly divorced, regardless of circumstances and it was impossible for that person to legally be remarried and blessed in church. Joyce could never consider marrying such a person when her local Church would not accept its legality.

Following the above episode and my years of trying and finally obtaining a divorce, my beliefs in the Law and in the attitude of the Church had crystallized into a jaundiced non-belief. From then on I also considered the opposite sex to be fair game and thought I would, in future, have no strings.

Chapter 10 - The RAF Plays Cupid and an Indian Adventure

Late that August I took part in another NATO Exercise and whilst flying at ten thousand feet I received an order by radio to divert to RAF Scampton near Lincoln. When we landed we were told we would not be taking off again until 07.30 the next morning so five of us decided to explore the City of Lincoln, a place I had not previously visited.

It was Friday night and we discovered that a dance was being held at the Assembly Rooms in Lincoln. When we entered the ballroom we were greeted by dance music from the Glen Miller era which boded well. Sitting back from the crowd, almost hiding, was an exquisite looking girl with a shape to make my Guardian Angel sigh. The five of us went up to her and asked her to dance and as I was in the centre, she chose me. That was it. Her name was JayeZara. She was a superb dancer and we danced every number until the last waltz, saying very few words. I put her in a taxi and said goodbye to her thinking she was a lovely girl but I knew we would be leaving Scampton in seven hours' time. I thought it was a pity but that's life!

The next morning we took off as scheduled but hadn't been flying long when we were once again ordered to divert back to RAF Scampton. When we landed we were told we would be there until Tuesday. I borrowed a razor, spruced up as much as possible (we had not expected an overnight stop) and caught the 'bus to Lincoln.

Happily I remembered the name of the road Jaye had given to the taxi driver the night before so I walked along the road calling at houses and asking if anyone knew a JayeZara until someone pointed me to the correct house. I rang the bell and a large lady with a non-too friendly look on her face (the reason for which I was to understand at a later date) answered the door. I asked for Jaye but before she could reply, a deep voice from inside the house called in a very friendly manner "Come in old lad." Her father, a very nice fellow, said I had better go into the garden as she was working there.

Jaye didn't look as sophisticated as she had the night before; she was in trousers and wore her long hair in a ponytail. She gave me a big embarrassed smile because her hands were in a bucket of fertilizer; she was building a mushroom bed. I thought she looked delightful and we spent a wonderful day together. We also spent Sunday together and I arranged to call for her after she finished work

97

the following day.

It was crazy considering my earlier convictions regarding women but I think it was then that my concept of the fairer sex reverted back. Jaye was the most desirable women I had ever met and was extremely intelligent. I later discovered she was earning twice my flying pay and was a highly qualified verbatim conference writer. I gradually learnt a little more about my new bird - she had had to fight TB as a child and only survived peritonitis in 1944 when the Army heard she was dying and supplied one of the earliest Penicillin doses to a civilian during the War.

At the time Jaye left school, Policemen could only communicate with their Police Station by using specially situated Blue Telephone boxes. They were just about to experiment with radio phones in police cars. Jaye answered an advertisement for Trainee Radio Operators and was chosen out of very many applicants, due to the clarity and lack of accent in her voice, to become one of the first but the youngest police Radio Operator at the Lincolnshire Constabulary. Later she specialised as a PA with verbatim shorthand.

On the Monday afternoon I once again travelled to Lincoln, bought the biggest bunch of Gladioli I could find (over three feet tall) and waited for her outside her business premises. I received strange looks from some of the girls and on the overcrowded bus on the way to her house I had difficulty protecting the giant flowers from damage. We spent another very enjoyable evening and Jaye agreed that as soon as we could both arrange a holiday, she would come with me to visit my very good friends Colin and Mich Carpenter who had retired from the RAF and were living in Ipswich.

After I returned to Base at RAF Shawbury we wrote and kept in touch by telephone and the fascination deepened. My Mother was very supportive and assured me that she and Sue could manage all right on their own so Jaye and I arranged our holiday for early

September.

The holiday was a wonderful and life changing time. On the drive there, we bought a basket of strawberries and a pot of cream and whilst we were sitting in a lay-by, feeding each other, a heavy goods vehicle pulled off the road. The driver gave us a look of disbelief and proceeded to eat his elevenses. Smiling, I took him a portion of strawberries.

We were smitten and couldn't take our eyes off each other, so much so that fifty miles later when I stopped on a hill at traffic lights, I eased my foot off the brake so that the car rolled forward and bumped into the back of the lorry in front of us. The driver looked at us through his driving mirror, shook his head, grinned and drove off. It was the same man we had met in the lay-by earlier that day.

When we arrived at my friends' house, Micheline came out, took one look at our faces and asked if she had to go to all the bother of making up separate beds. Jaye blushed, I made no comment but we enjoyed every moment of a superb holiday.

Having totally overcome my previous cynicism regarding women and marriage I invited Jaye down to Shawbury to meet Mum and Sue. They immediately took to each other and Jaye and Susan soon became great friends. I remember Mum saying, "She is very nice but so very modern."

Jaye also remembers that during their first meeting, my Mother had asked her if she liked dancing and when Jaye replied that she did, she was asked "And does he always sing whilst he's dancing?" When Jaye confirmed that he did, Mum replied "Oh! You poor child."

To this day I have a problem with rhythm, it seems to be part of me and just hearing a few odd notes so easily awakes the memory of a song. I just have to sing; my love of dancing must be linked to my psyche and my attitude to life. I sing wherever I am.

Unfortunately with advancing age, I've lost the top and bottom registers.

Some friends consider it to be an affliction, especially when we play cards but Jaye has always encouraged me to sing - we are obviously Soul Mates.

In October 1961 I volunteered to travel to India and help to fly back a Dove aircraft in sore need of a major overhaul as the Air Attaché for India and the Middle East had used it for liaison flights for no less than six years. It was too good an experience to miss. For the return flight, the Air Attaché (a Squadron Leader) was to be Captain of the aircraft accompanied by a Navigator with me as Communications and Second Pilot.

For this trip I had been promoted temporarily to Pilot Officer, without pay, and given a passport to prove it together with a Gooly Chit worth £1000 pounds sterling. This Chit was a document written in several Arabic languages, which could be used in case of accident or forced landing. It promised that anyone who gave the bearer assistance and returned him alive and unharmed to any British Embassy would receive a one thousand pound reward without question. We would be flying over some of the most rugged country where the native Arab tribesmen were at war with both the French forces and the French expat farmers who themselves treated any captured rebel tribesmen like animals. This Chit was necessary if we were forced to make an emergency landing amongst these unfriendly people as life would be very short lived particularly if they thought we were French or less than an officer.

Initially I flew out to Aden which took fourteen hours in an RAF Transport Command Avro York. It was a transport derivative of the Lancaster Bomber and a true workhorse which, during the 1948 Berlin Airlift, had carried out more than fifty-eight thousand sorties. Its wings gave concern to the unaccustomed air traveller because they flapped up and down more than any other aircraft I'd known; personally I thought it looked like a flying cartoon.

Much of the trip was over Ethiopia and I had not before appreciated what a variable landscape it had. We flew hour after hour over high hills, rugged rocks and sand. When we landed at Benina for a fuel stop, we were surrounded by farmland.

Then on to Aden, an unimpressive place, for an overnight stop at the Red Sea House in Maala.

The following day we boarded a Britannia for the last leg of our journey to Karachi.

We were received most graciously in Karachi and given accommodation at Boca's Speedbird House, the best hotel in the city with beautiful accommodation, excellent cuisine, immaculate service, breakfast in bed, shoes cleaned and suit pressed. I sent a 'Wish you were here' card to Jaye.

I met the Attaché and George the Navigator, an old acquaintance, and was accepted as a guest at the Embassy where the Ambassador's wife, a delightful lady, took me under her wing and spent a lot of time showing me the sights of the city. We were invited to an Embassy cocktail reception and taken to the Sindh Club, which is an exclusive place for wealthy Europeans and elite members of Pakistani society; you are only allowed into the Club wearing formal dress but I was given special  dispensation as I was in transit. Also, as a guest, you were not allowed to pay for anything at all. Lucky me, I would have needed a mortgage.

I spent a lot of time trying to get the Dove's old 1154/55 radio system working but it was absolutely clapped out and needed a total replacement. We were asked if we would be willing to take the aircraft in its present state and I replied that I would, provided I could complete satisfactory checks of the VHF Air Traffic Voice Approach Radio.

I thought about Jaye and then, completely out of character, made my first and only attempt at poetry.

My Dearest Jayzie:
To me you are just like a Rose
A scented thing that grows and glows
You'll always stay just like a bud
Instead of withering in the mud
But should your petals wane and droop
and water will not save your beaut
I'll plant you in some strong manure
and watch you grow up sweet and pure
Your Maurice

I think it must have been a strong test of her affection when she read this.

The decision was finally made to take short hops of about two hundred and fifty miles between overnight stopovers and that we would fly and rely on basic VHF communications. On reflection, this was possibly an unwise decision as we would be flying over some of the most desolate and unfriendly areas imaginable at that time in Algeria's history.

This was the period leading up to the French being forced to give Algeria independence. A process which incurred some of the most vicious treatment of Islamic Arabs by the French expats who had settled there and established farms. Had we been forced to land in this wild country due to engine trouble and thought to be French by the rebels, we would most likely have been cruelly treated or killed.

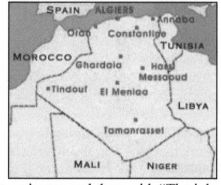

From my point of view it was a great trip. When we took off from Karachi, the Attaché asked me if I could fly. I told him of my experience, he watched me for twenty minutes and then said, "The job is yours." I enjoyed flying the Dove whilst he rested up for the next landing and reception, only waking him as we approached a town or refuelling point. Initially our Navigator was not too happy (he had known me only as a signaller) until he realized that I really could fly.

The Sahara Desert was an eye opener for me. It is not just one but many deserts. Its wastes are fractured by the sudden geometry of low, straight lines of hills, spiny ridges, vast flat depressions, escarpments and plateaux stepping up or down. There are red rock deserts, brown, yellow, black, grey and even blue. There are also deserts of small flat pebbles, of big black boulders, tiny stony hillocks, pumice, sparkling mica and also of tremendous shifting sand dunes.

Note: In the 1990s when elections were held in Algeria, the Islamists were poised to win but the French army annulled elections causing savage fighting in which nineteen priests, monks and nuns were murdered but the slaughter of Muslims by Muslims was on a catastrophic scale. Between 100,000 and 150,000 were killed including two hundred Imams.

Refuelling was taken very seriously by us and also by the security conscious native tribes in those rough regions as it gave slaves a possible opportunity to escape. At one stop high in the Ethiopian mountains, we found only a small building containing fuel where a tall black slave filled the aircraft's wing tanks by hand from jerry cans whilst a turbaned and picturesquely dressed Arab held a large drawn scimitar over him.

At another stop, a uniformed tribesman with an ancient six-foot rifle guarded a slave. It was all very impressive but in many ways discouraging.

Later, at a desolate stop in the middle of an arid desert, we landed on hard levelled sand near a windsock and a barbed wire fuel dump; there was neither building nor personnel in sight but on a hill overlooking us, we could see three Tuareg tribesmen warriors. They wore huge black turbans with their faces swathed in cloth up to the eyes and carried old muskets and ornate swords. They sat silently on magnificent horses and watched us. We called out but they gave no response. The very atmosphere was frightening. We taxied the aircraft right up to the side of the enclosure, it was unlocked, and contained an ancient hand fuel pump. We filled the barrels as quickly as possible and rolled them out to the aircraft, refuelled it by hand as fast as we could, then made a hasty take off.

We called at Tamanrasset which is located at an oasis set 4,333 feet up in the spectacular Hoggar Mountains although the peaks rise as high as 20,000 feet. It is the largest city in Central Sahara with a population of about forty thousand, mainly Tuareq. At night the temperature can drop to freezing whilst in the daytime it can rise to well over 100 degrees.

Whilst we were there, the French Foreign Legion had their Administrative Headquarters right in the centre of the town near the beautiful oasis but, needless to say, the local people were not overly well disposed towards their French overlords.

When we landed there we were met by a French Colonel and escorted to the Officers' Mess. It was siesta time and a batman showed us to our room and said he would wake us up for dinner. I dropped off straight away, only to be woken at about 8.00 p.m. by banging on the door. Without thinking, I leapt out of bed and opened the door, screamed, banged it shut and took a running Rugby dive under my mosquito net. It wasn't the batman knocking, it was thousands of the largest and most horrible flying creatures I had ever encountered.

Later that night, after dinner, I noticed one of the native bar staff with huge blisters on both his arms and was told he encouraged the tsetse flies to bite him and when the blisters were fully raised he used a straw to extract the fluid which was then dried and sold as the aphrodisiac Spanish Fly.

We found there was just one elderly English woman living in the town, a Dr Wakefield, a rather eccentric missionary in her eighties. She was something of a recluse, occupying a small hut packed with books and although she was very friendly, our French contact warned us that we must watch our Ps and Qs when we were with her as she was very religious and strait-laced. If she heard even the mildest swear word, she became extremely upset and would consider the perpetrator to be a partner of the devil. The French Legion Officers were more than a little wary of her and quite 'put out' by her strict attitude.

I also learned that Joy and George Adamson of "Born Free" fame had trekked through the town in 1953; a most arduous and dangerous example of their attitude to life. One of their main reasons for making this trek had been to visit a small isolated Church some forty miles distant from Tamanrasset which was the shrine of Charles de Foucauld, French aristocrat, soldier, explorer, hermit and lexicographer who was murdered during the rebel uprisings in the Sahara during World War One. He was beatified by the Pope in 2005 and is one of the main religious tourist attractions in Algeria, however, only the fit and hardy should ever consider trekking to the site.

Our next flight was to the Foreign Legion Fort of El Golia, some five hundred miles of high crags and desert wasteland into the middle of a disputed region dominated by the French. As we landed, the Commandant came out to greet us in his grand open tourer but we were interrupted when three large troop-carrying helicopters landed and from which about twenty rebel Arab prisoners were pushed, most of them covered in blood from their various wounds.

We looked horrified but the Commandant said "Take no notice, this is just an exercise" and then the Legionnaire escorts made the prisoners, regardless of injury, double into the fort. The temperature was over one hundred degrees in the shade.

For us, this was a so-called 'good will' visit with a little reconnaissance on the side and for the next three days we were entertained on a grand scale as the Commandant's guests. The Fort bore little resemblance to the Beau Guest films of Hollywood. It was much larger. The Officers' Mess was as big as some British mess buildings and the Commandant kept a full suite of rooms for himself, another suite for his mistress and the guest rooms we were using. Within the confines of his tropical garden he maintained a private zoo, pleasantly laid out with shrubs and trees and with a good selection of wild animals, all contained within the Fort itself. It was in this delightful shaded setting that we were served excellent meals.

Unfortunately I caused a discordant note at our first dinner together when I declined the wine offered by the Commandant. The Commandant stood up and said angrily, "No one dines at my table and refuses to drink." Recalling the way he had treated his Arab prisoners when we arrived, I acted the chicken and concurred and each night I was helped to bed.

Even so, his hospitality could not be faulted. He would rise early before the oppressive heat began and, with a motorized armed escort both in front and behind his car, he would either take us on a sight seeing tour or to the impressive Byzantine castle on a high hill some distance away. Each time we motored through the very large Oasis nearby, all Arabs within view of the cavalcade went down on their hands and knees and salaamed the Commandant. This gave an indication of the way the local inhabitants regarded the French. Ten days before we landed at El Golia, tribal rebels had taken some revenge when a French aircraft had force landed just a few miles short of the fort. By the time the Legionnaires' rescue force had reached the scene of the crash, every  member of the aircrew had been killed.

Another of our courtesy visits was to Khartoum where General Gordon was killed in 1885. It was of particular interest to me as my Aunt Annie used to speak of him affectionately as one of her family friends and possessed a number of books signed by him.

Unfortunately, I didn't get a chance to view the city because as soon as we reached our superb hotel, I collapsed with heat exhaustion and only recovered two days later in time for breakfast and an early take off. What a pity.

Our final call in the Middle East was Algiers but as we approached the Airport we found we were in the middle of a firefight between the Foreign Legion forces and the forces of the (FLN) National Liberation Front. We could see many explosions around the perimeter of the runway but we were in need of fuel and had no alternative but to land.

We taxied as quickly as possible towards the Air Traffic Control building, jumped out amid more explosions and the wizz of flying bullets and ran for cover. Later, during a lull in the fighting, we refuelled with haste, took off smartly and left the excitement behind us.

We then flew across the Mediterranean to France and landed at Marseille for yet another reunion. The next morning we flew on to the French Air Force base near Caen where the Attaché had many friends and where we all enjoyed our last, very noisy party where they enticed me to try Pernod but apart from the taste, the colour of it put me off.

We had reached the end of the adventure and left France on the last hop to the U.K. Considering the many doubts expressed regarding the un-reliability of our communications system and the need for the aircraft to suffer a complete overhaul, we had been very lucky. It had served us well. We landed at Shawbury in the late afternoon - it had taken the best part of four weeks to fly the Dove from Karachi to England.

The journey had been a diplomatic hand-over by the Attaché and we had visited the Governing Principal of virtually every Sheikdom, Emirate etc. covered by the Attaché during his many years of diplomacy. He was quite exhausted by all the entertaining; we had managed twenty overnight party stops and a further two when we arrived in France, all with no more than two or three hours flying time between each landing place.

Regretfully, I cannot remember the name of the Air Attaché but I shall always be grateful to him for giving me the opportunity to fly the twin engine Dove some four and a half thousand miles. It had been such an enjoyable and interesting experience. Unfortunately, I have lost my flying log and some fifty years later my memory of all the stops and sights we saw is somewhat vague but I do recall – Karachi, Oman, Masqat, Saudi Arabia, Shalala, Riad, Chad, Niger, Tamanrasset, El Golia, Khartoum, Alexandria, Algiers, Palma, Marseilles, Lyon and finally RAF Shawbury, and a great welcome home.

I bade the Attaché and George a friendly and appreciative farewell.

-0-0-0-0-

In August 1961 Russia built the wall across Germany. It was traumatic news for Western Europe and even more so for East German residents. It led to the loss of hundreds of lives as people tried to escape from the Communist regime which we heard was largely dependant on rules laid down by Stalin and controlled by many post cold war Heads of Government, Police and Security Services who had backgrounds linked to the wartime Gestapo and SS.

Chapter 11 – Crash Again and Get Married (Angel 9)

November 1961 - I took part in a training exercise where our aircraft played target for the trainee Ground Control Approach Controllers. As we prepared to land and attempted to lower our flaps, it became apparent from the instruments that our hydraulics had seized up which meant that our wheels were locked and unable to roll for a safe landing.

The Station 'Wing Commander Flying' was told of our situation and advised us that we had two options - to either go out to sea and bail out using the ejection seats or bring the aircraft in very fast, not to land, but just to touch the wheels down and pull straight off again hoping that the friction on the runway would free the hydraulics. We talked it over and thought that ejection could be problematic and a dousing in the sea wasn't encouraging so we felt that an attempted landing was better and possibly the least risky. We came in fast at about one hundred and fifty miles per hour, touched the wheels to the runway but found we couldn't pull off again. The aircraft came to a halt within about one hundred yards. The touch down friction had burnt off both tyres and had ground the wheels down to the hubs. What was truly amazing was the fact that the nose wheel did not collapse. We both got out of the aircraft thinking we had got away scot-free. This was my Angel's 9th visit.

I married the girl of my dreams on the 1st December 1961. The Civil Marriage Service was carried out with such sincerity and pleasure by two very earnest Registrars whom we dubbed Tweedle Dum and Tweedle Dee so despite the terrible weather, it was a very happy occasion. The rain ruined both of our cameras so we stopped at a small photography shop and had a few pictures taken.

We had an unusual honeymoon. I was totally broke after my divorce so we stayed in the Bedford van which had a full slide down double bed and cooking facilities. On the first night we slept outside the best hotel in Brighton, the Grand Hotel, but the entire honeymoon weekend consisted of helping two of my elderly Aunts who each had problems and for whom I was Executor. We arranged for Aunt Annie to be admitted into a hospital after a fall from a 'bus and Aunt Rosa to move into a private nursing home. Aunt Rosa was convinced we couldn't possibly be married because she said Jaye looked like a child. It was a memorable time and we have never had any regrets.

From the bedroom of our married quarters at RAF Shawbury we had a clear view of the Wrekin Mountain rising to a height of 1,335 feet above the Shropshire Plain. You may well ask "So what?" Well, it gave Jaye and I a major advantage on the days of early morning flying as we also had a direct view of the airfield's runway. If we couldn't see the Wrekin clearly and if there were no Vampires lined up near the runway, it meant there would be no flying that morning so we would snuggle down again, as some would say, purely for medicinal purposes.

Jaye took a temporary job as a shorthand typist at Chubb Engineering. Working conditions were not the best and she was asked by the female staff to represent them. She did so with considerable vigour and obtained for them greatly improved working conditions. This immediately brought her to the notice of the management and she was offered promotion which she declined with thanks.

Life at Shawbury was great and we became a happy family. One surprising thing was Jaye's immediate affinity with Tanya. As I have mentioned, the dog had always been very protective of our Bedford and only family could enter. No one, not even well known friends, could get in or out of the vehicle unless I was there to say so. One day I went off on an early flight and when I returned later in the day I found the vehicle shining brightly, inside and out. I asked Jaye who had let her into the car. She said, "I let myself in but the dog stayed very close to me." Perhaps the dog had foresight!

After we left the cinema one evening, Jaye and Sue got into the Bedford and I took Tanya for a walk. About two hundred yards away I met an enthusiastic policeman and we stood talking about dogs when suddenly Tanya growled furiously, left me and rushed off towards our vehicle. The policeman and I saw a man running for his life with a purposeful dog chasing him. Luckily Tanya stopped when I shouted, however, when we reached the car Jaye explained that a man had been

110

flashing himself at them but with Tanya's rapid attention, he'd been lucky to retain his essentials.

On the 17th January 1962 I was posted to RAF Stradishall to fly in Varsity aircraft and again I was flying as a Signaller and Safety Pilot.

Until we were able to find somewhere to live, Susan went to Boarding School in Shrewsbury. Happily it was a place she enjoyed. Jaye got a job at one of Sainsbury's Production Centres situated between the RAF Base and Haverhill and spent her working hours taking and issuing minutes until during a meeting attended by Lord Sainsbury, it was discovered that she was a verbatim conference writer and he almost doubled her earnings over night.

When we had been married about three months, Jaye received a solicitor's official Breach of Promise letter (this was quite a common practice in those days). Her ex-fiancé was suing her for breaking off the engagement. She packed up every piece of jewellery he'd given to her for birthdays, etc. and sent the packet to the solicitor with a letter explaining that she was already married and didn't have any money.

She told me later that she had always been afraid of marriage having seen too many married friends and family members who were either miserable or downright unhappy. She had been engaged five times but always backed out, on one occasion getting as far as the Registry Office and then running away.

She then explained to me that the Sunday after we met, the second Banns had been called for her wedding but after meeting me, she couldn't go through with it. Somewhat fearfully, on the day I had returned to Shawbury, she had arranged to see her fiancé for lunch in a large well-packed restaurant. There she had returned the ring to him, apologised and said that it just wouldn't work.

He had exploded, voiced his feelings in the centre of the restaurant, thrown his Anthony Eden hat onto his brief case and jumped up and down on them. One could hardly blame the fellow. Jaye said she just ran out of the restaurant as fast as she could, irrespective of the very tight skirt and three inch heels of the day, and caught the train back to her parents' place. Apparently she and her fiancé had already put a deposit on a house, furnished it and arranged a honeymoon in Sorrento.

I think he had fair cause for his explosion but it also explained her Mother's uninviting attitude when I first visited her house and the strange looks from her office friends when I had met her from work. What can I say - Jaye gave up a financially secure chap with an established and highly paid career for me. I must have had something but I know it was the best thing my Angel ever did for me.

Life was good but it took us about two months to find accommodation. It was difficult to find a house to rent from the avaricious landlords in Haverhill (pronounced Avril by the locals) but finally we found a very run down end terrace house and the landlady promised that if I repaired and redecorated the property to make it comfortably habitable, she would greatly reduce the rent when the work was finished. I agreed. Jaye said I shouldn't trust her.

The bathroom was the only modern room in the house but it was on the second floor under the roof and although it contained new fittings, the rest of the attic was in poor repair and full of junk. When our guests wanted to use the bathroom, we would direct them up to the attic and advise them to ignore any flying birds they might meet. They would smile thinking we were a bit odd and then we would hear a wild shriek as a sparrow swooped past a disbelieving friend.

Until I carried out the repairs, birds could come in through gaps between the window frame and the wall; in fact, I could have shaken hands with a window cleaner without opening the window.

After six months of working every spare moment, I asked our landlady for the promised reduction in rent. She smiled and refused and added that if we didn't like it, we could move.

This annoyed us so much that we took her to the local Rent Tribunal. At the hearing, the Chairwoman read out our complaint, stopped the procedure and announced that all members of the Tribunal would walk to our house (which was nearby) and inspect the property, top to bottom, carry out a proper survey and upon their return to Court the Members would assess the case and give their verdict.

After the hearing was reconvened, the Chairwomen made the following statement "It isn't that there isn't a lot of furniture in the property, it just isn't worth anything, whilst the renovations Mr

112

Hamlin has carried out are excellent. We therefore reduce the rent from five pounds per week to ten shillings per week and no rent increases will be allowed without further inspection".

The story was widely reported in the local paper and we had total strangers stopping us in the street to congratulate us. It transpired that the landlady in question had a bad name in the town.

This turmoil had another affect on our lives. I had always kept a little red notebook containing details of my financial commitments and worries. One day Jaye saw me puzzling over this book and asked to look at it. She studied it for a few minutes and then threw it onto the fire and said, "No more worries like that, I will sort it out." And she did. She looked after the money from that time onwards and whatever the problem, she used her magic to solve it. I was even more convinced that I had found a gem.

Another friend, Tommy Thompson, was an unusual character and like myself was an Air Signaller. He flew with a crew who appeared to be prone to having their aircraft become unserviceable when on the odd navigational exercise overseas. Each time this happened, his wife was left to look after their two very young and boisterous children. This continual occurrence was getting her down and she was very upset when, yet again, he returned late after another trip. She opened the door and said "Hello Darling, I've just asked the Forces Favourites radio programme to play a record for you." He replied, "That's a wonderful idea. What was it?" She replied, "Hit the Road Jack" and told him it had to stop or else.

Tommy decided to improve home life for his family. Like Jaye and I, they wanted to live off the Base and started looking for a rented property close to Haverhill. They answered one particular advertisement for an 'Airy three bedroom house for rent at £5 per week' and arranged to view the following evening. The outside of the house looked all right but as Tommy's wife stepped into the entrance, she fell through rotten floorboards. The prospective landlord said, "There's no problem, the floor can easily be repaired." He then invited them to go upstairs to view the rest of the property. The master bedroom looked satisfactory but when they went into the second bedroom they could see the starry sky through a hole in both the ceiling and the roof. Again the comment was "Soon be fixed."

With two RAF Airfields, an Army Barracks and an American Base close to Haverhill, these properties were typical of the available rentals.

Once again Tommy's wife received a message from the Air Traffic Control saying that his aircraft had been delayed for several days in the Middle East because of servicing problems.

She dressed the two children, walked them down to the Station Commander's rather impressive married quarters, knocked on the door and told the C.O.'s wife, "These are yours until my husband returns," turned on her heel and walked away.

A somewhat chastened Tommy was brought back on the next available British Airways flight and this incident could have ended with great trouble for Tommy but then fate took a hand.

His next escapade was of a very different nature, proving the versatility of our training as Safety Pilots (even if not officially recognized). Tommy took off on a flight as co-pilot with our Commanding Officer sitting in the pilot's seat. As the aircraft left the ground and started climbing, the C.O. collapsed with a major heart attack and died. Tommy took over the controls, brought the aircraft round and landed it safely. I never did hear what commendation he received but he certainly saved both the aircraft and crew. The C.O.'s death was particularly poignant as the previous week he had won eighty thousand pounds on the football pools.

Photo shows Jaye and I jiving at the Tramps Ball, RAF Stradishall.

In October 1962 Jaye and I decided to take the plunge. We took out a mortgage and moved into a new house in the small village of Keddington (locally known as Kitten) just outside Haverhill and only five miles from the Base. The house was in a nice setting and the people were friendly but insular; we were told there were only three surnames in the village of one hundred and twenty people, except the Vicar of course. The property was nicely decorated, spacious and had three bedrooms, lounge, dining room, kitchen and a full bathroom. Also, it had a detached garage, a small garden at the front and a huge garden at the rear and all for £3,400. Life was very different for young couples in those days.

By the end of June 1963 Jaye was feeling very poorly and was receiving conflicting observations from the local Doctor. For three weeks he prescribed various tablets until one night I came home and found her in tears because the Doctor had told her that the trouble was in her head and he was arranging an appointment for her with a private psychiatrist.

I told her the Doctor was the one who was crazy in the head and the next morning took her to my RAF Station's Senior Medical Officer. At first he somewhat abrupt and told her that the consultation was unorthodox as he was only allowed to treat service wives who lived in married quarters but said, "As your husband is worried about you, he can't do his work properly and my job is to keep him fit. What did your Doctor say when he examined you?" Jaye replied that she hadn't been examined. The M.O. was sceptical but gave her a thorough check. When he called me in, he said "There's nothing wrong with your wife's brain, I believe she has a problem with her kidneys, she is

diabetic and also pregnant and should go into hospital immediately." Jaye was sent to the RAF Hospital in Ely where she stayed for the next six months.

15th January 1964 was a Red Letter Day. Steven our first son was born. Mother and baby were in excellent health but the specialist considered Jaye would become a full diabetic by the time she was forty because eventually her intermittent pancreas would cease to work altogether, however, Jaye was particularly lucky because a few years later it did the opposite and actually started working normally. Picture of Jaye and Steven.

We had just bought our first new house at Keddington and after Jaye's illness with the baby, I was determined to make sure she had a beautiful home. We saw a splendid solid teak dining suite in Maples of London so we placed an order with them on the assurance that the

115

furniture would arrive well in time for Steven's christening party. When the dining room suite was delivered, we found the legs were made of deal wood dyed to match the teak. Letters and many telephone calls brought no satisfactory response from Maples.

I travelled to London one Saturday morning and found the store crowded and the salesmen all too busy to hear a complaint. In desperation, I stood on a chair in the crowded furniture showroom and called out very loudly in best parade ground manner "You have delivered a solid teak dining suite with stained deal wooden legs and ignored all my complaints. If it is not collected by next Tuesday, I am going to put it out into the garden with the other rubbish." There followed a deathly hush before the Manager rushed up to me and assured me it would be attended to immediately; it was collected on the Monday afternoon with profuse apologies.

This felt satisfactory but it left just one problem. Where would our guests eat on the evening of our son's christening? Jaye found a solution which turned the evening into one of the best dinner parties we ever had. The guests were chatting and enjoying a pre-dinner drink and commenting on how well we had furnished our home when Jaye announced that dinner was ready and opened the doors into the dining room. There was a hush for a moment - the dining room was furnished with carpet and curtains and lit by dozens of tea lights in baby food jars. Each guest had a wooden apple box covered by a bath towel for a seat and for a table had an upended orange box with a few sheets of newspaper covering it. Conversation recovered with considerable animation - the first person asked "Does anyone fancy a caravan in Yarmouth for the second week in August?" quickly followed by "I say, have you read about that Vicar in London?" etc. It was an unforgettable evening. And the wine flowed.

Whilst Jaye had been in hospital, I started having a problem with walking and severe back pains. X-rays showed that the massive deceleration caused during the Vampire crash had compressed my spine and the three bottom vertebrae had fused together. I was almost an inch shorter. My mobility deteriorated so badly that I could barely walk and the Medical Officer sent me to the Remedial Hospital at RAF Headley Court near Leatherhead.

On arrival we were told that, irrespective of seniority, rank was void during instruction because everyone was a patient and must carry out all orders regardless of the rank of the instructor. The remedial

116

instructors were mostly non-commissioned and some quite senior officers and civilian patients took exception to this order and made difficulties by refusing to comply. The Wing Commander Medical Officer interviewed such people and reiterated that they were in hospital as patients and they must comply with all orders given by the staff and if this was unacceptable, they would be discharged. Some were sent away.

The Headley Court treatment and staff were superb. The therapy incurred an eight-hour schedule from Monday to midday Saturday and, in my case, included a lot of physical exercise to build up my back muscles to overcome the spinal damage.

Our day started at 8.30 a.m. with gentle warm up exercises, then more exercise on the mat followed by yet more in the pool although we were not allowed to swim. Then we took a very short walk which became longer each day, gradually building up muscles and stamina. In the afternoons we played a relaxing game of croquet or did therapy work with wood or other materials. When I was discharged four months later, I was able to lie down on my back and lift my whole body off the ground supported only by the balls of my heels and my head. I was also able to walk sixteen miles around Leatherhead and return feeling as though I had just had a gentle stroll. Incredible!

It was a wonderful feeling to be so fit and healthy and I kept myself at this level of fitness for a great many years. I owe a lot to RAF Headley Court and their professional and caring staff.

When I returned to the Squadron I was told that my eyes were falling below flying standard for someone using glasses which I had been allowed to use due to my many years of experience, however, they said I could continue to fly for a further six months up to the end of my contracted service but if I wished to continue my RAF career I would be grounded and have to take a technical position in signals.

I wondered whether or not this ultimatum might be attributed more to the fact that I had not always followed orders than to my eyesight. Even so, I must admit that those days when I occasionally got the opportunity, I found landing the aircraft was a little hazardous, as I had to waggle the stick to find the last few feet.

One bitter, snowy day I was driving to the Base for an early morning take off when I saw the Station's civilian Boiler Man walking to work so I stopped and offered him a lift. He accepted the offer and said "It's too dangerous for a bicycle this morning." I replied that there would be no problem in the Bedford van and, within seconds, I lost control as the vehicle skidded, went through a hedge and down into an icy ditch. A friendly farmer pulled us out with his tractor. Luckily we were unhurt and able to see the funny side of the incident.

On another evening I was driving to the Base from home for a late evening take off when I came upon an accident that had just occurred. A car had left the road, turned over and smashed into a ditch, badly injuring all four male occupants. They were all unconscious and there was a lot of blood. Three of them had been thrown from the car whilst the driver was huddled over the wheel. Luckily a local farm hand on his way home from work arrived on the scene and I got him to dash to the nearest farmhouse to telephone for an RAF ambulance stationed only four miles away. I did what I could to staunch the worst flow of blood. They were all so badly hurt, two of them were almost scalped with ghastly head injuries and broken bones.

Thankfully the RAF ambulance arrived promptly but it was the only one available so the Medical Officer asked if I could take the two less seriously injured men to hospital in my vehicle. We let down my double bed and placed them on it then, with lights flashing, I followed the ambulance. Once the injured men were safely in the hospital I hurried to the Squadron and changed into flying gear ready for our sortie. As we walked to the plane, I collapsed and was taken off to hospital.

I felt like a total wimp when I woke up but the Doctor saved my pride by saying that shock hits people in many ways. The injured men had been very lucky because as I had acted so promptly I had probably saved their lives. Many people in such accident situations keel over with shock before they are able to help.

I was away on another overseas exercise when two-month-old premature baby Steven was taken very ill. The doctor called and left a prescription for antibiotics but Jaye didn't have transport. There were only two buses a week from our village into Haverhill so she asked our neighbour, who had just returned home for lunch, if he would collect the prescription on his way home that evening. He declined saying he couldn't possibly do that in the evening rush hour. He was talking about a town with a laid back population of three and a half thousand people where you rarely saw a car exceed 25 mph. Jaye was naturally frantic with worry and stepped into the road and flagged down the first vehicle that came along. It happened to be a bread van and the roundsman was pleased to help and returned in less than an hour with the prescription. A true Christian. By the time I arrived home the baby was well on the way to recovery.

Incidentally, the only way Jaye had of weighing the baby each week was to use the scales of our friendly travelling Green Grocer.

April saw the end of my carefree RAF flying career and despite various clashes with RAF authority, it had been a wonderful life which I would recommend to any young person; I believe it is a pity the Government stopped National Service. Regardless of some petty confrontations, it taught me team spirit and personal discipline. Whatever the service, reliance and trust can mean the difference between life and death and it is usually difficult to find such a close team spirit in civilian occupations except perhaps, the Fire service and some divisions of the emergency services.

Although the RAF had given me the option of a ground crew job in signals, I considered my somewhat lax attitude to everyday non-flying discipline would not have been happily accepted and I was too old at thirty-nine to change my ways. At first glance the future looked bleak.

Our house was only seventeen miles from Cambridge so Jaye said she intended to take up thesis typing for the University so that she could work from home and help supplement our income whilst I sorted out my future. I knew that finding a job in Civvy Street was not going to be easy. I was not an academic by any stretch of the imagination and had little worthwhile experience in any occupation that would support a family. I had, however, applied and been accepted for a short University course at Liverpool which would lead to employment as a Probation Officer but the course didn't begin until five months after my RAF discharge.

I obviously couldn't sit idle for months wasting our savings so I asked Jaye, who had always held down well paid jobs, to type an application to every company advertising in the Telegraph for people without previous experience for highly paid sales jobs. How hopeful can you get? However she soon had me lined up with a half dozen interviews in London, the first being with Pitney Bowes, a major office equipment manufacturer.

The interview went well in some ways but their Sales Director said,

"Well you are not really what we are looking for but we have a course starting in two weeks' time and we have just lost one entrant. If the RAF will release you in time to take that course, we will give you a three month trial." The position they offered was for a salesman of small office machines to work in Central London but knowing that Jaye didn't like the idea of living in or near London, I replied "I will accept your offer if you will agree to my one condition which is, if I am successful, you will transfer me out of London after six months."

The Sales Director was rather shocked but also seemed to be impressed and he agreed to my terms. The RAF were very understanding and allowed me to have leave to take the training course so long as Pitney Bowes didn't pay me. I passed the course with flying colours, had a friendly discharge from the RAF and looked forward to my new life.

Chapter 12 – In the Money   (Angel 10)

Dressed in my new three-piece city suit complete with soft grey tie, bowler hat, briefcase and furled umbrella, I joined Pitney Bowes in Tottenham Court Road (May 1964) with some trepidation. My only previous experience had been selling three-penny ice cream cornets and raffle tickets and my indoctrination into the world of professional salesmanship came as a shock.

My first impressions convinced me that it was undignified. After the negotiations when I actually had to ask for an order, it felt like begging. In my first week with them I was taken out and shown the ropes by a superb salesman, Bob Bache, a true gentleman. He was one of the Company's top equipment specialists, well spoken, highly educated and earning a great deal of money. He rarely started work before 9.30 a.m. and at 12.30 p.m. always stopped for pink gins and lunch, usually finishing work by 5.00 p.m. but he greatly impressed me with his sales technique. And I learned fast. Within three months I had doubled my RAF pay and with my first salary cheque I also received an ex gratia payment and expenses for the time I had spent on the PB training course.

The photograph shows my introduction to my PB team; Bob with his glass raised in the centre and another Mr Peter Hamlin (no relative) next to me on the far right.

One sunny morning during my second week in London, I was walking along the South Bank admiring the view to Waterloo Bridge when an elegant lady stopped me and said, "I am a Canadian tourist and this is my first visit. I would really like to take a photograph of a real English business gentleman." Smiling, I replied, "I should be delighted to oblige." She took her picture and thanked me. I raised my bowler and, highly elated, carried on walking towards my client's premises. I felt as though I had arrived.

I usually arrived for work at 9.00 a.m. on Monday mornings and left at 4.00 p.m. on Fridays to travel back to Suffolk. The Company allowed me to have a key to the office premises so during the week I arrived at 7.30 a.m. each morning and didn't leave until 10.00 p.m. Outside normal selling hours I was always on the premises, studying and dismantling their whole range of equipment, researching how they worked and learning how to modify them to cope with a wide variety of applications. Although I was selling the lower range of equipment, I was continually on the look out for clients who could use the larger machines and thereby earned even more commission for passing leads on to the Major Equipment Division.

When I had been with the Company for six months, I reminded my Sales Director that he had agreed to transfer me to an office outside London if I had proved successful. He tried to dissuade me from moving by offering me a position which he thought I would reject; it was as a Systems Salesman covering a small part of Hampshire, Dorset and Somerset and all of Devon and Cornwall. My new friends at the London Office advised me against taking the offer because that particular area was well known as "the salesman's graveyard", however, it turned out to be a gold mine. It appeared that due to the distances involved, not many salesmen had tried selling equipment in those areas and I found few businesses there had heard of either Pitney Bowes or the equipment they supplied. Most of them were pleased to see me.

In September, with Sue and nine month old Steven, we moved to Bath and bought Thornham Villa, a beautiful Georgian house high on the hill at the end of Camden Crescent and overlooking the City which had been built in a shallow bowl. The house boasted two palm trees in the front courtyard and at the back had a peach house and an orchard. There were some mornings when the city was shrouded in

122

mist but from our house on high we could see above the cloud, pink in the early sunlight, with only tall church spires peeking through and reflecting the light. It was a magical sight.

It must be agreed that I am not usually nervous or given to flights of fancy but the first time I saw our ghost I was quite startled. I walked down the stairs leading to the dining room when a woman in a brown full length frock with two lines of darker braid around the bottom of the skirt and a small bustle at the back, walked past me from the dining room, into the kitchen and disappeared. At first I thought it must have been a trick of the light but this same figure appeared many times during the eighteen months we lived there, always walking through the hall and into the kitchen. Yet this was a friendly apparition. The house always felt welcoming. I obviously said nothing to my wife as I didn't want to cause alarm.

At this time I usually spent three days a week in the far reaches of my Cornish territory and the rest in and around Salisbury, Bournemouth and Weymouth. All very lucrative. Our social life in Bath was excellent with dinner dances at the Assembly Rooms and many other places, also concerts of all kinds. Once a year we were allowed to swim in the Roman Baths and afterwards dine in the Pump Room, always accompanied by a well-known band of the day. (This annual event later became named as The Roman Rendezvous). Ladies beware: the natural chemicals in the hot spring at the Roman Baths can temporarily change the colour of any beautiful swimsuit into a horrid dirty orange.

During my first six months working in Cornwall, I sold one of the company's largest systems (£10,000) to a photographic company based at Lands End; they flew all over the country from their private airfield to take school photographs. The place was so out on a limb that PB (Pitney Bowes) tried to kill the sale by quoting a £2,500 delivery and installation charge. I told the client there would be no delivery charge and hired a three ton self drive van, collected the equipment from the factory and drove it to Lands End where I had arranged for a hire crane and operator from Redruth to meet me at the site. An engineer was also waiting there for me and we installed the system together. After this, PB had to provide permanent service cover for the area which greatly helped to enhance my future sales.

From the start of my career with PB, I adopted my own specific sales philosophy; it was the honesty which had been ingrained in me by my Dad. If I could prove to a prospective client that the equipment I offered to sell him was both needed and cost effective, I would pull out all the stops to close the sale, however, if I found neither of these was correct, I backed out gracefully. This policy led to many satisfied and friendly users and a large number of referrals to new prospects.

When Jaye became pregnant again, a house on four floors was too much work so we decided to move to a more modern and easily managed house. Thornham Villa sold within two weeks of being on the market for £8,000 to a Director of Robertson's Jam. Within a day of agreeing the deal we had a crazy offer of £12,000 from an art collector enamoured by our views of the city. Unfortunate, but I kept to my Dad's teaching – a handshake is a contract.

We next moved to a house in Sladebrook Road in Bath and once we had settled in I told Jaye about the ghost I had seen going into the dining room at Thornham Villa. She replied "Oh! Yes, I frequently saw her but didn't mention it to you because you might have thought I was imagining it."

Jaye is something of a psychic and this has come to light many times during our life together and it is always totally unexpected. The first time I became aware of this aspect of her character happened whilst she was at the dentist having a tooth prepared for a crown. In those days there were no high-pressure drills and it was a long, slow treatment usually taking the best part of a morning. Jaye used to have what is known as 'out of body experiences' and could close her mind to what was happening and literally watch things from outside her being. My simple mind boggles at the thought but it terrified the dentist when he told her "All done, rinse please" and she could neither move nor answer. He was about to call an ambulance when Jaye sat up, grinned and said she had been looking around the area and it had taken a while to get back. She has had many such experiences.

At nine o'clock one morning I walked into the offices of a recruitment company in Plymouth. The Director was very interested in the PB systems and explained how he ran his business. I immediately saw a way to increase his efficiency and greatly reduce his overtime costs. I was with him for seven hours and every time we came to the point of signing the order, he would turn the conversation to another subject.

At three o'clock, when I thought I had him, he suddenly changed the conversation and talked about genealogy and brought out a printed family tree stretching ten feet across the office. His name was Hamblin and we found we were distantly related. He showed me his researches into the Hamlin-Hamblin-Hamelin-Hamlyn family name going as far back as far as 1060 which showed that we both originated from Hamelin Town in Brunswick, Germany.

Unfortunately, I was slow and didn't grasp the opportunity to negotiate to buy a copy of the document so I have no idea just how correct his research had been. This discussion kept going until half past five when his staff said it was time for them to go and we realized the day had gone. He suddenly exclaimed. "I have a friend in the garage business just round the corner who should also buy this." I said, "Right, sign here and we'll go straight away." We did and I obtained two sales.

In the same week I visited the local newspaper in Falmouth. They had enquired about addressing machines because once every week they had to stop a large press and use it to print off labels for their extensive newspaper delivery rounds. I quickly arranged to demonstrate an addressing system to them and one week later proved how simple it was to create an address card for each clients and to operate the system which proved to the owner that the weekly leasing cost of my system on a three-year lease would save twice the amount he lost every week on downtime and re-setting the printing press. He agreed with me but was still humming and harring until at 5.30 p.m. when one of his office staff asked if it was it all right to lock up and leave. As before, this seemed to trigger him and he signed the contract.

I was amazed when three years later both the Recruitment Company and the Newspaper business wrote to PB asking for the loan equipment to be collected. It was even more surprising when the engineer picked up the systems and discovered that although both machines had been paid for, they had never been used and were still in their original delivery boxes.

As they say in Yorkshire "There's now't so queer as folk."

The Death of a Legend:

On the 13th January 1965 Sir Winston Churchill, our greatest statesman, died and was given a state funeral. I believe the world has never truly acknowledged the debt we owe to this great man. He made mistakes, but who could have been perfect with such a wide spectrum of responsibilities.

To me, and many others, it appeared that in 1940 many of those people high in Government were far too ready for appeasement or even favoured the Nazis. This of course included the ex King Edward who, as Duke of Windsor, toured Nazi Germany in 1937 when he and his Duchess were feted by Adolf Hitler. They were photographed partying with senior Nazis seemingly ready to accept Nazism.

Churchill kept democracy alive whilst others dithered until it was almost too late. Had Britain folded in those early days, Hitler's victory over Britain would have meant Russia being overwhelmed by all the land, sea and air forces released from fighting in the West. Undoubtedly Russia would have fallen without support and President Roosevelt of the USA would have been powerless against the mass of isolationist sympathisers in America.

On the 8th March 1965 we were thrilled to hear of the first spacewalk. A Russian, Alexei Leonov, had actually walked outside the USSR spaceship Voskhod 2. This was the first step in a great adventure and the beginning of the miniaturisation of a plethora of multi purpose computer hardware. It was a tremendous achievement.

That spring Jaye was in the throes of learning to drive. She had ten lessons with an excellent professional instructor but we also had great fun together. I took her along the narrowest country lanes with stone walls either side, up the worst of the City's narrow steep hills with sharp left hand turns at the top then around a crazy hair pin bend leading onto a main road and finally through the rush hour traffic in the centre of Bristol. She was confident and passed her driving test the first time.

The following week I took delivery of a brand new company car and told Jaye to take it out for a run. She stopped at a junction in the centre of town, just a little too far over the line, put on the handbrake and watched a massive ten-ton ERF lorry quietly crunch in the bonnet. The impact was so gentle it didn't wake up the toddler on the back seat.

The next day we went shopping and I bought her an old banger to allow her to gain experience. Built like a tank it was complete with running boards and idiot sticks (old fashioned direction indicators). Later in the year when she was backing it out of the drive, the brake seals failed and the car rushed forwards, butting the house and leaving permanent indentations in the stone where the headlights made contact with the wall. There was no other damage. Actually she was extremely lucky because had she managed to get the car out onto the road before the brakes failed, she would have been on a very steep hill and there would have been no way of stopping the vehicle. Do you think my Angel may have been watching?

The following week we went shopping again and this time I bought her a new MG and she never looked back.

The 30th January 1966 was another great day when our son Philip was born in the Forbes Frazer Clinic in Bath.

My introduction to the Conservative Party:

I had been introduced to Edward Heath shortly after he became Tory Party Leader in July 1966 and when he visited Bath the following year, I was so impressed with his apparent sincerity and honesty, I agreed to stand as a Tory Councillor in the Bath local elections. It was a great experience for both of us. We learned how difficult it was to judge anyone's political opinions by outward appearances and found some of the most "Tory-minded" people living in lowly circumstances and many on poor housing estates. In one instance, Jaye was canvassing an estate whilst toting a toddler and a baby in a pram when she had a scary encounter.

She approached a house with a broken gate, a garden growing only pieces of scrap and knocked on a battered door, which was standing ajar. A harsh voice shouted, "Come in." She hesitated. It didn't sound inviting. She knocked again and had the same response in a louder voice. She gingerly pushed the door open and found four ladies playing cards on a coffee table, the only furniture in the room except a pram containing a young baby. She introduced herself and said she was canvassing for her husband who was the Tory Candidate running for Twerton East. They were very friendly and explained that few people around there bothered to vote as the Ward had had the same Labour Councillor for years and no one had ever stood against him. They said complaints got nowhere with the Labour man and promised they would vote for Hamlin and tell other people who lived nearby.

On one of my calls, I canvassed an ex-RAF Air Gunner who said that whilst his communist beliefs wouldn't allow him to vote for me, he would not vote for the opposition and he also volunteered to be a driver to bring people to the polling station to cast their votes.

We worked extremely hard, visiting almost every household in the ward. Instead of the usual fund raising coffee mornings, Jaye instigated evening sherry parties which became very popular and highly profitable for Party funds.

On polling day the vote was so close that after the third re-count it was found that Labour had won by just thirteen votes. When I tried to congratulate the other candidate and shake his hand, he turned his back towards me.

Fortunately for me I produced another good sales result at work and once again won a place as top Systems Salesman at the Annual Sales Convention, which was to be held in Jersey the following spring.

I arrived in Jersey to beautiful weather and the Sales Convention started well, however, on the second day I collapsed and was taken to hospital with a suspected heart attack. Fortunately a doctor who had recently been practicing in the Far East recognised that as I was obviously extremely fit, the problem was unlikely to be the heart. He believed I was suffering from virus pneumonia. It was a correct diagnosis and his intervention almost certainly saved my life. Pitney Bowes were very good; they brought my wife and two children out to Jersey and put them in a first class hotel. After two weeks in hospital, the  Doctors believed I was well enough to join Jaye in the Hotel but at dinner on the first night, I collapsed again and was rushed back to hospital and stayed there for another week. Just before my discharge, the Doctor asked me to carry out a final lung test with a new machine. I was asked to blow into a tube with as much pressure as possible but, when I did, the machine exploded. He said, "Well, your lungs are obviously all right but this machine will have to go back to the makers." This was my Angel's 10th visit.

The guests and staff at the Hotel Savoy were wonderful in the way they supported Jaye and the children. During the evenings when the boys had been put to bed, Jaye was able to visit the hospital because the Porter would switch the baby alarm to loud speaker and many of the guests took their pre dinner drinks into the reception area and enjoyed listening to the boys singing and chatting before they fell asleep.

At lunch one day, an elegant lady sitting on her own asked Steven if he would like to taste her wine. He took a sip and said, "Thank you very much but I prefer a white wine." (As I am not a drinker, this had to be the result of my wife's more cultured influence.) However, this lady was so impressed with the boy, she took a delight in taking him out whilst Jaye visited me. Philip at just two years old was taken care of by a wonderful Irish couple who were on their honeymoon.

By the time I was finally discharged from the hospital, the illness and the length of time I had spent in bed had caused a recurrence of the spinal problems incurred by the RAF Vampire crash. The hospital doctor wrote to the RAF who agreed to take me back to the Remedial Centre at RAF Headley Court where I spent another three months and, once again, they succeeded in returning me to superb fitness. As before, I owe a great debt to the RAF staff for their wonderful care and also to Pitney Bowes who paid all hospital and hotel expenses without a quibble.

 Early in 1968 the "I'm Backing Britain" Campaign was a brief patriotic effort aimed at boosting the British economy. It started spontaneously when five Surbiton Secretaries volunteered to work an extra half an hour each day without pay in order to boost productivity and they urged others to do the same. This invitation received an enormous response and the campaign took off spectacularly becoming a nationwide movement within a week.

Trades Unions were very suspicious of the campaign and some directly opposed it; they took it as an attempt to surreptitiously extend working hours and to hide the inefficiency of management. After a few months without any noticeable effect on either individual companies or the economy in general, interest flagged amid much embarrassment about some of the ways in which the campaign had been pursued and supported. Eventually it was regarded as an iconic example of a failed attempt to transform British economic prospects.

During the morning of the 9th April 1969, we were startled by a tremendous roaring in the sky. It sounded like a flying cement mixer. We rushed into the garden and were amazed to see the magnificent British Airways Concorde 002 flying overhead on its maiden test flight from Filton Aerodrome near Bristol. Jaye told the children to remember what they were seeing because it was history in the making.

It was the 1st October 1969 before Concorde completed its first supersonic flight, flown by test pilot Brian Trubshaw (I felt it was a preliminary to the space age), however, it wasn't until the 21 January 1976 that British Airways flew the first commercial flights from London Heathrow to Bahrain and Air France flew from Paris to Rio.

Unfortunately Concorde was launched at the height of the fuel crisis and the combination of its small fuel tanks and heavy consumption meant it could not enter the lucrative Trans-Pacific market and this made it uneconomic. Even so, it was a tremendous boost for British/French aviation technology and worldwide esteem.

I was promoted to Systems Manager for the Nottingham Region in 1969 and with her usual zeal, Jaye took on the job of house hunting. She contacted several estate agents and told them we required a large house with five bedrooms and preferably a wood panelled hall with a fireplace. One agent took her to a lovely property with a large garden situated in a good area and which appeared to tick all the boxes. When she stepped into the beautiful hallway she exclaimed "Oh! No! This wouldn't suit my husband at all, he can't stand oak panelling" and she walked out of the house. Understandably the agent was upset and asked angrily "Whatever was the matter? That property was exactly what you asked for." Jaye agreed with him and then explained that she couldn't live in that particular house under any circumstances because something terrible had happened there. He then asked, "How did you know about the tragedy?" and when she enquired "What tragedy? He told her that the late owner had committed suicide there.

Jaye's intuition cannot be explained. We finally found an excellent home and settled down happily in Ribblesdale Road, Nottingham where we enjoyed three happy years.

Chapter 13 – The Politics of Business (Angel 11)

I have always enjoyed driving and on one of those lovely sunny days in the Spring of 1969 when all seemed right with the world, I drove my new top of the range, two tone, Ford Cortina through beautiful countryside to see a very positive client whose office was about eighty miles from my home.

When I reached Market Harborough, it was market day and as I travelled through the centre of town, a vehicle reversed from a road side parking area straight into the side of my car causing considerable damage. After exchanging documents I travelled another twenty miles to my client, made a sale and then drove back to Nottingham. Unfortunately, my mind had completely blotted out the fact that I had been involved in an accident.

All was well until we sat down to dinner that evening and I began to get the most intense pain in my head. The Doctor came to see me and prescribed tablets. An hour later, my wife called him again and he gave me an injection. The pain increased and I thought my head would explode, it was almost midnight when Jaye called an ambulance and I was taken away to hospital screaming with pain.

In the hospital I was sedated for two days whilst they tried to find the cause of the problem but it was only when Jaye went into our double garage and walked around my car that she found it was badly damaged on the driver's side. She then looked into my briefcase, found my appointments diary and immediately saw an entry written in scrawled, inch high characters giving the name and telephone number of the person who had caused the accident. There was also a short sentence admitting his responsibility, which had been signed.

Jaye immediately contacted the Hospital and gave them the information. I had apparently banged my head against the side of the car and bruised the brain which resulted in the loss of all knowledge of the crash. The hospital said I had 'suffered a hard blow to my right temple with undiagnosed damage'. The pain subsided and I was soon back at work but on my first day in the office I found I had lost part of my memory although I retained my technical knowledge. I couldn't remember simple facts such as talking to a client on the telephone, making an appointment or where I had put a file and it meant that for some time my wife, with two children in the back of the car, drove me everywhere and when I was in the office, my Secretary kept tabs on me.

One day when I was on the Company's stand at a major exhibition in London I met some old friends. One of them asked "Where are you living these days Maurice?" I um'd and ah'd for a few minutes and then took out one of my business cards, read it, and told him I lived in Nottingham. This was highly amusing but later that day when I saw another old friend and said "Hello, I haven't seen you for ages." He looked astonished and replied, "What the devil are you talking about, we had lunch yesterday." At times it was embarrassing but I laughed it off.

Some weeks after the accident, I was sitting in my office believing all was well when a salesman knocked on the door. I asked him to come in, looked up and couldn't see him.

Other than seeing shadows I was virtually blind for four days and when I saw a specialist he said I had obviously injured the part of the brain that controls the optic nerves and that the outcome was uncertain.

The accident had another affect; it caused me to transpose my words. I was quickly becoming a contender of the Reverend Spooner although I didn't say anything quite as funny as "Our Lord is a shoving leopard."

Things improved and some months later on my last visit to the neurologist he asked, "How are you feeling Maurice and how is the word transposition?" I replied "I feel fine, and I was just saying to my wife as we left the 'par cark' how much I had improved." Ah well! Life goes on and except for the odd lapse, we progressed and prospered, once again getting all of my sales team qualified for the next Annual Convention.

Six months later I lost my sight once again and the Specialist said there was nothing I could do but wait and rest. I was on tenterhooks until some six days later my sight began, very gradually, to return to normal. It was a truly frightening experience.

On the 20th July 1969 the Apollo 2 lunar Module Eagle touched down on the moon and as Neil Armstrong and Buzz Aldrin stepped onto the lunar landscape, Neil stated "That's one small step for man and a giant step for mankind." The Command Module was controlled by

Michael Collins who waited anxiously for their successful landing and return; his job was every bit as important as theirs but he shared little of the limelight showered on the other two, however, it was a spectacular achievement for all, including the workers behind the scene.

In 1972 we went to Podgora in Yugoslavia for our summer holiday and I introduced Jaye and the boys to snorkelling and the fascination of under water sea life. The whole time the boys were in the sea I had to wear my own flippers because Philip lost his from time to time and would yell "Help" as he submerged and I would leap to his rescue.
At that time it was impossible to buy flippers in a very small size.

The hotel was excellent but Philip created an amusing incident - he had been practicing a few words in German and the first time we entered the dining room (Phil leading) he had said to the head waiter 'Guten morgen mein freund'. Without looking at us, the family were led to the area in the restaurant reserved for Germans.

That evening after the children were in bed, we returned to the restaurant for the evening dinner dance. There was an excellent band and we were swinging round, entirely in our element, when one unpleasant person in an English group exclaimed quite loudly, "There go those blasted Krauts again." The next time we passed them, I called "What Ho' Old girl!"

One beautiful morning we climbed the mountain at the back of the town and met a friendly elderly couple who lived in a cave. They had moved there some years earlier when the old town sited a mile above them had been devastated by an earthquake and still stood in ruins. They insisted we stopped and took refreshment with them; a light pink wine served in the only two glasses they possessed which, before serving us, they washed in a stream running beside the mouth of the cave. They had so little and yet wanted to share what they had with us.

The meeting made a great impression on our family. Later in the week we climbed the mountain once again and took them a box of tea bags and some chocolate. They were delighted.

Another evening we were strolling along the promenade, looking at boats and the mountain scenery when we met a Serb who had just returned to his own country after living in Australia during the war. He invited us to visit his family who were extremely hospitable. It transpired that whichever drink you accepted, its fresh fruit equivalent always accompanied it. For instance, if you drank wine you were served grapes, peach brandy, you had a peach and so on.

The family owned a seventy foot sailing boat which they were overhauling but under Tito's laws, they were allowed to work on it only one half day each week. They also owned another property about which they had to keep quiet as it was illegal to own two.

Their opinion of Marshall Tito was mixed; they felt he was ruthless but that his type of dictatorship was the only way to keep Yugoslavia together but they were very worried about their future, convinced it was only his background of mixed Croatian and Slovenian descent which maintained comparative harmony between the various regions. Marshall Tito was a towering figure in Yugoslav politics for more than thirty years. Unfortunately history was to prove our friends right.

In 1971 towards the end of our stay in Nottingham, we heard that one of the oldest hotels in the centre of the town was to be demolished to make way for a new shopping centre but to mark the part it had played in the history of the area, it was going to host a spectacular fancy dress ball when everyone had to be dressed in the style of 1902, the year the hotel was built. The dinner was an extravaganza and included Crab Bisque, Quails in Aspic, Lobster with Mustard Sauce, a Baron of Beef and luxurious puddings.

136

A classical pianist entertained us during the meal and this was followed by a top swing band for dancing. The whole affair was magnificent in every respect. We hired our clothes from a costumiers but Jaye made me an evening shirt in keeping with the period. She also trimmed up her hired gown and a hairdresser gave her the correct style of the period. After the success of the ball, the hotel was reprieved and I understand it is there to this day.

In 1972 PB asked me to move to Manchester and take over as Systems Sales Manager for the North West Region which was experiencing major difficulties. Whilst this was one of their largest branches, it was a dubious promotion as it had a badly failing sales team with extremely low profitability, a factor that would have a major affect on my overall salary but I like a challenge and accepted. After assessing the potential of the sales staff, I found most of them were totally inefficient with neither aptitude nor initiative. I sacked those who were hopeless and recruited new people. The whole team was taken on with the understanding that they must be willing to be trained to sell and that they must understand the technicalities of the equipment they were to market. They began by learning how to strip down the machines, reassemble them and, when needed, modify them to suit any client's specific requirement. The training had to be attended by all members of the sales force at my home and outside normal working hours. The Region's annual turnover doubled within the year as did the salary of each salesman and they all qualified for the overseas convention, a target not previously reached nor, to my knowledge, since equalled in any region of the company.

When we moved North with the three children and my invalid mother we needed a five bedroom house so we bought a two hundred year old Coach House on the outskirts of Bolton, just eight miles from my office in Manchester. The property was situated down a private drive, which led to two other modern houses, one belonging to the Managing Director of Tube Investments, an extremely pleasant family and the other to the Chairman of the Ferranti Group.

We named our house Woodstock Lodge. It was in a magnificent setting and stood in half an acre of garden but required a total renovation. Fortunately my hobby was DIY but this was understandably my most exacting challenge as the previous owners had made some unusual conversion attempts and then abandoned them. One amusing feature of the property was a semi transparent glass brick wall separating a bedroom from the corridor - we were told the room was for a youthful au pair.

Originally there had been six bedrooms, three reception, two bathrooms, four shower rooms, eight toilets, several utility rooms and a large double garage, all left unfinished and without services.

Whilst the property had been empty it had been visited by vagrants and left in a total mess, however, we could see the potential if given careful redesign and a great deal of work. The biggest challenge was the thirty five by twenty-four foot sitting room which was dominated by a twelve foot long by eight-foot high Cumberland slate fireplace. A week before we were due to move there, our Estate Agent rang us in some distress to say that thieves, posing as the new owner's builders, had taken out a ten foot wide window and used a fork lift to strip out the huge fireplace. When we arrived a week later we found an enormous hole in the front of the house. The police were informed but they could not be expected to do anything. Loss of the fireplace was a great relief to us and we replaced it with another picture window, which gave a wonderful view of the trees and garden.

House conversion and modernisation of old property was my hobby and I found it very relaxing after my work in an office environment, however, this house was uninhabitable so Jaye took the boys to South Wales for two months of the school holidays whilst I made the property safe and carried out the massive job of moving walls, fitting new windows, internal doors, rewiring, heating, etc and removing two of the eight toilets. I designed and built a four-foot wide sweeping staircase in teak, which led from the hall to the upper floor, underneath of which I built a library in the same wood.

I spent all my spare time and, with help from various tradesmen, made a superb house but it took eighteen months to complete. Jaye was an understanding and resourceful wife bringing up two small children in the middle of this chaos but she had the design flare to make the house into a beautiful home as well as doing much of the painting, curtain making, acting as a general dogs body, looking after the family, delivering seven pups to our beautiful standard poodle bitch, Sheba, and setting out the large garden.

On completion, I sometimes used the huge lounge for training my sales team. With hindsight I think this was one of the factors upsetting some of the Company Directors. I had a spectacular house in wonderful surroundings with prestigious neighbours and earned a great deal of money.

The boys were six and eight years old when we moved to Bolton so they had to attend a new school. They had been there only a few days when the Headmaster, Mr.Caulderbank, rang Jaye in some distress and asked her to come to the school immediately as Steven had been very rude to a teacher. As it was so unlikely that our quiet son would do this, Jaye hastened there to find the Headmaster, the French teacher and the boy together.

It transpired Steven had said he didn't want to learn French but when the Headmaster had told him that many children of his age would give their right arm for such an opportunity, he had replied "I want to learn Latin, not French, Sir. I want to be a Doctor not a Head Waiter."

Woodstock Lodge had a huge lawn surrounded by many forest trees. Both boys leant to drive on the motorised lawn mower with its forward and reverse gears but Philip liked to climb trees. One Saturday morning he came into the house crying because the neighbour's gardener had told him he had no right to be up a particular tree and had ordered him down. His Mother explained to him the importance of caring for the trees and plants and of always being polite to grownups but, she added, as the tree was on our land, he could continue to climb there. Shortly afterwards Mr Hill himself saw the boy swinging upside down on a low branch of the same tree and ordered him down but Philip replied in a sing song voice "My Mummy says - these twees are in our garden - and so long as I don't hurt them - and am not wude to anyone - I can stay and climb."

I

Mr Hill steamed up to our house, hammered on the front door and angrily told Jaye "Your son has just been extremely rude to me," so Jaye asked him quietly "Were you rude to him, Mr Hill?" He immediately turned on his heel and stormed off and our paths rarely crossed again.

There was just the once when his wife rang to ask us to keep our garage door closed as it spoiled the aesthetic beauty of the place. This time Jaye explained that a robin was nesting in one of her husband's Wellingtons and until the fledglings had flown, the garage door would be left ajar during the hours of daylight.

We spent Christmas 1973 at the Imperial Hotel in Blackpool. Steven, dressed in a Frank Usher cocktail dress, won first prize as Miss World, Jaye dressed as a Bumble Bee and I was Sheik a Lotte. Mum Hamlin, by now well into her eighties, was with us and actually danced each night in the ballroom. We have many lovely memories.

Pitney Bowes entered the field of computerised Point of Sale equipment which gave me a new view of the future. Regretfully they sold it off just as it was becoming really interesting. But again, it was another good year for my branch and all of my sales team qualified for the next Convention

By 1974 I had turned the Manchester branch into a happy, efficient and very profitable arm of the Company. All was going well until someone dropped a very heavy machine on my foot and crushed my big toe which suffered eight breaks. It was in a plaster cast for six weeks.

I was unable to walk and had been off work for a month when, in March, I was summoned to PB's Head Office and informed that I had been sacked. No reason why.

Just bluntly and with no recourse. I had turned Manchester into the most profitable branch in the country. Was the big house and my lifestyle the problem?

It was so petty I took them to Court and won my case. The Court decreed that the Company should reinstate my pay to cover the short time up to ten years of service, pay compensation and grant me the pension into which I had paid; here I slipped up badly as I should have insisted that the pension was index linked.

Pitney Bowes itself was, and is, an excellent Company and I was very sorry to leave but it showed how personal jealousies and politics invade every phase of life. Looking back, I think PB did me a favour. The unfair dismissal gave me new energy to widen my horizons and I believe it was the birth of ambition within me and the beginning of conceiving the unique idea of using a computer to evaluate the computer supplier market.

I was immediately recruited by AML Machines Limited as their Northern Regional Manager based in Manchester. When I arrived at the office, I found many irregularities and at least half of the sales orders were either fictitious or fraudulent. I sacked all the salesmen involved, recruited new and set up strict order verification controls. However, after fighting a losing battle with a Head Office that was not only unethical but downright dishonest, I resigned and shortly afterwards the Company went into liquidation only to re-open the following day under another name. I was better off out of such a devious organisation.

Chapter 14 – We Fight the Print Unions

My wife's company, OKOS Limited, had a Graphic Art Division, a Print Department and a Direct Mail Service.

She was able to supply a client with a design and printing service and had the capability to mail up to one hundred thousand letters a day.

She had a good staff and suggested that I should join her and add a Systems Division, buying and selling "end of lease" equipment. I thought it was a great idea. She had built her company into a successful office services provider with a reputation for quality work, carried out efficiently and on time. She knew more than I did about business management and financial control whilst at the same time being fully conversant and efficient at most jobs within the direct mail business and happy to get stuck in where an extra pair of hands was needed.

My job was to build up the business using Mercantile Leasing who had a problem disposing of equipment which had reached the end of its lease period. They would advise me when they had a specific piece of equipment available, give me the details of the manufacturer, model number, original price, etc. and where it was situated. Without sight I would estimate whether or not the equipment could be refurbished to a high enough standard to obtain an original manufacturer's maintenance contract. I would then make an offer to the Finance Company and my word was accepted as a firm contract. I arranged collection and paid their account.

Finally I had to find a suitable buyer and make a profit covering the cost of collecting the machine and its restoration. Sometimes the equipment was beyond upgrading, or useless, and I accepted there was no come back and wrote it off to experience. It was stimulating work.

It was our policy to scrap anything for which we could not acquire an original manufacturer's maintenance agreement and during our first year I bought up all kinds of equipment and modernised and re-equipped OKOS so that it was fully automated. Jaye's larger clients were British Steel, the National Coal Board, G.U.S., Littlewoods, etc. We did very well.

Some say that all good things must come to an end and for us this happened in 1977 and was due to the Print and Graphics Unions, SOGAT and NGA, when they started their dirty tricks campaign. The NGA had always dominated the labour intensive world of paper and ink and SOGAT was the union of print machine operators and assistants.

The introduction of microprocessors revolutionised the industry. It reduced the time spent on many lengthy manual tasks particularly in the field of type setting and graphics and thereby greatly improved productivity and profitability. It became a business based on electronic devices and in which the NGA had little influence but they were happy to break a company if its employees would not join their organisation.

We were a non Union Company providing good working conditions and paying above Union rates, however, when the print war began, they brought it to our doorstep which meant we had difficulty obtaining printing ink and other supplies. They pressured our staff to join one or other of their organisations and this resulted in a great loss of revenue. All the work we did had to carry a Union acceptance sticker to prove that a paid up member had actually done the job. It also meant that we could not use a client's own graphics if the work was not Union approved. Likewise we were not allowed to accept printed work for mailings if it didn't carry the stickers of both Unions. It was farcical.

It appeared that almost overnight a happy Company without demarcation was turned into an 'Us and Them' place of work. The problem came to a head one day when a major client gave us an exceptionally large rush job which had to be completed by a specific date. We needed staff to work over the weekend and on previous occasions this had not only been acceptable but welcomed as we paid bonus rates and we enjoyed working together. Not this time. The Union Representatives said the staff would not work, irrespective of the fact that if the job was not completed on time, we would not only let our client down but also probably do irreparable damage to our future business, not to mention losing our reputation.

We put these facts before the Union and offered extra money and time off in lieu but also said that if we were forced to let our customer down we would close the Company. The Unions called our bluff and said "No."

Family and friends rallied round and after working a weekend without sleep, we completed the job on time.

We then refused all new business of any kind until we were sure that all outstanding work had been completed and delivered. We paid all outstanding debts, paid the staff off and put the Company into voluntary liquidation. We vowed never again to have a business that could be controlled by Unions.

Goodbye Unions,
Goodbye Staff and
God Bless Maggie Thatcher.

PART 2

CON-sultancy

Chapter 15 - Computer Consultancy Re-invented

*It must be remembered that there is nothing more
difficult to plan, more doubtful of success, or more
dangerous to manage than the creation of a new system.*

*For the initiator has the enmity of all who would profit by
the preservation of the old institutions and merely lukewarm
defenders of those who might gain by the new ones.*

Niccolo Machiavelli 1513.

In October 1978 whilst Jaye and I considered our long term future,
we moved to a small suite of offices above a dress shop in the centre
of Bolton where we concentrated on our association with Mercantile
Credit and the selling of the higher end of office equipment including
the early VRCs (visual record computers) and word processing
systems. It was lucrative and enjoyable and kept us financially stable.

After so many years in the Air Force I had developed a preference
for holidaying in the British Isles but this particular summer had been
wet and cool and Jaye rebelled.

She took off on her own and joined a safari party of French
tourists for a holiday in Tunisia to find sunshine and to investigate
museums and ancient mosaics.

The first part of the adventure was by Land Rover to a large oasis
but when there, the travellers were presented with camels and native
dress and told it was essential to
wear this because of the attitude of
the local tribes they might
encounter. The French ladies
chickened out but Jaye, dressed in
flowing robes, continued with the
rest of the party. The first stop was a

hotel built in a large hole in the ground where she had to spend the
night in the women's quarters wedged between two large Arab
ladies.

Whilst Jaye was away I continued to improve the coach house and thought about our future and how to solve the problem of choosing the correct computer for the needs of each particular business. My research proved to me that a computerised library of information on the total market was the only possible solution and that this information should encompass all the equipment made by every computer manufacturer together with details of each software developer and the packages they had written.

The main obstacle was to find a computer search engine with cross-relational 4GL capability.

I wanted to offer a totally unbiased computer advice service able to match any client's computer requirements against the total UK market place and produce the ideal solution.

All that remained was for me to explain my ideas to Jaye when she returned from holiday and to get her opinion of its feasibility.

Jaye returned from Tunisia with a lovely tan and a beautiful smile.

As she stepped into Arrivals, I said, "Hello Darling, I want to sell Woodstock Lodge and buy a small house so that I can buy a big mini computer. If you agree we are going to solve the computer selection problem and form a consultancy company."

She replied "Okay." Just like that! "What a girl!"

When we announced our intensions to the media, the Consultancy Industry laughed and threw scorn on my solution saying that there was no such in-depth IT information library and even if one existed, there was no computer with an operating system or application software capable of such intricate cross relational matching.

I clarified my thoughts and produced a specification which showed how to develop such an information research facility.

The first major task was to start creating a vast database of all information relating to manufacturers and developers of computer hardware, software and application packages available within the UK and then to create a cross-relational search engine of our own.

I wanted a consultant to be able to key every aspect of a client's specification of requirements into the database regardless of the type of business, commerce or industry, and for the system to match it automatically against the thousands of details available. The system should then produce an itemised report showing which suppliers products and services most closely matched the client's needs and in particular, identify those suppliers who had experience of installing their system into a similar type and size of business as that of the enquirer.

My target was to obtain such high accuracy with our selection system that we would be able to offer every client who used our advice a one million pound guarantee (underwritten by Lloyds of London) to replace the system if our recommendation failed.

At this time in 1978 almost all information retrieval systems were based on a Boolean Text search. A method that, in my opinion, allowed only the poorest search and selection. Boolean search results depended upon the data capture of vast quantities of textual information which, even after the matching process, left a lot of work to be done manually by sifting and evaluation. This was highly labour intensive taking days, not minutes, for each enquiry and I believe had less than a 20% ability to produce an appropriate list of suppliers which more often than not missed the best solution.

From our earliest analysis of the problems facing us, Jaye and I agreed that the whole project relied upon finding a "multi-user", cross-relational mini computer with the ability to develop into a bespoke bibliographic multi-relational search engine.

Months passed and all my enquiries failed to find such a computer and the continuation of our project seemed doubtful.

We continued in business as Maurice Hamlin Associates (MHA) to keep our heads above water whilst also putting maximum effort into finding such a beast. After weeks of demonstrations and assessments we had to agree that there was no such fully advanced animal on the market, however, we did find one mini incorporating most of the right basic elements and which would allow us to modify and integrate it into the first fully inter-relational cross matching search engine.

It was a Molecular 18 mini computer from BCL (a part of the Trafalger House Group), which came inclusive with its operating system. It was a demand paged, multiuser, virtual memory, time-sharing computer operating system based around a unique "multivalued database" (advertised as the first 3.5 GL). It also came together with report writing software called SIMPLE. We considered it to be the only possibility and decided to take the plunge.

It was sink or swim.

Woodstock Lodge was put up for sale because we needed all the resources we could summon to sustain us for a long period of time and to finance our daunting venture. We bought our Molecular and started creating my vision.

Our next task was to recruit software specialists conversant with the Molecular and SIMPLE so that we could start the huge task before us.

We found a buyer for our house almost immediately, the Deputy British Consul of New York who was about to retire. He paid a deposit to our Bolton Estate Agent and it was understood that completion would be delayed until he retired to England nine months later.

In the meantime we employed twenty researchers with experience in information library search and retrieval. Their job was to seek out every supplier and manufacturer of computer hardware and/or software application packages and then record each facet of the information against a specific four-character code.

I devised a library of criteria codes relating to every meaningful item, feature or function I could think of. The Researchers linked every item of their research to its appropriate code and also cross related the code to every supplier who sold or maintained the product.

If, during their work, they found something for which no criterion had been issued, I was advised and a new individual code was created and this in turn was cross-related to every relevant supplier's record. It was an ever-expanding function. When we began, all areas of research and development were a matter of trial and error but following many months of disappointments, our search and match capabilities started to offer hope.

We named our new search engine 'SystemSearch'.

We promised our new clients that their specification would be matched against every integrated computer system and application software package available on the UK market and whilst SystemSearch allowed Boolean text searching as an additional facility, it approached information retrieval from a totally different concept. It allowed every definable attribute of a company, its software products and services, to be given our four-character code e.g.

> Simple Stock Control - A004
> Stock with Colour, Size and Style - A397
> Stock Traceability - A395
> Quarantined Stock - D478

There were 44 criteria covering all aspects of Stock Control and altogether 4,629 coded criteria created, any of which could be linked to any supplier and each of their relevant hardware, software packages or services.

This meant that instead of having to ask the system for all textual references on a subject, supplier, industry or product and then having to read much that was totally abstract and meaningless, we had only to enter the attributes essential to the requirement i.e.

1. Every Industry/Business type - Architects, Broking, Construction, Dentists, Energy, Farming, Investment, Petroleum, etc.

2. General Application area - Manufacturing, Animal Feedstuffs, Analogue Control, Accounting, Production Control, Sub-contractor, Control, Risk Analysis, etc.

3. Special Application functions - Multi Lingual, Desk Top Publishing, Digitiser, Crop and Resize, DTP, Compositor, Headers, Footers, etc. and where geographical support is available (worldwide).

4. Maintenance support – 2, 4, 8 hours etc. or via modem availability.

5. Support - single source, turnkey or otherwise.

6. Languages - which computer language available.

7. Operating systems.

8. Spoken language - is the package available in French, Arabic, Chinese, etc.

9. Hardware - any or all the above may be matched to run on any specific hardware.

10. Research into which specific services or expertise each company held.

11. List of all companies with a specific expertise and who are VARs (value added retailers) for each application area.

12. A client's specification could also request that all suppliers selected must conform to any one or more of the following:-

   a. Specific software, hardware or operating system platform.

   b. Each aspect of the client's particular manufacturing or business accounting requirements.

   c. Where suppliers offer hardware and software support - in which county or specific country, and if staff are fluent in the language of that country.

   d. If the supplier must have a turnover exceeding X £Millions.

   e. The number of years experience the supplier has had in the client's business/industry application function area.

As the months ticked by we were getting concerned over the sale of the house. We had had several communications from the Consul to say that all was going to plan but then when eleven months had passed since he had paid his deposit, we were told that he had bought elsewhere and wanted his deposit back (English law makes this acceptable). Disgusted, we put the house back on the market.

We kept our faith in SystemSearch and development continued whilst I worked as a salesman for MHA.

We uncover an International Con Man:

A few days after the American Consul's disastrous stab in the back a large car pulled into our circular drive. The caller said his name was Black and that he was interested in buying the house. He took a long time inspecting the property and at the same time mentioned he worked for the Saudi Arabian Government. He said he was currently negotiating with British Leyland for one hundred massive vehicles which were designed to unload barges in shallow shore waters and each vehicle would cost £200,000. He added he was also arranging to purchase 100,000 tins of biscuits from Nabisco (later to become part of Rank Hovis). He added that he liked the house and wanted to show it to his family. On parting he commented he was about to take over a vacant block of offices previously owned by our local newspaper and said there would be no need for a mortgage for the house.

We were delighted and arranged a further viewing three days later. On the second visit, accompanied by his wife and children, all went well but this time he brought up the fact that he needed to fit out his offices with equipment and furniture adding that he was so busy with his other negotiations, it would be a great help if I could take on the contract for the office and that money would be no problem. We discussed his needs and I agreed to obtain quotations and delivery dates. He smiled and again said he wanted to go ahead with the purchase of our property.

Jaye remarked that the clothes the wife and the children wore did not reflect the money Black portended to have. His family had been totally overawed with the size of the house and particularly the luxury of the bathrooms.

Mr Black contacted me by telephone to ask how quickly I could get the orders placed and the office ready for his occupation. I replied this could be done as soon as he agreed the quotations and advanced a retainer.

The next day I visited a small but efficient printer I used for business cards and whilst chatting, I noticed a Litho Press running off letterheads. I asked if business was going well and picked up one of the prints and was surprised to see the high quality of the paper and what appeared to be the official letterhead of the Bank of Riyadh, Saudi Arabia. I asked him who he was printing the letter heads for and he told me that the Bank's representative was in Bolton and that if the sample printing met their quality and price requirements, he would get all their printing work.

The penny dropped. I said, "Whatever you do, don't let him have this work. Make an excuse. This isn't right. I will contact the Bank in Saudi." I immediately sent a copy of the letterhead to the Bank by express and the next thing I knew, Scotland Yard was breathing down my neck and Mr Black was in prison awaiting trial for fraud.

We were later informed that he lived with his wife and children in a caravan at the bottom of his mother's council house garden on the other side of Bolton. I was disgusted with the Saudis, Leyland and Nabisco. Not one of them had the courtesy to thank me for unmasking the man's duplicity. It also showed that I should always trust Jaye's instincts. Some months later we sold the house to a genuine buyer.

Life can be hard for a young boy:

We moved from Woodstock Lodge to Chorley and a few days later the boys came home on exeat. Philip clanked up the wooden stairs and rushed around the bedrooms, came downstairs somewhat horrified and said "Mummy, there appears to be only one bathroom." My! Oh! My!

Mummies can be misjudged:

In late December, Jaye and Philip took the two standard poodles for a walk beside the stream in the silent winter wood. It was a lovely clear day and the snow was crisp on the ground. They had walked for about a mile when they found that someone had fixed a stout rope fixed over a branch of a huge tree so it was possible to swing from bank to bank across the wide stream.

This delighted my son and he had swung there and back several times before the rope gave way and he landed on his feet in the middle of the stream with the water lapping over the top of his Wellingtons. Jaye asked him to climb out quickly as they should hurry home but he said he would like to walk in the water for a few minutes. She watched his knees between his short grey school trousers and his Wellington boots turn blue and told him they must definitely leave now. Then a man with a Labrador came along the path walking towards them, Philip immediately turned to his Mother, put his hands together as if in prayer and said, "Please, please Mummy. Can I come out now? I promise I will be a very good boy."

The look the stranger gave Jaye was beyond description but I wonder what he thought of the laughter he heard after he had passed by.

SystemSearch was launched on the market in 1980:

SystemSearch was now capable of matching any enquirer's requirement against every aspect of over 7,400 computer manufacturers and suppliers (excluding retailers) and the 26,250 Hardware/Software products they marketed.

Below is an actual printout of the results of a match carried out for a major Shoe Manufacturing and Distribution Group which necessitated SystemSearch matching the eighty seven specified functions required by the Group so they could control their wide financial, production and vehicle distribution management operation.

The left hand side of the page shows the specific functions and at the top of the matrix, each four-character number relates to a specific supplier's identity code. Each column containing a 'Y' showed that the software included the required feature but where a 'dash' is shown, it meant the feature was not available. Each supplier's ability to meet the total requirement is shown as a percentage at the foot of each column.

The actual time taken for the system to produce and print out this analysis was never more than two or three minutes.

We would then contact the listed suppliers whose score was over 50% to enquire the name of a user of the system they had installed and ask for permission to contact the customer to obtain a reference of how the system had met his requirements and its expansion capability to cope with projected company growth.

Next we would arrange for the three most successful suppliers to give a demonstration at the user's installation.

Over the following years Systemsearch never had a failure or a single complaint about the accuracy of its recommendations. A guarantee was never required.

Here follows an actual example of a clients match showing his eighty seven specific systems requirements.

Member : 490001   Client Ref : LOTUS

	Suppliers					
	7184	7208	7249	7313	7602	7849
Multi-Currency	Y	Y	Y	Y	Y	Y
Ledger - Sales	Y	Y	Y	Y	Y	Y
Ledger - Purchase	Y	Y	Y	Y	Y	Y
Payroll	Y	Y	Y	Y	Y	Y
Production Control	Y	Y	Y	Y	Y	Y
Multi Cost Centre	Y	Y	Y	Y	Y	Y
Payroll - Casual Labour	Y	Y	-	-	-	Y
Critical Path Analysis	-	Y	-	-	Y	Y
Ledger - General/Nominal	Y	Y	Y	Y	Y	Y
BOMP - Bill of Materials Processing	Y	Y	Y	Y	Y	Y
Invoicing	Y	Y	Y	Y	Y	Y
Pensions	Y	Y	Y	Y	-	Y
Sales Analysis/Statistics	Y	Y	Y	Y	Y	Y
Picking List	Y	Y	Y	Y	Y	Y
Production Scheduling	Y	Y	Y	Y	Y	Y
Stock Costing	Y	Y	Y	Y	Y	Y
Cash Book	Y	Y	Y	Y	-	Y
Credit Control	Y	Y	Y	Y	Y	Y
Statements	Y	Y	Y	Y	Y	Y
Trend Analysis	-	Y	-	Y	Y	Y
WIP - Work in Progress	Y	Y	Y	Y	Y	Y
EPOS/POS - Point of Sale	-	-	Y	-	-	-
Works Order Processing	Y	Y	Y	Y	Y	Y
Waste Optimisation	-	Y	Y	-	Y	Y
Distribution Planning	-	-	Y	Y	Y	Y
Order Processing - Sales	Y	Y	Y	Y	Y	Y
Order Processing - Purchase	Y	Y	Y	Y	Y	Y
Vehicle Route Scheduling	Y	Y	Y	Y	-	Y
Diary/Reminder System	Y	Y	Y	Y	Y	Y
Tachograph Analysis	-	-	Y	-	-	-
Prospect Control	Y	Y	Y	Y	Y	Y
Multi-Company	Y	Y	Y	Y	Y	Y
Production Forecasting	Y	Y	Y	Y	Y	Y
Quality Control	-	Y	Y	Y	Y	Y
MRP I - Material Requirement Plannin	Y	Y	-	Y	Y	Y
Salesmen Control	Y	Y	-	Y	Y	Y
Traceability to BS5750 Standards	-	Y	Y	Y	Y	Y
Vehicle Fleet Management	Y	Y	Y	Y	Y	Y
VAT Analysis	Y	Y	Y	Y	Y	Y
Commission Processing	Y	Y	Y	Y	Y	Y
Multi-Location Stock Control	Y	Y	Y	Y	Y	Y
Bar Code Reading	-	Y	Y	Y	Y	Y
Bar Code Printing	-	Y	Y	Y	Y	Y
Personnel Management	Y	Y	Y	Y	Y	Y
Expense Accounting	-	Y	Y	Y	Y	Y
Costing and/or Estimating	Y	Y	Y	Y	Y	Y
Product Costing	Y	Y	Y	Y	Y	Y
Subcontractor Control	Y	-	Y	Y	-	Y
MRP II - Manufacturing Resource Plan	Y	Y	Y	Y	Y	Y
Piece Work Control	Y	Y	-	Y	Y	-
Multi-Branch	Y	Y	Y	Y	Y	Y
Retailing	-	-	-	-	-	-
Distribution	Y	Y	Y	Y	Y	Y
Footwear	Y	Y	-	-	-	-
Clothing/Garments	Y	Y	-	-	-	-
Warehouse Management	Y	Y	Y	Y	Y	Y
Promotion Marketing	-	Y	-	Y	Y	Y
Stock Valuation	Y	Y	Y	Y	Y	Y
Demand Forecasting	Y	Y	Y	Y	Y	Y
Raw Stock	Y	Y	Y	Y	Y	Y
Allocated Stock	Y	Y	Y	Y	Y	Y
Finished Stock	Y	Y	Y	Y	Y	Y
Shift Work	-	Y	-	-	-	Y
Vehicle Loading Schedules	-	Y	Y	-	-	Y
Consolidation of Accounts	Y	Y	Y	Y	Y	Y
Batch/Lot Traceability	-	Y	Y	Y	Y	Y
Stock Control - Style/Colour/Size	Y	Y	Y	Y	Y	Y
Rejected Stock Returns	Y	Y	Y	Y	Y	Y
INTRASTAT - VAT & Statistics Reporti	Y	Y	Y	Y	Y	Y
Stock Transfer	Y	Y	Y	Y	Y	Y
Minimum/Maximum Stock Levels	Y	Y	Y	Y	Y	Y
Bin Location Stock Management	Y	Y	Y	Y	Y	Y
Multi-Warehouse Control	Y	Y	Y	Y	Y	Y
Vehicle Utilisation/Performance	-	-	Y	-	-	-
Graphics - Design	-	-	-	Y	-	-
Graphs & Charts	Y	Y	Y	Y	Y	Y
Pattern Generation	-	-	-	-	-	-
WP - Word Processing	Y	Y	Y	Y	Y	Y
Percentage Capability of meeting above Criteria	75	90	85	80	77	87

"Y" = Available   "-" = Not Available

158

The family enjoy the delights of caravanning:

We bought a caravan big enough to accommodate two dogs, two boys and two adults and had some wonderful adventures. We were members of the Caravan Club and were amazed at the friendliness of the other travellers. Whenever we arrived at a destination in the dark or in the rain, there was always someone who would leave the comfort of their own van to help total strangers. We usually headed for Scotland and stayed in Ardfern but sometimes travelled as far as Oban or Sky.

The first year we stayed in Ardfern we parked on the moors where we could watch the otters playing in the Loch. We had a visit from a very young bull, a strawberry blonde with curly hair, however, when we saw him the following year we couldn't believe our eyes. He was huge, magnificent. Needless to say, this time no one attempted to stroke him.

One year our moor was invaded by TV filmmakers and Philip upset them by peering over a rock just as Moira Anderson was miming to a song. Her second attempt was foiled when a sheep wandered in front of the camera. They were not a happy band, bored and in a bad mood because the star kept them waiting so long.

Down in the village we were introduced to the Laird, an impressive figure in kilt and woolly socks complete with dagger. With his red hair, beard and sturdy figure, he looked as though he had just left the film set of Rob Roy. He was a true party animal and local gossip said that on wild nights in his ancestral home, he had been known to enjoy taking pot shots at portraits of his forebears.

Another year we arrived at Ardfern in the midst of the Guinness Regatta. About a dozen yachts had sailed over from Norway to join in the festivities and I found my smattering of Norwegian quite useful, however, I don't advise the feint hearted to try boisterous Norwegian dancing to Scottish music. The weather was perfect and the Laird had bought bottles of sweets for the children's Regatta.

-0-0-0-0-

By 1982 we had twenty-two franchised ComputerScan Consultants offering advice in line with my concept that "No single person could be a specialist in all areas of industry, commerce and services."

159

To this end we had developed specific questionnaires to cover the whole spectrum of business. The Consultant's job was to visit each client, complete all aspects of the relevant questionnaire and obtain a detailed description of the client's business practices together with any special needs.

On receipt of the questionnaire from the Consultant, Head Office would convert the completed specification into criteria as per the example above. After analysis, a recommended shortlist of three or four suppliers who were considered to be the most appropriate were returned to the Consultant who would arrange for the client to see demonstrations in a live working environment which had a similar workload to that of our client. Finally, we would advise the client which system we considered to be the most appropriate for his purpose but the final choice was the client's. We never had a failure.

The Falklands War:

April 1982 began the same as any other normal working day and it was only whilst listening to the BBC news that we learned Argentinian forces had invaded the Falkland Isles, a place few British people had ever thought about. Even so, we knew it was inhabited solely by Brits who wished to remain under the British flag so when Mrs.Thatcher declared war on Argentina and swore to send a force to regain it, most of us were in favour of the action, however, we were all very pleased when the war ended in June with the surrender of the Argentinians. It had lasted seventy-four days with three civilian Falklanders being killed and also 255 British and 649 Argentinian soldiers, sailors and airmen.

The political effects of the war were strong in both countries. In Argentina a wave of patriotic sentiment swept the land but the heavy casualty figures prompted protests against their Military Government which hastened its downfall and the process of democratisation. In the United Kingdom, Margaret Thatcher's Government was bolstered up and it helped them to gain victory in the 1983 general election which prior to the War was thought to be uncertain. Personally I believed the war was justified but I felt that the distant Atlantic mineral rights helped the UK to accept the tremendous costs involved.

On the 26th November 1982 we obtained our Consultancy Guarantee Policy underwritten by Lloyds of London:

DELEGATED AUTHORITY

MINI AND MICRO COMPUTER INSURANCE POLICIES

BRITISH ENGINE INSURANCE LIMITED of Longridge House, Manchester (hereinafter referred to as British Engine)

authorise

of
(hereinafter referred to as the Broker)

to sign and issue Mini and Micro Computer Insurance Policies as supplied by British Engine to the Broker on their behalf subject to the Terms and Conditions annexed to this Authorisation

Signed on behalf of the parties hereto

for British Engine Insurance Limited
Branch Office: 8 Exchange Street, Manchester M2 7HA

The terms and conditions upon which the Broker is so authorised are hereby accepted by the Broker

for the Broker

Date 26 Nov 82

This proved we were able to offer a quality service, which was unbiased, and had never before been considered possible by any other consultancy.

Even so, getting accepted by the business community was not an easy task for such a small Company particularly when Government departments showed no interest whatsoever. They appeared to wear blinkers against progress.

In 1983 A.T.Kearney produced a report (backed by the DTI), which stated that the UK Government and Industry were losing £800 million per year by buying the wrong computer systems.

Another report gave an example of what the losses featured in the Kinsey Report could actually represent i.e. if that wasted £800 million was spread over four thousand companies it would equal, on average, £200,000 per company and businesses spending that sort of money on computers have about two hundred employees. That equates to placing 800,000 jobs at risk through insolvency or through loss of major contracts due to the poor efficiency of management control.

In conjunction with the Kinsey report we took part in the annual Manchester Business Exhibition and used a coffin surrounded by useless and inappropriate computers as the centrepiece to emphasise the seriousness of buying the wrong computer system.

It made a somewhat startling impression on some of the more imaginative attendees.

Hospitals in particular were one of the major victims of the lack of Government policy and guidance as shown in the following story of my experiences with the Isle of White Health Authority.

162

Internal hospital politics were chaotic.

The Senior Administrator of the Isle of White Health Authority asked me for advice because neither he nor the Senior Surgeon, both members of the Hospital Computer Committee, were particularly computer literate but they knew that the Hospital Purchasing and Usage Policy was wrong. I was asked to do an honest and factual survey of what their overall policy should be.

I found they had made a fundamental mistake because they had not established a computerised Hospital Master Patient Index. Instead of this, every Head of Department was investing in a stand-alone micro or mini computer, all running under different operating systems and none of them were able to communicate with each other. Every department was creating its own separate record for each patient they treated. Almost without exception, each Head of Department was determined to buy the particular computer he preferred for his requirements with no thought of mutual benefits or efficiency to the Hospital in general.

Not one system knew, or was able to record, if a patient had also attended another department in the Hospital. Each computer recreated its own Appointments Register and Patient Records showing the patient's personal details but, each time that patient attended a different department, all the information had to be recorded again on their system.

Imagine the time wasted re-entering the thousands of patients' personal details, the lack of management statistics and the confusion from incorrect entries caused by poor data entry. The Hospital did not have the ability to print off a total record of patients treated either at the Hospital or within the Group.

I was particularly disillusioned with the Pathology Department which had installed an £80,000 system only to find that the word processing module was unable to print out understandable textual reports on their research. Yet they were recommending the local Group Purchasing Office to order a further five similar computers for other Group Hospitals despite knowing that they would be unable to communicate with each other or compare patient records.

I sent an extensive and somewhat critical report to the Administrator and he arranged a meeting so I could explain all aspects of my findings in detail to the full Committee.

It was rather intimidating to express to their faces just how badly I considered they had managed their IT but I presented the cold bitter truth. It was a lengthy report describing the failings of each department and I pointed out that their thinking was illogical and wasteful of both money and resources.

I impressed on them that they were all being insular, considering only their own direct needs and not what the Hospital and patients required. I ended by saying they needed to scrap their current plans, appoint a single person with computer knowledge to control and manage the overall installation, build a Master Patient Record system to which all Departments would be linked by either a terminal or integrated micro/mini computer and with each having the ability to produce intelligent departmental reports. I closed by saying that no department should be allowed to order any hardware or software without agreement from the proposed System Controller because it should be his responsibility alone to ensure that, where possible, new requisitions should be able to integrate into the Master Patient Records system.

The meeting closed in a sombre atmosphere. My two initial contacts thanked me, privately delighted, but said the Committee would no longer need my services. They paid me quite happily.

The problems of fatherhood:

After leaving the RAF, my good friend Collin Carpenter worked as an Air Traffic Controller at an American Base in Norfolk. His wife, Mich, had recently had a baby at home so we visited these old friends to congratulate them on the birth of a lovely daughter and they relayed the following story:-

The morning after the birth of the baby, Collin had assured Mich that he would take care of everything. He would prepare breakfast, take young Adrian to school, put the washing in the machine and make sure everything was clean and tidy before the Midwife's visit. How difficult could that be?

He put the clothes into the twin tub but didn't close the lid, put a saucepan of milk on the cooker and popped the bread into the toaster. Simple! The back doorbell rang announcing the early arrival of the Midwife so he removed the saucepan of milk from the cooker but the handle was hot and it burned his hand so he threw it up into the air. The pan landed squarely in the washing machine just as the toast caught fire. He rushed to open the back door, slipped on the spilt milk and cannoned across the kitchen banging his head on the wall.

When he opened his eyes he saw two sturdy legs encased in thick stockings and wearing heavy black shoes and heard the voice of doom saying "Poor Mrs Carpenter. Poor Mrs Carpenter."

Colin also brought us up to date about Brian, another ex RAF friend of ours also working for the Americans. He had an ancient Riley Pathfinder with a fuel pump which was always giving trouble. As the pump was located in the boot of the car, it meant that each time the Riley stopped, the driver had to get out of the vehicle, open the boot and thump the offending pump with a sturdy hammer. They lived deep in the country and had to get the car to the garage so Brian came up with a brilliant idea. He put a rug into the boot of the car and told his wife to get in there and every time she felt the engine stop, to bang the pump. None too pleased, she crept into the boot, however, unbeknown to them, the Police had roadblocks on all minor roads in the area because someone had escaped from the local Borstal Detention Centre.

The Police stopped Brian and asked for identity but an insistent banging was coming from the back of the car so the Policeman asked if he had anything in his boot. Brian replied "No. Only my wife." When the Police opened the boot they found Pauline crouching down, wielding a hefty hammer. She looked up and said, "What's up Bri?"

An embarrassed girl was liberated but they were both held at the Police Station for some hours until their identities were confirmed.

Chapter 16 – NHS Scandal

In the early 1980s computing was still almost a foreign language to most senior directors of companies or heads of organisations such as hospitals and Government departments and certainly to most ministers and departmental heads.

It was also a golden opportunity for computer manufacturers, software suppliers and their agents to Sell, Sell, Sell whatever they had available to an unknowing audience regardless of suitability.

The Kearney Report and my open criticism of the Isle of White Hospital's IT policy was widely reported in "Computer Weekly " and other journals which prompted many letters of agreement and requests for help from Regional Hospital Managers and IT staff who realised they were totally out of their depth when searching for appropriate systems and software. No one in Government appeared to appreciate the massive effect computerisation was going to have on either improving or holding back our Country's industry and commerce.

It was equivalent to another Industrial Revolution, and Britain missed being at the forefront.

The Government's top priority should have been to install an IT El Supremo with Ministerial authority but one who had real IT knowledge and in particular, if one could be found, a person who was not susceptible to the gifts and pressure of lobbying by vested interests. Industry, business and hospitals alike all needed specific guidelines.

Computer suppliers should have been made responsible for training their salesmen to understand the capabilities of the computer systems they were selling and the suppliers should also have been responsible for damages if their salesmen sold systems which were incapable of carrying out a client's specified job.

Computing was so new that many salesmen, and consultants, had little understanding of the plethora of needs that such a variety of business, commerce and industries required – in fact the computer industry itself was only just realising what a bonanza of new business opportunities had just been created and also the need to create hardware and software to satisfy the thousands of new applications. All too quickly, however, many realised they could sell almost anything in this fertile market. Without bothering to give salesmen proper training or laying down any sales ethics, all they asked of their staff was that they obtain orders and collect their commission.

Most buyers had little knowledge of computing or the rights and wrongs of taking the supplier to Court for misrepresentation.

Suppliers, consultants and lobbyists should also have been made accountable when they recommended systems and unattainable deadlines for completion of major computer/software projects. If they failed, they should have been named and company directors and/or political figures held responsible for their mistakes.

Computer Weekly reports my comments on IT Ministers:

Kenneth Baker (top left) John Butcher (top right) and Geoffrey Pattie: unlikely to solve problem

It is time for legislation on systems specifications

From Maurice Hamlin

Manufacturers or suppliers of business computer systems should be obliged by law to give a specification of what is being supplied.

I have suggested this to successive ministers responsible for technology, including Kenneth Baker, John Butcher and Geoffrey Pattie. Their references to voluntary arrangements are not, alas, likely to solve the problem now clearly established.

What is happening is that purchasers rarely ask for a specification of the applications and capacity required. Inappropriate installations follow the temptation to make a sale. Business seems unable to protect itself: it needs help.

We think that sales worth £80 million a year soon have to be replaced. It is a huge waste when the disturbance to industry is taken into account.

A bill should be drawn up to enforce the supplier to put into writing a description of what is supplied, and the cost, covering hardware, software and modification. Finally, the supplier should sign a statement to say he understands the client's needs and can implement them.

On hardware, specification should include reference to the following:
● Expansion capability without processor change
● Whether or not the system is true multi-user multi-function

● Whether or not the system can spool and includes spool interrupt
● Whether or not the system has background printing
● What response time can be expected for an average VDU enquiry when the system is expanded to the foreseeable requirement
● Full maintenance costs and whether or not one can use an alternative maintenance source.

Specifications for software should include confirmation of the availability of software extensions proposed for the future.

Maurice Hamlin, Atlas Computer Consultants, The Guild Centre, Preston, Lancashire PR1 1QR.

I wrote to Technology Ministers Geoffrey Pattie, John Butcher and Kenneth Baker warning them that computer sales were made with little or no restraint from each computer company's management on whether or not the system sold was fit for the purpose for which it was intended.

I highlighted the harm this was doing not only to the businesses involved but also to British industry's efficiency and expansion capabilities.

No one listened.

Financial Times:
MICHAEL WILTSHIRE talks to Maurice Hamlin regarding his revolutionary Computerised Computer Consultancy service and about the high cost of making the wrong choice

AROUND 80 per cent of office computer equipment is on lease. But while this arrangement clearly offers many advantages, one of the worst leasing mistakes a company can fall into is to make a hasty choice of equipment and find itself stuck with the wrong computer system.

The cost each year of such computer disasters is estimated to at least £60m in the UK alone. This is the view of Atlas Computer Consultants, which recently surveyed 200 UK computer installations.

According to the consultancy, 20 per cent of the 30,000 business systems supplied each- year in the £10,000 to £100,000 price range later proved to be inappropriate - and have to be replaced.

The chaos resulting from selecting the wrong system can sometimes lead to bankruptcy, especially if the company concerned is a small business which sees computerisation as the answer to a make-or-break situation, says Mr Maurice Hamlin, Managing Director of ComputerScan.

"Literally every week we hear of another disaster," he says. People who have got it wrong are often very reluctant to admit it. Even people with in house computer management expertise can be fooled or led astray by financial incentives from unethical sales perks.

While Britain had the highest per capita use of computers in Europe, many potential users did not really know what computer equipment and software was best suited for their needs.

"You need the right advice," adds Mr Hamlin.

The main mistakes are:

1. *Evaluation which overlooks essential aspects of the user's business.*
2. *Purchase of single user systems when a multi company accounting system is required.*
3. *Equipment and software, which proves to be a poor fit for the business concerned.*
4. *Inadequate capacity either at the time of installation or for expansion which should have been foreseen.*
5. *Programmes not written in an appropriate commercial, technical or scientific language.*

Not taken into the reckoning are the many selections and functions, which could have been improved upon. So many users make the best of a poor selection due to lack of knowledge, poor or unscrupulous salesman's advice.

Similar mistakes are also made sometimes in purchasing larger computers priced well above £100,000. According to Hamlin, a computer department director or manager may be so set on the prestige of saying he has installed or controls a main frame (which needs a controlled environment room) when in fact a large mini distributed system would be more suitable. Empire building by computer departments buying a main frame has harmed many companies.

In thirty years from now, if anyone remembers, they'll look back and say, "Hamlin was right."

The joys of parenthood:

Early one Sunday morning we were woken by a policeman ringing the bell with some urgency. When I opened the door he asked if I was the owner of a blue Audi. I confirmed that I was and asked if he wanted to look at the vehicle as it was on the drive with my wife's car. He said "No, Sir. It's not on the drive, it has been crashed a mile away at the top of the hill." I stood there in my pyjamas and dressing gown and said, "As you can see, I haven't been out this morning."

He then asked if my sons were in. I confirmed that the eldest was away in London and the younger, Philip, was upstairs in bed but he didn't have a driving licence. The Constable then asked, "Would you mind if we just checked Sir?" We traipsed up the stairs and found Philip's room in darkness and my son curled up under the covers, fast asleep.

The Policeman then took me to the place where the car had been found. The front had been crashed through a hedge and he commented that it couldn't have happened long ago because the engine was still warm. I could only say that it must have been stolen.

By the time I arrived home, a tired and anxious Philip was dressed and eating a hearty breakfast. No more was said and the insurance company paid up without a murmur.

However, two weeks later I received a telephone call from the Mother Superior of the local Convent who said "Our gardener has recovered a car number plate which the Police tell me belongs to you. Would you like to collect it?" I declined and said how sorry I was that the stolen car had damaged their property and she replied "Oh! Please don't worry Mr Hamlin. The car demolished our front fence and gates, which were in a very bad state of repair, but they have all been replaced by the insurance people and look very nice. The Lord works in many ways his wonders to perform."

My son, Philip had developed an interest in flying and after considering the RAF (he was a most physically active person) decided the Parachute Regiment was more to his liking. His first attempt to join up at sixteen years of age was turned down and he was told to join the Territorial Army to prove himself and to re-apply again in a year's time. He did this whilst taking an apprenticeship in general building.

At seventeen he was accepted into the Army and thoroughly

enjoyed himself. He telephoned us to say he would be making his first live practice jump the following week. He jumped, landed correctly but found he could not move.

After a back X-ray in hospital, he was found to be suffering from Scheuermann's disease which, unknown to us, he had taken in his stride. However, the Army gave him a medical discharge. What a blow! He was devastated. He then became an IT and office equipment specialist whilst also excelling as a landscape gardener.

Winchester House rear gardens during landscaping by Philip

-0-0-0-0-

In 1984 computer failures were becoming ever more prevalent and I believed one of the major problems for the Government Purchasing Officers was that they paid scant attention when they confirmed terms and conditions of contracts. They also appeared to place little importance on finding out about the abilities of each contending company i.e.

a. that both the client and supplier fully understood and agreed the Requirement Specification and that the supplier had sufficient fully experienced staff in the required project environment,

b. that the supplier fully understood the complexity of the on-site staff required and the time and cost elements of the task in hand,

c. that the supplier fully agreed with the costs relating to the resourcing and maintaining the scheduled completion date

d. and that suppliers and purchasers had had full discussions and both sides totally understood the bonuses to be paid for early completion and also appreciated that fixed penalties for failure to achieve the scheduled completion date, would be strictly adhered to.

I am positive many contenders for major Government contracts (remembering the size and costs of some were in the multi millions) considered that accurate cost estimating and time scheduling was less important than actually securing the contract.

The premise was to get the contract because once the work had started, the thought of cancelling a project which had already had so much money spent on it, and the disruption and cost of rethinking and going back to the drawing board, would be unthinkable because the political fall out would be so great - and more money would always be found.

To this day, you rarely hear of anyone being blamed for failure.

Jaye has some light moments:

Much of our consultancy work was in the South which made it economical for us to rent a flat in Clapham. We had arranged to carry out a survey for London Weekend Television so the previous evening Jaye travelled down to Euston. I rang our son Steven who was studying Sacro Cranial Osteopathy in London and asked him to meet his Mother off the train as she was tired.

Apparently Steven arrived a few minutes after the train and whilst Jaye stood on the Euston concourse waiting for him, deep in thought about the job the following day, a clean and warmly dressed woman broke into her thoughts and said, "Excuse me Madam. I haven't slept in a proper bed for months. Could you spare me the price of a meal?" Jaye, brought back to earth with a jolt said automatically "Do you take Amex?" (Our accountant had always impressed on us the importance of paying for everything this way.)

When Steven arrived he said, "You look a bit flustered Mater. What's wrong?" and when he heard the story and had eventually stopped laughing, he explained that the beggar was a regular at the station.

And yet another time as Steven approached his Mother at Euston, Jaye noticed that his thick dark hair was a bright shade of red. When she enquired if he was following the fashion of the day by dying his hair, he replied "I went to a fancy dress party last night dressed as a punk. I used red vegetable dye on my hair and gelled it into style, I tore a tee-shirt and wrote 'Guy Fawkes was right' on it, borrowed a garden chain, padlocked myself into it and went to the party. I had a great time but unfortunately lost the keys to both the flat and the

174

padlock. At 9.00 o'clock this morning I was sitting outside the Ironmonger's waiting for them to open so they could saw me out of the chains. By the time I showered the dye wouldn't wash out of my hair."

Back to the real world of failing computer systems:

In March 1985 the Minister of Technology, Geoffrey Pattie, spoke on computerisation at a meeting in Bolton. My earlier letters to him had been whispers in the dark so I bearded the Lion in his Bolton Den and pointed out that mine was the only Computer Consultancy Company whose recommendations were covered by a Lloyd's Guarantee of Effectiveness.

I also tried to impress upon him the serious lack of control over computer purchase by Government Agencies and in particular, those within the NHS. I sighted some of my experiences of stupid Health Service failures due to lack of guidance and of leaving decisions to people of literally no experience but with the possibility of personal gain.

I asked him why the Government did not tighten up the rules making their Departmental Purchasing Officers responsible for wrong or "lobbyist-pressured" computer purchasing disasters. Also, when it was proved that poor decisions were the fault of outright complicity, misrepresentation by the lobbyists or computer suppliers, why one or the other of these parties was not brought to book?

He asked me to write with details of our service and I did so immediately.

The following letters show an almost total lack of urgency by the Government in dealing with the harm caused to the nation by unscrupulous computer sales ethics, also losses to industry, commerce and within the health service due to the purchase of inappropriate computer systems.

In the first letter the Minister says the problem is well known but makes no mention of possible corrective action and in the second letter says they have a list of consultants.

Why did they make no move to make 'Connery' and 'Un-Fit for Purpose' against the law?

DEPARTMENT OF TRADE AND INDUSTRY
1-19 VICTORIA STREET
LONDON SW1H 0ET
Telephone (Direct dialling) 01-215-
GTN 215 5947
(Switchboard) 215 7877

From the Minister of State
for Industry and Information Technology

GEOFFREY PATTIE MP

M R Hamlin Esq
Atlas Computer Consultants Ltd
The Guild Centre
PRESTON
Lancashire
PR1 1QR

29 March 1985

Dear Mr Hamlin

Thank you for your interesting letter of 8 March.

The problems you spoke about in Bolton and outlined in your
letter, are indeed well known to my Department. The relative
lack of impartial advice available is certainly a difficulty for
any prospective purchaser of computer equipment.

I am not sure that there is any need for a meeting on this
subject, but you can rest assured that the appropriate officials
will be in contact with you if the need should arise for a
discussion.

Yours sincerely

Geoffrey Pattie

GEOFFREY PATTIE

AP1/AP1AAD

MANAGEMENT AND PERSONNEL OFFICE
Great George Street
London SW1P 3AL
Telephone 01-233 - 4146

CABINET OFFICE

Maurice R Hamlin Esq
Managing Director
Atlas Computer Consultants Ltd
The Guild Centre
Preston LANCS PR1 1QR   17 April 1985

Dear Mr Hamlin

GOVERNMENT PURCHASING - CONSULTANTS

The Cabinet Office (Management and Personnel Office) has recently
set up an index of management consultants. This index provides
a service to all government departments enquiring about the
specialisms of consultancy firms.

As a result of the report to the Prime Minister about Government
Purchasing, departments are now charged with significantly
improving the value for money they obtain in their procurement
of goods and services. Some departments may therefore wish
to employ consultants specialising in procurement related
studies to help them with this task.

At present the index lists only a few consultants with expertise
and experience of procurement and related subjects. It would
clearly be useful if the index was expanded to include more
consultants specialising in this field.

I therefore wonder whether you would be willing to put your
firm on the index. If so, please fill in the enclosed proforma and return it to me.

Having your firm on the index does not, of course, guarantee
that you will be approached by departments to undertake any
work. However, I think you will agree that it would be useful
for both 'buyer and seller' to make use of this scheme.

Yours sincerely

R D J WRIGHT

ME1 Division

(Room 60A/3)

Naturally I completed and returned the proforma immediately.
We heard no more.

Early in May 1986, the DTI advertised that they were offering grants for innovative IT companies but intimated this was only linked to manufacturing. Considering the constant reports of Government and private company IT disasters, I felt there could hardly be anything more innovative than a system able to dramatically reduce this wastage so I complained to John Butcher, Minister of Technology.

The following letter again show how little attention they paid to the problem or the urgency they placed in seeking solutions.

JB5AEW

From the Parliamentary Under Secretary
of State for Industry

JOHN BUTCHER MP

DEPARTMENT OF TRADE AND INDUSTRY
1-19 VICTORIA STREET
LONDON SW1H 0ET
Telephone (Direct dialling) 01-215) 4302
(GTN 215)
(Switchboard) 01-215 7877

Jeremy Hanley Esq MP
House of Commons
LONDON SW1A 0AA

21 May 1986

Dear Jeremy,

Thank you for your letter of 7 May to Michael Howard with the enclosed correspondence from Mr Maurice R Hamlin of Atlas Computer Consultants (UK) Ltd, of The Guild Centre, Preston, Lancs PR1 1QR. I am sorry if Mr Hamlin encountered a negative attitude in his dealings with the Department.

Mr Hamlin suggests that DTI grants are available only for manufacturing. I can assure you that our standard Support for Innovation provision is available for developments in both the service and manufacturing sectors. However, we clearly have to apply the same criteria across the board, particularly with respect to the degree of innovation and the need for our funds to bring forward projects which would not have happened without support.

If Mr Hamlin feels that his bureau development is at a sufficiently early stage that it might qualify for support in this way, I would advise him to discuss it with the relevant official in the Department's Information Technology Division. The contact is Dr Peter Rothwell, at 29 Bressenden Place. His telephone number is 01-213 4650.

Thank you for drawing this to my attention.

Yours

John

JOHN BUTCHER

As suggested, I contacted Mr Peter Rothwell outlining the services we offered and the fact that our recommendations were guaranteed by Lloyds of London. I also told him we would be willing to extend our research into any area the DTI felt would be of help to the Country.

We heard no more.

Why did the Government Purchasing Officers and the Department of Trade and Industry have closed minds?

Mr Den Dover, my MP, also tried his best but no one showed any interest. There appeared to be no one in Government who was really computer literate and who also had an open mind.

Another light moment:

At an early age son Steven was a Master War Gamer and a student of Greek history so when he left school he took a three-month holiday in Greece so he could visit sites of ancient battles, etc.

When he arrived at Marathon, he asked some English students to look after his backpack whilst he ran the original course, however, when he returned he found they had stolen everything except his maps, underwear and small camping cooker.

He decided to trek over the mountains to the coast but misjudged the level of the water plain. On the first night of his journey he had to climb to the top of a ruined building to escape the attention of a pack of feral dogs and the next day he had neither food nor water until he reached a monastery where he was made welcome.

On the second morning when he woke up in his cell, he found his freshly laundered clothes by his side. It was time to leave the security of their hospitality and they gave him water, cheese and rice to help him on his way.

When Steven reached the ocean, he saw a young boy casting a

very large fishing net into the sea so he waded into the water and gave him a helping hand.

Later that evening as he was boiling some rice, the Greek boy returned and said, "You have worked. You must come and eat with the family." Steven stayed with them for several weeks and worked on the family's trawler catching octopus. He told us that whilst they were fishing, they didn't have coffee but instead ate freshly caught sea urchin.

Steven had left home a young man with hair cut with short back and sides, horn-rimmed spectacles and clean-shaven. When he returned and rang the bell, my wife didn't recognise the tall, bronze, yellow haired, bearded stranger standing before her, until a deep voice said " Hi, Mum."

Before he returned to Greece the following year he bought a computerised backgammon set and when he could beat it on all nine levels, he reprogrammed it to cheat and still learned to beat it. He also wrote a lot of music for the bouzouki.

On his next visit to Greece he confounded the locals in the cafes – how could a young English chap play their national instrument and what's more, play backgammon the Greek way?

Quite amazingly, the Greek Embassy in London had learned of his expertise with the bouzouki and invited him to play for them. He gracefully refused feeling not proficient enough for an expectant audience.

Chapter 17 – A Russian Surprise

One morning when I arrived at the office Jaye said "Don't make any appointments for the first three weeks in August because we are going on holiday." When I asked her where were we going to, she replied "Russia." Rather startled I said that we couldn't go there because we would need visas. She laughed and said "Don't worry, you signed your application six months ago. Everything has been arranged." She managed all our affairs, business and personal, and I signed everything put in front of me; my head was always in the next stage of development of SystemSearch. How could I complain?

Note: Mikhail Gorbachev had been elected General Secretary by the Politburo on 11 March 1985.

That August we flew by Aeroflot to Moscow and upon arrival there, all three hundred passengers were placed in one room for an hour or so whilst the authorities checked our luggage. We then had a long, slow coach drive over badly maintained roads to the Hotel Rossiya, which was situated just off Red Square and was, at that time, the biggest hotel in Europe, now sadly demolished.

When we arrived it was dark and although we were tired, we were not allowed into the hotel reception but had to wait outside for almost an hour whilst the Tour Representative registered each member of our party. We were not even allowed to go to the toilet and some of the ladies were getting quite distressed. Jaye, who had recently had a bladder operation, was obviously suffering badly and was surprised when a lady wearing a Dirndl skirt rescued her and said "Come with me dear, behind that bush" and spread out her ample skirt.

During the rest of our stay in Moscow, members of our party would sometimes smile and comment that a particular shrub didn't look well.

The food in the hotel was adequate but basic. At breakfast each person was allowed only two slices of bread and asking for more was fruitless. Meal times were strictly adhered to  and food would be placed on the allotted table at exactly the scheduled time whether or not the guest was sitting there.

On each floor, close to the lift, was a desk behind which sat an unsmiling guard who checked everyone in and out, coming and going.

Our room was large and elegantly furnished and had an amazing view of St.Basil's Cathedral and the Kremlin. The bathroom was modern and stylish but both the sink and bath were without plugs. In those days it was essential to provide your own toilet paper because that supplied by the hotel was rather like thin woodchip wallpaper. The cloakrooms on the lower floor of the hotel always had a sour looking attendant sitting in the doorway handing out one sheet of paper per person.

Before leaving home, Jaye had learned about the shortage of tights, ballpoint pens and scented soap in Russia so went prepared. Almost every child we met received Biros in black, blue, red and green.

In the centre of Moscow a supermarket was drab with many empty shelves. There were no fruits, vegetables or eggs on show, just dried fish and tinned foods, which all carried white labels with black writing. Next door was a Dollar Store which was brightly lit and had an armed guard on the door but in there one could buy washing machines, toasters and most of the goods we accepted as normal household items but also different types of foodstuffs and whisky, vodka etc. It dealt only in Dollars and Sterling and was solely for senior party members and visitors. It was hard to understand why the people accepted this as normal, but they did.

We were assigned a very pleasant young guide who spoke excellent English and who took us to Lenin's Tomb, Red Square, the Kremlin, etc. however, she could not understand why, of all the party, we wanted to  slip away and look around on our own. We found that in Moscow we could always get our bearings by using the Metro; all stations appeared to be decorated alike but when we saw a different design, furnished with sparkling copper panels, we knew we had arrived under Red Square. We also travelled on the riverboat which was rather like a 'bus and we would get off when we saw something of interest. A big smile and sign language worked wonders.

The people we encountered were very friendly and frequently stopped us to ask about Britain and the working conditions there. Also about our health service but in particular, they asked about our freedom of speech and the right to travel. Many believed our miners were living in abject poverty with little food and that their children were without shoes. It must be remembered that only very senior members of the Party were allowed access to world news and films; the Russian television showed only what was deemed necessary for them to know.

The Police in central Moscow were smart, efficient and correct. One day I noticed an old and poorly dressed woman asking a policeman to help her to cross a busy main road; he saluted her and stopped the traffic whilst she crossed. But, woe betide anyone who set a foot over the painted curb line because he would screech on his whistle and, waving a heavy truncheon, run towards the offender.

Marriages in Moscow were conducted at weekends and one delightful custom was for the wedding party to walk across the Moskva River Bridge where the happy couple would kiss before returning. We were told it represented 'walking into a new life'. It was then traditional for the party to first visit the tomb of Lenin, walking to the front of the queue, where the bride would leave one of her flowers. After this they would walk to the memorials or statues of

their favourite Russian heroes and each time, leave a flower. We noticed that the brides always dressed in a long white frock, usually with a beautiful picture hat, and the groom wore a suit but there was rarely another suit or hat in the party; it was very touching.

We visited many historically interesting places and parks with magnificent sculptures. At one large and opulent church a funeral was being held. Inside it was full to capacity but outside the walls were surrounded by peasants clothed in black, with one hand placed on the stonework as they prayed and mourned. It was unbelievably moving, however, a discordant note was struck when the distinguished procession and coffin left the church and was besieged by a large group of Japanese tourists whose behaviour was appalling. They literally pushed the mourners out of the way to take photographs. We were astonished.

We wanted to visit the famous Moscow State Circus and Jaye did a superb job obtaining tickets from the hotel management. She first had to stand in a long queue to obtain a slip of paper giving her permission to stand in another queue to get tickets but, before handing them over, the clerk asked how she intended to get to the Circus and Jaye responded, "How do you suggest we get there?"

The clerk replied, "You must go by the designated bus." When we left the hotel to actually go there, we hopped on the first "Circus" bus we saw; it was full of Czechs but they didn't appear to mind.

When we arrived at the Circus we were placed on the front row with several small children either side of us. This was a blessing in disguise as each person was allocated only a small space on the narrow plank on which to sit (or balance a cheek).

During the interval, a Magician walked around the audience palming sweets and money out of ears, hair and pockets. Everyone was in party mood. When he reached me, he said "Ah! English. Come with me" and led me out into the centre of the main ring. There was a loud roll of drums and he asked me if I had anything in my pockets. I was wearing slacks and a short sleeved sports shirt and replied "No, just a handkerchief" and being an idiot, I turned round pulling out my pockets for all to see.

He then asked me if I was sure my pockets were empty. I replied, "Of course, I'm sure" and put my hands in my pockets and found they were full of playing cards. I swung round, scattering the cards. The Magician asked again "Are you sure they are empty?" I checked my pockets and once more they were full, so I pranced around again disposing of the cards. He then asked if I would make sure I had nothing left and then I realised my shirt pocket was bursting with cards so I spun around tossing them in the air.

He introduced me to the audience, thanked me, shook my hand and I started walking back to my seat but the crowd were screaming and pointing. I turned round and the Magician was smiling and swinging my watch. A watch fitted with a new strap which I had difficulty undoing. Amazing!

During the next interval, several people were talking to my unresponsive ears when a young Danish girl said in English "They wish to know if you are part of the act." I laughed and replied that I was a tourist from England.

We visited the famous GUM departmental store but found it was a series of individual shops on the style of a large shopping mall.

We also visited the Resurrection Gate, which Stalin had actually knocked down, modified and rebuilt so his tanks could pass through it into Red Square.

During our whole visit to Moscow the temperature was one hundred degrees in the shade but the air was so dry we felt no discomfort. It was a delight.

We next travelled to St. Petersburg, which was formed by Peter the Great in May 1703 since when it has changed its name to Petrograd, Leningrad and finally back to St. Petersburg. It was approximately three hundred miles by road from Moscow and the city still appeared to be recovering from its tragic wartime siege. Many main roads had potholes. There were long queues for apples etc. Everywhere looked shabby and yet amazing reconstruction was being carried out on some ancient buildings. In one particular instance the huge roof and ceiling were suspended by cranes to allow for preservation work to be carried out.

We visited the Hermitage and then the Winter Palace, which was unfortunately closed for renovation, but we were greatly impressed by the ingenious gravity fed system of fountains flowing downhill through the gardens.

St Petersburg suffered greatly during the war and was under siege from September 1941 until January 1944. In January and February of 1942, 200,000 people died of cold and starvation in Leningrad. The city suffered 900 days of bombardment and a total of 641,000 people were either killed or died during the siege.

A week of our adventure was spent in Yalta but when we arrived at the Moscow Airport and started walking towards the aircraft, we found the way lined with many high-ranking officers, all smartly attired and carrying bunches of flowers. We made the usual jokes saying that we didn't realise that they knew we were coming, etc. but after we were settled in our seats, we saw the officers being presented to Mikhail Gorbachev (a very impressive man) accompanied by his wife, Raisa.

Jaye and I, together with probably another two hundred people, travelled on the top deck of the aeroplane whilst Mikhail Gorbachev and his entourage used the lower cabin. Throughout the eight hundred mile flight the refreshment consisted of one small plastic cup of lemon scented, ice-cold water.

We stayed at the Yalta Intourist Hotel, which was situated close to the golden sands of the Black Sea, however, if you wished to swim in the huge pool, a physical examination was mandatory. Men and women were separated for this and about twenty intending swimmers lined up in a row whilst a doctor examined certain parts of each person, after which a clerk awarded every one with a small pink card.

To access the beach, we had to take a lift to the bottom of the cliff and walk through an underground passage at the end of which were two turn styles and a police checkpoint. Western tourists and the top categories of Russians went to the left and all others to the right.

We emerged onto a superb golden beach but we were divided from the average Russian holidaymakers by a twelve-foot high wire fence extending well into the sea. Security helicopters flew along the coast at least every hour with their loud hailers blaring but we had no idea what they were saying. On our part of the beach we were mixed with well to do Party Members and other tourists. We met a lot of friendly people but the two I remember most both held prominent positions in the party.

The first was a Consular Official who had recently returned to Russia after working for several years in Paris and who had frequently travelled to England and knew it well. He was holidaying without his family and every time a helicopter approached whilst he was talking to us, he would hop underneath the umbrella, laugh and say "Just a joke." When he found out about my love of singing, he said he would like to take us to hear the Red Army Choir when we returned to Moscow but that evening he rang us at the hotel to say he would be unable to take us to the concert because of political reasons and knew that we would understand.

The other person I recall was a tall, very attractive woman of about thirty-five who took a great liking to Jaye. She was a producer of children's television programmes and always dressed in designer clothes with a preference for Dior. She arranged for us to meet some of her friends and we spent a rather wild evening together proving that Russians really can party, but that's another story.

The hotel was extremely pleasant but a fair walk from the centre of Yalta which at that time was the main holiday resort for the more favoured Russians. We were surprised how many spoke English, many of whom approached us wanting to hear our impressions of life in the West. We met several academic people, one a Physicist who was on holiday with his two children. He told us that his wife would be taking her holiday at a later date because parents who were also senior technical or scientific specialists were not allowed to go on holiday as a family. He explained that it was to prevent them trying to escape together as a unit. He also said that because of their position, they were able to have a television and a stereo and could watch news and films from the West, hence their excellent English.

One day we visited a delightful park in the centre of which was a small but beautiful building approached by wide marble steps. It housed the toilets. Jaye and her new friend went into this place and returned giggling and quite embarrassed; the loos were a line of individual holes arranged side by side and divided by handrails.

We also visited an Arboretum some miles away in the hills but beside the sea. It was beautiful, a pure delight. We walked close to the cliff and heard joyful voices below and noticed a path leading down to the beach where there was a busy café and places to picnic. We climbed down to the beach and I went into the wooden construction to buy cakes and drinks but when I entered I saw dozens of sparrows sitting on the food and pecking away until they were shooed off because that particular item had been ordered. We unanimously decided against eating there and caught a sleek

hydrofoil to Yalta. It was an exhilarating short sea trip and even our non-seaworthy Jayebird was able to enjoy the ride.

One evening before leaving Yalta we took a battered taxi into town pretending not to notice the state of the tyres. The road downhill was narrow with an incredible camber; it twisted this way and that, and the whole time the driver's foot was pressed to the floorboard. We all hung on for dear life and the girls giggled nervously the whole way into the city as the four of us were flung from side to side in the car. My friend, sitting in the front, remarked, "Thank God, it's only one way."

We visited the Casino Hotel and were stopped at the door by two guards bearing automatic weapons. My wife and I were allowed to enter the hotel immediately but our friend, who bore a remarkable resemblance to Fidel Castro, was stopped, questioned and his papers scrutinised before he was grudgingly allowed to join us. It appeared the Gorbachevs were staying there for a working holiday break.

The hotel was superb with a wide sweeping marble staircase leading to the first floor. The downstairs nightclub could only be described as 'plush' and boasted an incredible music system. It was slightly let down when I visited the cloakroom to find that although it was well appointed with the most modern furnishings, the floor was awash with water and the lavatory paper was neatly cut up pieces of newspaper threaded on string. Perestroika had only just arrived.

After leaving the Casino we queued for some time for a taxi. When it was our turn, Jaye was just getting into the car when a young woman carrying a three-year-old girl rushed up to her and said, "I have a child." Jaye smiled sweetly at her and said, "Don't we all dear." The taxi driver laughed as we started our journey and he explained that it was the law that anyone with a child in arms had precedence and could walk to the front of a taxi queue.

As the journey continued we realised there was only one road to and from the hotel. It was not one way.

When we returned to Moscow we spent our last evening in the Hotel's Dollar Bar where people of many nationalities had gathered for a drink. It had a small but superb dance floor and shortly after we arrived the music changed to a Glen Miller tape. Jaye and I were in our natural element and went to town but to our surprise the other dancers left the floor. When the music ended we had a standing ovation; everyone clapped and shouted for more. I must admit, we lost all restraint and let ourselves go. It is a wonderful memory of dancing at our very best.

Chapter 18 – Investment

Back at work after a wonderful holiday, I was amazed to read in 'Computing' that the complaints I had expressed so often about the major computer suppliers' unethical sales marketing policies were actually having some affect. IBM was at last acknowledging its poor ethics regarding selling boxes instead of systems.

Antoine Colboc: 'IBM staff lost sight of what users v

Industry-angled switch for sales

IBM this month reacted to criticisms that its sales staff are too blinkered by adopting a new industry-based marketing structure.

For the past six years, the company has had an aggressive product-oriented sales and marketing force that has helped it to grow rapidly.

But it has also resulted in sales staff with little knowledge of or interest in selling another group's product line, even though it might better suit a customer's actual needs.

Antoine Colboc, UK managing director of leasing company, ECS, said: 'IBM sales staff concentrated on selling one product and lost sight of the sort of applications users were doing.

'One salesman might be pushing a mainframe when a network of minis was a better option or vice versa.'

Colboc said IBM went halfway to tackling the problem when it merged its two major sales force divisions at the turn of the year.

This month IBM followed up by reshuffling marketing staff into industry groups and starting the transfer of many headquarters marketing personnel out into field offices where they will be closer to their customers.

Typically for a company of IBM's size, the reshuffle will take months to complete and details are still unclear.

But IBM UK is expected to form three main industry groupings covering government and public bodies, financial institutions and general industry users.

In July, IBM caused surprise when it set up a new London-based sales group, General Office Systems Marketing (GOSM). This is now seen as a first step towards the company's new organisation.

10 COMPUTING   OCT 1986 ~

191

There was more woe for the Government over what appeared to be total mismanagement of the controversial system, which was supposed to solve the Department of Social Security's accounting problems.

MPs slate computer costs mess at DSS

Accounting systems at the department of social security came under attack in the Commons after it was revealed that the cost of the country's biggest computerisation scheme was allowed to soar out of control.

The public accounts committee was highly critical of the monitoring of the £1,036 million strategy following a 145% increase in cash estimates since 1982, when it was begun as several different projects.

The MPs said: 'We t it most unsatisfactory having adopted the conce overall financial control the strategy in 1986 the of accounting weaknesses such that the depart could not produce a fina base line strategy until 1988.'

MPs were staggered to that in the early days the control was the assessme viability of each project.

'Adequate financial co can only be exercise the establishment of sou based budgets for each pr followed by monitorin expenditure in sufficient to enable effective an of all the reasons for variances from budgets undertaken,' they said.

They were 'seriously cerned' that the depart did not have ade arrangements until July 1

1988 saw little improvement in computer sales ethics particularly in the area of the major software development companies and in the quality of Government purchasing.

This year the Metropolitan Police placed a £30 million order for the development of a crime reporting system named CRIS.

I would like to ask why the authorities were totally unwilling to talk to other developers of such a system? In particular to ComputerScan, the designer and developer of the first cross-relational multi data information retrieval system, SystemSearch, and who had also designed a crime detection system named 'CrimeSearch'.

All our requests to talk and demonstrate to Police Authorities regarding a system that was already proven fell on deaf ears.

Our name was unknown, we had no one lobbying for us and we could offer no grandiose inducements.

What a crime for the UK Tax payer.

```
oooooooooooooooooooooooooooooooooooooooooooooooooooooooooooooooooooooooooooooo
Screen No....              CrimeSearch                        14 June 1992
                      SUSPECT/CRIMINAL MATCHING
oooooooooooooooooooooooooooooooooooooooooooooooooooooooooooooooooooooooooooooo
```

Note: Enter known Suspect/Criminal's description and modus operandi, aliases, etc.	Crime Nos. matching Criminal's modus operandi					
	6661	7774	9120	9154	9140	9155
Code DESCRIPTION						
2008 Educated Accent	Y	Y	-	-	-	-
2114 Age 50/60	Y	Y	-	Y	Y	Y
2010 Aggravated Assault	Y	Y	Y	Y	Y	-
2092 Previous Convictions	Y	Y	Y	Y	Y	Y
2072 Hair Grey	Y	Y	Y	Y	Y	Y
2064 Tall	Y	Y	Y	-	-	-
2121 16 stone	Y	Y	Y	Y	Y	Y
2071 Muscular	Y	Y	Y	Y	Y	Y
2068 Ex Army	Y	Y	Y	Y	Y	Y
2123 Trained Unarmed Combat	Y	Y	Y	-	Y	Y
2034 Drives Lamborghini	Y	Y	Y	Y	Y	Y
8638 Profession - Ind.Estate Agent	Y	Y	-	Y	Y	-
2082 Walks with Limp - left knee	Y	Y	Y	Y	Y	Y
2044 Pale Complexion	Y	Y	Y	Y	-	Y
2109 Tattoo - left arm	Y	Y	-	-	Y	-
2126 GBH	-	-	Y	Y	Y	-
2024 Moustache	Y	Y	-	Y	Y	Y
2116 Smart business like appearance	Y	-	Y	-	Y	Y
2144 Sideburns	Y	Y	Y	-	/	Y
Percentage Capability meeting above Criteria	90%	90%	76%	71%	81%	67%

```
COMPLETE TEXT DISPLAYED
WHEN FINISHED, USE <ESC> TO ACCESS QUICK MENU
oooooooooooooooooooooooooooooooooooooooooooooooooooooooooooooooooooooooooooooo
Suspect  Crime  Criteria  Text  Print  List  Match  Exit  Menu  New  Off
oooooooooooooooooooooooooooooooooooooooooooooooooooooooooooooooooooooooooooooo
```

1. The above is a match of one criminal's details matched against all crimes to produce a shortlist of likely crimes committed

2. The opposite is the matching of a crime's details against all criminals to produce a shortlist of likely suspects

My sons were always surprising me:

While Steven was studying in London he played in several musical groups - Indian, pop and classical. He was tall, wore his hair in an immaculate ponytail and dressed in an Errol Flynn type white shirt with fitting black trousers and riding boots, the whole outfit covered by an enormous blue cloak with a gold trim. He looked a little eccentric but always elegant.

One day I met him off the train in Preston and as we walked down the main road towards the car park, we saw on the other side of the road an extremely hairy tramp looking rather like a scarecrow. He suddenly stopped, held his hands above his head and crossed the road and stood in front of Steven. Moving his hands in a circle with the palms towards us, he looked up at Steven in awe and said "Wow, man! Wow!

Wearing a smart business suit, I was a bit embarrassed at the time but in retrospect I realise my son looked spectacular.

The year the IBM Whale called on the Minnow for help:

Jaye took a call from a man at IBM who asked "Is it true your database holds details of every application software package that has been written for IBM hardware by our third party suppliers?" Jaye confirmed that it was true and that we also had the names of all their suppliers, details of all of their packages and the businesses for which they had been written. She then asked how she could help him. He replied, "Just send us a printout of them all." Jaye then explained that it would be a big job and would have to be costed out and asked to whom she should send a quotation. There was silence at the other end of the telephone. Jaye then added that the information contained on the SystemSearch database had cost hundreds of thousands of pounds and over ten years to research. Finally, he said, "We are not paying for it"

Jaye replied politely "In that case, I am sorry but I am afraid you are not getting it."

At that time IBM, in common with many of the major computer manufacturers and suppliers, did not keep records of the thousands of applications that had been developed (using their hardware) for industry, commerce and services. They had been solely interested in selling boxes.

Barbour Index plc replied to our call for investment:

In January of this year after the Government declined to help us with a development grant, Jaye and I decided to advertise for major financial investment so we could have an equipment update and major software rewrite to take us into further marketing avenues which would be essential if we were to realise the true potential of SystemSearch's unique capabilities.

Barbour's sent one of their senior Directors, Mr Jack Dunn, to investigate our potential. He was an astute Scot, most likeable and negotiations began to take place due to his recommendation.

They were a non-computerised specialist Information Source Company for the Building Industry and held all their building product information on Microfiche. They were highly impressed by SystemSearch and our ability to back our findings with a Lloyds of London guarantee of accuracy. They were also interested in our ability to advise them on the computerisation of their own somewhat out-dated Building Industry Information Library.

Barbour's took a controlling interest in SystemSearch and in exchange they paid all the company's operating and redevelopment costs and placed a Director on the Board on behalf of Barbour's who exercised control on all policy issues. They spent some £890,000 on updating our computer hardware and rewriting the software.

We recruited Paul Brown, a first class innovative Pick software systems analyst who, together with my son Steven (also a Pick specialist), redeveloped and transferred our software systems and programs over to a new large C.Itoh mini computer system with eighteen interactive terminals plus printers whilst at the same time also continuing our applications software redevelopment under the Pick operating system.

Regrettably, for some unknown reason but mainly due to the Barbour Index Board's lack of familiarity with computers, they would not allow me to recruit salesmen or have a sales or advertising budget. In particular, we were not allowed to use the Barbour name either in sales contracts or in editorial sales marketing.

They did, however, pressure me into employing one of their own Microfiche salesmen who knew nothing about computing. He proved to be totally useless and was unable to assimilate either the concept of SystemSearch or our marketing strategy. During his employment he obtained not a single firm contract.

Barbour's strategy was that I should personally find and convert prospects to orders and prove the system's profitability before they would be identified as owning the company, yet at the same time I had to oversee and control the development and expansion of the new system and services. I considered this cautious policy to be a storm anchor to our marketing policy but as they were so generous with funding, I had little option but to agree with them.

The next two years were an intensive period for our IT Specialist Team and our twenty-five Researchers. Little sales or marketing effort was possible other than wide exposure via the media (mainly in Computing and Computer Weekly magazines) due to my constant battles over the computer industry's poor ethics and my communications to the Government about its total lack of direction in IT, especially regarding the NHS with its practice of allowing every individual department to buy its own preferred computer i.e.

   1988 - Guys Hospital suffered a £20 million fiasco. Costs rising and no end in sight.

   1988 - Department of Social Security slated by MP's over the costs of the Country's biggest computerisation scheme, which was allowed to soar out of control.

Bulgaria, a delightful interlude:

We spent our summer holiday in the Communist country of Bulgaria and whilst exploring the ancient city of Varna we came upon the Cathedral and noticed that all the windows had been boarded up; religion was discouraged. Inside the building, the nave was roped off and the high dome appeared to hold but a single light bulb. As Jaye looked around, she put one foot beneath the rope separating the nave from the transept and to my horror, went rigid and had great difficulty in breathing. I had to physically pick her up and take her outside and it was several minutes before she regained her composure and was able to speak. She just said that she felt something really terrible had happened there. No one was in attendance and we didn't go back inside the building.

As always, wherever we went on holiday, we found good music and a dance floor and Bulgaria was no exception. The Intourist Holiday Company provided vouchers for all meals and these could be used in any restaurant or hotel, however, due to the highly beneficial exchange rate, every evening we dined a la carte accompanied by pink champagne. One evening I had a glass of the special pink bubbles myself and to my surprise found it tasted like lemonade, however, the second glass went straight to my brain and we had to return to our hotel before eating. Jaye told me I giggled all the way back to the hotel repeating over and over again, "It only cost forty Stratinki."

There were many building sites in the resort where new hotels and apartment blocks were being erected but to our amazement there was not a man to be seen; the bricklayers, hod carriers climbing ladders and drivers of dump trucks were all women. We were told that the men worked in the factories.

Note: The oldest gold treasure in the world was discovered by chance at Varna in 1972. It consisted of coins, weapons and jewellery dating back to 4,600 BC and is said to be as important as the discovery in Turkey of the great treasure of ancient Troy some one hundred years earlier.

Airborne invasion creates havoc:

One Sunday Jaye was preparing lunch when she heard a loud huffing noise. She ran out into the garden and saw a huge red Post Office balloon just skimming the rooftop of a neighbour's bungalow and thought it might try to descend onto our lawn.

The dogs were terrified. So much so that the young one, Scooby Doo, scrambled over an eight-foot beech hedge to escape the dragon. He ran blindly for almost a mile and was killed as he crossed a main road.

Once again Jaye's inbuilt insight proved itself. I was rushing out to start searching for him but she said, "No, get the car, he's dead" and took me to where he was lying. What a terrible blow!

It was only after the story was featured in the local paper that the GPO paid for another puppy but it couldn't replace the lovely animal they had killed.

1989 – At last the DTI recognise industry is losing millions:

The Department of Trade and Industry horrified by reports on the £Millions being wasted by companies buying the wrong computers, launched OSTT (Open Systems Technology Transfer).

The intention was excellent. Directors of commerce and industry were offered short courses to educate and alert them to changes in information technology transfer and to instruct them on the use of Open Systems software programs which were used by alternative software houses to modify or integrate new applications to meet their needs. This had been made possible by the introduction of UNIX, an operating system that allowed a source code to be used by software houses other than the originator. I offered our help but they showed no interest.

By no means did the computer salesman cause all the misunderstandings. Most company directors or senior management went into computer purchase wearing either blinkers or with an enhanced belief in their own minuscule knowledge of computing which they mistakenly thought made them experts. When they failed, they rarely admitted their faults and many hid the problems they encountered and even recommended the system they had bought to directors of other companies.

This total lack of understanding or appreciation of the complexity of requirements between different companies was one of the reasons for the proposed Government OSTT initiative but sadly the DTI did not have the ability to put the message across. Their instructors were almost too professional; they could not understand that although they were talking to highly intelligent beings, they were teaching totally uninitiated students. It was the same as bright teenagers learning a new language without the basics.

Most attendees who completed the course came out saying that it left them more confused than before they entered.

The courses were cancelled.

-0-0-0-0-

Barbour Index, our Investors, authorised a six-month sales exercise prior to sanctioning a high cost advertising campaign. I personally had to prove the viability of our service by offering to install a terminal in the offices of computer consultants, accountants and user companies so they could link directly to our SystemSearch database and carry out their own researches. This was chargeable on a 'time on line' basis. During the six-month period, enquiries built up to seventy-nine in the final month. Profitability had been achieved by my cold calling and without advertising of any kind.

By mid 1989 the re-development of SystemSearch was complete. Paul and Steve had surpassed all of my expectations. The system was working like a dream and I had to wrack my brains to envisage possible further improvements. We had a meeting and I announced the next task was to devise a means to reverse the matching process so we could ask the system why it had not chosen a specific supplier i.e. ICL, IBM, Bull, or XYZ company.

Later that day, as Jaye returned from the bank she found Paul outside the office on the tenth floor landing, standing with elbows on the high window ledge, puffing a small brown cigar and gazing across the city with deep concentration.

She said "Anything wrong Paul?

He answered "I feel like Michelangelo after he's just finished the Sistine Chapel. The Pope comes to see it and then he says, "Very nice my boy, but I would have preferred it pink." It was typical of Paul. Within a week the new feature was up and working.

Germany celebrates:

On the 9th November 1989 and after twenty-eight years, the Berlin
Wall was torn down.
The world celebrated
as we watched
television pictures of
the historic
destruction of the
Wall. Due to a
peaceful revolution,
the border between
East and West
Germany was
rescinded, the Cold
War ended and

Germany was reunited. The Brandenburg Gate was open.

It must be remembered that 171 people who were either killed or
died attempting to escape over the Wall between the 13th August
1961 and the 9th November 1989.

SystemSearch proves itself once again:

Late in 1989 a Consortium of five haulage companies had been
searching for two years to find a proven software package to control
their accounting and the operational management of their Transport,
Commodity Trading and Warehousing Group. Two U.K. blue chip
system suppliers had convinced them that no such package existed
and the only way forward was to have bespoke software written at a
cost of £100,000.

The order was being put together by Assistant Managing Director,
Malcolm France, of H.Burroughs and Son Limited of Bressingham.
However, before the deal was signed, Mr.France had been advised of
our company's reputation and asked if we would carry out a full
check to find out if there was such a thing as a Pick based package
compatible with the Bull hardware already in use. Within two days I
gave him a shortlist of three suppliers of suitable haulage packages
and demonstrations were arranged. Using our recommendation, the
installation cost many thousands less than anticipated and in Mr

France's words "The business was revolutionised." Our charge for this work was only £200.00.

Air Crew Association's Summer Ball ends with burglary:

When we attended we had taken the dogs with us (wearing their velvet bow ties) as we would be away for more than six hours. We had a wonderful evening with our good friends Maureen and Peter Howells and arrived home at about 1.30 a.m. to find the house had been ransacked and vandalised. My wife's jewellery had been stolen, mirrors broken, china and glassware smashed and my suits torn. We were told the house had been targeted by an experienced team if burglars.

One man for jewellery, one computer expert and the third man as a lookout.

The Police said the lookout would have done the damage to relieve boredom. They found a three foot long iron bar outside our bedroom door and said that had the dogs been left at home, they would almost certainly have been killed.

In the garage, the burglars found our huge fireproof safe, which contained our security tapes and unique system source codes. Luckily we had invested in a safe that proved to be beyond the robbers' ability to open.

The next day in the office I told the staff what had happened and warned them to be alert for any peculiar telephone calls in case the robbers had found anything pertinent to our software development.

We employed one very clever, security conscious young man whose sole job was to try to hack into our computer security files and to identify any possible weaknesses.

Over two years he had succeeded only twice and each time was well rewarded for his efforts and each time we changed the encryption codes.

He was a most enthusiastic lad, keen on his job and one evening when he was working late he received a telephone call from someone enquiring about the type of computer we used and he replied, "Dunno mate, I'm just the cleaner."

-0-0-0-0-

In February 1990 one of the items on the Agenda of Barbour Index's Group Board Meeting was to approve a major advertising campaign for ComputerScan which our Director thought was a foregone conclusion.

Not so!

On commencement of the meeting Barbour's auditors released news of major disasters within the Group. They had found problems in three of their Associated Companies and the Board had voted to pull out of all businesses that were not part of their core business of Building Information.

a) It was revealed that one part of the Group had dropped £9 million in profit,
b) the Managing Director of another Group Company had been arrested for an £800,000 fraud and
c) in yet another Company, a Director had been found laundering stolen electronics.

This devastating news was reported in the Times Newspaper.

What a disaster for Barbours! What a disaster for us! We had proved our capability and profitability yet were forced to close down. Our

Barbour Index Director was very upset at the situation we faced and did all in his power to assist us in our negotiation to take back the full hardware assets and software rights.

We had to vacate our luxurious Preston offices and find a new base. At home I had just completed building a large extension. It had been my ambition to have my own snooker room, a game that both Jaye and I enjoyed and watched on TV. The extension also included a bathroom and storage room.

Looking on the bright side, I converted the billiard room into an

IT complex and we were up and running again within two weeks trading under the name of Maurice Hamlin Associates.

Chapter 19 – DTI corruption

1993 - In tandem with six major IT manufacturers, the DTI thought up OSIS (Open Systems Information Source), which sounded like a brilliant way to overcome all IT misunderstanding.

Sponsors sought for Open Systems service

CHARLOTTE DELAFORCE

The search is on for industry sponsors to fund an Open Systems Information Service planned by The Department of Trade and Industry (DTI).

The estimated cost for start-up and first-year running is £300,000 and the DTI has already staked £100,000 in promotion money, said Warren Greaves, open systems unit manager at the DTI. 'We do not want to be the host (to the operation); we would like it to be industry-led.'

The programme is a 'signposting service' which co-ordinates and collects existing information on open systems and points users to the relevant path.

The main areas covered will be: product & supplier information; standards information; commentary and guidance; and planning and procurement guidelines. There will also be practical demonstrations, quality assurance and local services.

A pilot service will run from November for a year to assess demand, confirm resource requirements and plug any holes in the sources of information. The service will then officially start up in 1994. The operation will be non-profit making and is viable only if sponsored, said the DTI.

Greaves believes Groupe Bull has the facilities to navigate users through the information service with its recently opened £2.4 million Open Systems Centre. He added that Bull 'is an excellent example' of the sort of company that could help run the service.

Bull's centre provides free demonstration and training for Vars, as well as for Bull manufacturing partners and customers.

George McNeil, CEO of Bull UK, said the centre will help the company grab a bigger chunk of the software and services market: 'We want to provide systems integration and solutions.'

The Open Systems Centre at Hemel Hempstead consists of a systems integration centre, porting facilities, benchmarking centre and demonstration centre.

It did, however, also appear to be an attempt to justify the millions spent by the DTI on the OSTT (Open Systems Technology Transfer) programme launched in 1988 which ended with company director participants stating that it left them more confused than before.

I believe this new initiative, OSIS (Open Systems Information Source) was inspired as an answer to A.T.Kearney's 1990 report (backed by the DTI) which highlighted the disastrous £17 Billion losses suffered by Government and British companies because they bought the wrong computer systems.

The above advertisement was the first indication I had of OSIS and I immediately contacted the DTI and explained that we already had a proven IT information retrieval library and multi relational search engine. I was told to write in and send details so I asked what had happened to the data the Minister had assured me was held on record.

They could find no such information so I immediately wrote again but as before, it elicited no response. It was not until the 30th May, almost two months later and after several letters, telephone conversations and finally the intervention of my Member of Parliament, that they agreed I could demonstrate our unique SystemSearch.

At the time I failed to understand the DTI's reluctance to evaluate a system offering everything they had advertised they wanted to create, but I would eventually learn why.

When I attended the DTI's London offices to demonstrate SystemSearch's capabilities, I was introduced to the Level-7 company experts who were to be the host mainframe computer agency chosen to handle the thousands of anticipated enquiries when OSIS was launched. The number of people invited to see my demonstration gratified me. I set up an on-line terminal to our Lancashire based office computer after which each person there thought up every possible outlandish question they could imagine, and to every request SystemSearch responded correctly and within seconds. I was able to prove that the database held information on every aspect of eight thousand and six hundred suppliers and the seventy thousand software products they marketed in every possible business area - furthermore, any enquirer could match his company's complete IT requirements against this mass of information in the knowledge that he could expect a guaranteed solution underwritten by Lloyds of London.

All those at the meeting were completely astonished at the system's capabilities and despite trying to think up all manner of trick questions to beat the system, it passed every test and they had to agree that it was the perfect tool for OSIS.

It was agreed that Maurice Hamlin Associates (our new name) should be the main provider of information and client enquiry evaluation using the SystemSearch search engine and that we would develop an interface to the DTI-Level 7 mainframe computer. To this end, a member of their staff would spend considerable time in our offices acting as a co-ordinator.

The DTI carried out a survey of company directors to find out what they really wanted the OSIS service to provide. The vast majority of users said what they wanted was - *reliable, unbiased, up to date information with independent guidance on the available software packages in each specific business area.*

I was surprised by the following statement which appeared to the Press.

Press Statement issued by Martin Greave of the DTI
He stated that he believed the IT company "Group Bull" has the facilities to navigate users through the information service with it's recently opened £2.4 million Open Systems Centre; Greave added that "Bull is an excellent example of the sort of company that could help run the service." Bull's centre provides free demonstration and training for VARs (value added retailers) as well as for Bull manufacturing partners and customers.
This free service only covered Bulls products, how does this equate to unbiased advice?

Statement to the press by George McNeil, CEO of Bull UK.
"The centre will help the company (Bull) to grab a bigger chunk of the software and services market".

We then received the following memoranda:

---

1) In June we received the following memo from the DTI:-

"Formal proposals have been formulated to place OSIS onto a firm footing showing the business structure and financial management

Founding Vendors - ICL, IBM, DEC, BT, BULL, SEQUENT

Founding Users - M&S, BASS Brewers, Courtauld's Clothing, BP, ICI, Thorn Lighting and Lucas Aerospace

Management Board - ICL, IBM DEC, DTI, M&S, BASS Brewers

Proposed Founding Service Providers - NCC, Level-7 Ltd.

Proposed Initial Associate Service Provider - Maurice Hamlin Associates

---

2) The next memo read:-

FOUNDING VENDORS June 16th 1993 – ICL, IBM, DEC, BT, BULL and SEQUENT. Benefits per vendor:-

1 share of profits
1 member on board
1 vote

a) All pay service set up costs of £20,000 in 1993, £30,000 in 1994 which will be repaid out of service income.

b) All Founding Vendors to have FREE ACCESS to primary service (other than connection charge)

FOUNDING SERVICE PROVIDERS – NCC & LEVEL 7 (not MHA), Benefits -

1 share of profits
1 member on board
1 vote

a) Each would commit resources to value of £20,000 in 1993 and £30,000 in 1994

b) All Founding Service Providers to have FREE ACCESS to primary service (other than connection charge) and free access to SystemSearch.

DEPARTMENT OF TRADE & INDUSTRY benefits –

1 member on board
Attend General Meetings

a) Commit £100,000 for start up costs and promote service.

b) DTI to have FREE ACCESS to primary service (other than connection charge) and free access to SystemSearch (MHA)

ASSOCIATE SERVICE PROVIDER, MAURICE HAMLIN ASS, benefits

No share of profits
No member on board
No vote

MHA will not have access to primary service free of charge.
MHA to be offered assistance with development costs to meet service needs but all such costs to be repaid by MHA.

All services provided by Founder Vendors and Founder Users to be paid for by The service at £4/500 per day.

Shareholders to receive all MHA income in excess of operating costs for a defined period.

I was horrified at the negative terms offered but accepted them as the price of getting our capabilities known.

Ray Whitehouse wrote asking me to advise them of all costs that would be involved in bringing MHA and SystemSearch on line to offer the agreed service to the Nation via the Level 7 interface.

July 7th 1993 - To Mr Ray Whitehouse from Maurice Hamlin
The following is an appraisal of the costs involved to bring SystemSearch in line to offer the proposed service under the DTI Signpost scheme.
1. Software development - programming would take a minimum of 66 days. 7 hours per day at £45 per hour = £20,790
2. Application areas - defining application areas to be linked to each of the 351 highlighted industries would take approximately 34 days.7 hours a day at £45 per hour = £10,710
3. Data input - inputting of information into database and checking at 30 minutes per industry would take approximately 25 days. 7 hours per day at £20 per hour £3,500
Equipment Requirement: Two PCs would be required, one for each systems man to be directly on line to SystemSearch to carry out development work from home. This would cut out travelling time and expenses.
For the CTTOH/M300 Main Hardware System Upgrade, CPU upgrade including 25 Mhz R91 Pick RDBMS-4MB Memory and Disk the cost would be £17,782.

TOTAL COSTS:		
Software programming		£20,790
Industry System update		£10,710
Information update		£3,500
Hardware, Operating System etc.		£17,782
Total		£52,282

Plus purchase or hire of two PCs, and move to new premises prior to launch of new service.

The costings were acknowledged without comment. We assumed they were acceptable.

In the autumn of 1993 the DTI issued to all businesses the following Winter Brochure extolling the coming of the OSIS Service which was to begin in February 1994. They quoted extracts from their huge research campaign which had ascertained what business leaders expected from the service.

The new programme was put forward as a 'Sign Posting Service' which would co-ordinate and collect all existing information on Open Systems and point users to the correct path.

As you will see, the initial launch advertisement stated, "The main areas covered would be product and supplier information, standards information, commentary and guidance, planning and procurement guidelines."

It further stated "The operation will be UNBIASSED and NON-PROFIT MAKING."

They said a pilot service would run from November for a year to assess demand, confirm resource requirements and plug any holes in the sources of information. The service would then officially be approved to start in 1994.

Open Systems

BULLETIN
WINTER 1993

IN THIS ISSUE: ■ COVER FEATURE — OSIS – THE TIME HAS COME ■ PAGE 4 MINISTER TO LAUNCH INFORMATION SERVICE ■ TAKING THE HEADACHE OUT OF COMPUTER SOFTWARE SELECTION ■ PAGE 5 BROKERAGE SERVICE UPDATE ■ PAGE 6 MINIMISING COSTS IN AN OPEN DISTRIBUTED SYSTEMS ENVIRONMENT ■ PAGE 7 CRITIQUE CITES DTI'S OPEN SYSTEMS PROGRAMME A SUCCESS ■ PAGE 8 UNIFORUM UK LAUNCHES CODE OF PRACTICE ■ OPEN SYSTEMS FACING THE FUTURE

OSIS – THE TIME HAS COME

The next phase in the onward march of Open Systems begins in January when a unique, new service will be launched by two of the UK's leading Open Systems organisations, NCC and Level-7. Provisionally known as the Open

Systems Information Service (OSIS), it will continue the vital promotional work of the three-year Open Systems Programme. More importantly, however, it will bring tangible benefits to users and represents an important shift in emphasis away from Government initiatives towards industry leadership.

The need for an Open Systems information service was first identified in market research commissioned earlier this year by a group of leading IT companies, with support from DTI. The commissioning group included Bull, IBM and ICL – OSIS's three sponsoring vendors. The research results revealed some thought-provoking facts about the state of the Open Systems market. The

vast majority of users, it appeared, wanted independent guidance and felt that they lacked the appropriate information to guarantee trouble-free implementation of Open Systems. A major impediment to the adoption of Open Systems for many users seemed to be the absence of reliable, unbiased and up-to-date information on which to base their choices. "It would be of great help to industry if a body could provide information on the applications available in specific market areas," one typical respondent commented. "We are not able to digest all the detail of the multitude of standards which seem to exist today," said another.

OSIS was conceived with such comments uppermost in mind, and the idea has been developed with the close involvement of several large IT users. OSIS has been devised as an easy-to-use information resource – a simple dial-up service offering on-line information and help on Open Systems. The research showed that users want an independent service and, accordingly, OSIS will be run by two organisations with unparalleled reputations for independence in the Open Systems field. NCC is a respected world leader in the development and supply of third-party Open Systems testing technology and services,

while Level-7 is a major vendor-independent European supplier of management and consultancy services relating to Open Systems. Both NCC and Level-7 are active within the international standards-making process and, in particular, as members of the European Workshop on Open Systems (EWOS).

John Perkins, NCC

Under the direction of these two organisations, OSIS will provide information about products and services as well as 'signposts' to sources of other useful information. "We see it as a gateway," says John Perkins, NCC's

EDITOR'S NOTE

This is the penultimate edition of the Open Systems Bulletin to be published by DTI. Our main story features the Open Systems Information Service, due to be launched in

January. This initiative is an example of several of its type: initiated, supported and operated by industry to enable further promotion of Open Systems in the UK. In our final

issue, due for publication in early February, we will have a round-up of these initiatives and also report on ongoing and future DTI activity in this area.

During the months of July to November we were in constant communication with OSIS via their in house co-ordinator, advising them of our progress towards full integration with the DTI and the Level 7 mainframe system. We were not paid for the work we did for the DTI but carried on in good faith so that the launch would be able to go forward as promised. We then received the following cancellation letter:

Letter received in November 1993

To: Maurice Hamlin
From Richard Hinckley, ICL

Dear Maurice,
DTI INFORMATION SERVICE
First an apology for not getting back to you earlier, I have been on leave and the arrangements were at a delicate stage

Basically I do not have good news. For reasons which I am reluctant to go into in writing, the other vendors did not want to take up the proposal for system in the way I had envisaged, and which they had been happy to go along with up to now.

A further proposal by one of the sponsors is to be made, which if not accepted is likely to be the end of the idea. Unfortunately this does not include attaching the Hamlin system at this time, although possibly there may well be an opportunity in the future.
I can quite understand if you feel you have wasted your time following this up. I feel let down too as the organisation mainly concerned with rejecting the idea could have blown the whistle a lot earlier. Such is life?
Regards,
Richard Hinckley, ICL

Our company was dumbfounded. When I asked Mr Hinckley why this had happened, I was told that some of the Vendors considered our system and information database to be illegal. He said he was sorry but it was not his decision.

How could it be illegal? We had been running the service for years; our services were guaranteed and used by many of the most prestigious financial institutions in the country.

There was to be no remuneration for the mass of research and development requested and work carried out for the DTI to meet the agreed time schedules to link up with the DTI Level 7 mainframe computer.

At no time had we received any indication that any of the Founding Vendors were not impressed with the service we were offering and no word from their in house liaison man.

Without doubt there was no other system available that could possibly replace the versatility and breadth of information held on SystemSearch.

What was truly astonishing was the fact that the DTI continued to support the Vendors' failure.

A fictitious and unfounded excuse:
In December of that year the DTI wrote to me and said that the reason for our exclusion was due to legal reasons.

They then told us that they had to go ahead with the launch of the service using the NCC/Level 7 database because of the money already spent and because of the advertised commitment. The service was to be launched on the 27 January 1994. A formal invitation for me to attend the meeting was included with the letter.

I wrote to the Minister, Patrick McLaughlin MP, and Under-Secretary of State for Trade and Technology, pointing out that when the DTI asked its own Research Team to find out what it was that business most needed from the OSIS service, the answers had come back loud and clear *"**reliable and unbiased advice**"*.

The DTI's own research was now to be ignored:

1. Only suppliers who paid a high fee to Level 7 were to be included within their searches.
2. Less than one hundred suppliers had signed up to be included.
3. Almost all suppliers who paid to be included were linked to one or other of the Vendors - IBM, Bull and ICL
4. At that time SystemSearch held over 7,500 suppliers (not including retailers) and over 30,000 software products in 340 different business areas.
5. There was no other such IT information library in existence.
6. Without our information library and search engine, OSIS was unable to offer any of the promised essential requirements.
7. How was it possible for the DTI to continue placing money and support behind a Manufacture/Supplier marketing scam?

The DTI replied to me saying:

1. Firstly, that I had taken statements out of context and that the service was never intended to be non profit making.
2. Secondly, that they had always intended to charge suppliers to advertise their products and

3. Lastly that the launch could not be deferred as all arrangements had been made.
4. Also that they were sure that the NCC-Level 7 OSIS had adequate capability to make the service a success. (This was totally false.)

The above DTI explanation together with the various memoranda and the insulting terms of the original agreement offered to MHA by the DTI and Vendors enhanced my belief that it was never their intention to actively use my service.

It all points to the fact that they had already tied up with the main Vendors but didn't know how to refuse me after having seen a demonstration which proved that SystemSearch was capable of instantly answering any question keyed into it as it covered every aspect asked for in their initial advertising campaign. There was not one honest reason for them to refuse to use SystemSearch other than their personal agreements with the major computer vendor companies.

I believe the statement at the beginning of the project given by Martin Greave of the DTI in conjunction with George McNeil CEO of Bull UK (one of the main Vendors) who gave the most honest answer about what was intended. He said, **"We will be able to grab a bigger chunk of the UK software market."**

There was no question of the Vendors' final solution being unbiased.

Likewise, if you study their proposed contract to my company, it offered us virtually nothing. We were to have: -

No member on the Board
No voting rights
No unpaid access to our own system once it was set up
No attendance at policy meetings
No share of profits
The share holders were to receive all MHA's income in excess of operating costs for an undefined period.
Any financial assistance given to MHA during its further development to satisfy the OSIS requirement was to be repaid by MHA once the system was running.

I accepted these ridiculous terms because I felt that British companies so badly needed proper unbiased advice. I also felt it would place Britain in front of the rest of world.

Money wasn't so very important to me but what an epitaph for SystemSearch it would have been.

Again I would ask - were these the actions of an honest Government Department whose mandate was to work for the good of the country?

DTI MANDATE described in 1992: -

*The DTI drives our ambition of 'prosperity for all' by working to
    create the best environment for business success in the UK.
We help people and companies become more productive by
    promoting enterprise, innovation and creativity.
We champion UK business at home and abroad.
We invest heavily in world-class science and technology.
We protect the rights of working for fair and open markets in the
    UK, Europe and the world.*

The OSIS failure makes a joke of this Mandate.

Open Systems

BULLETIN SPRING 1994

A ROYAL LAUNCH FOR OSiS

London's Café Royal was the venue for the January launch of OSiS, the independent information service for Open Systems, managed by NCC and Level-7. Over 100 representatives of vendor and user organisations attended the event, chaired by George R. Sidey, head of the Technology Promotions and Services Branch of the DTI. The meeting was addressed by Patrick McLoughlin MP, the Parliamentary Under Secretary of State for Trade and Technology; Mike Fisher, IS director Bass Breweries; and NCC's chief executive, Nigel Banister.

Patrick McLoughlin discussed the achievements of his department's Open Systems programmes to date, and observed: 'Today we are seeing both the successful completion of DTI's promotional activities and evidence of the industry's continued determination to respond to key market demands, especially from small to medium sized companies'. This determination had inspired the development of OSiS, an on-line service embodying the new approach to independent information provision offered by IT itself.

Announcing the formal launch of OSiS, the minister congratulated all those organisations who had been involved in its establishment: NCC and Level-7, the service providers; the three sponsoring vendors, Bull, IBM, and ICL; and the small group of influential user companies which had advised and supported the venture – Bass Breweries,

Nigel Banister, NCC

Courtaulds Textiles, Marks & Spencer, Thorn Lighting, ICI Chemicals and Lucas Aerospace. 'This is truly a working partnership', he said, 'in which DTI has been happy to play a part'.

Nigel Banister summed up the general feeling. 'I believe OSiS will prove itself to be of vital importance in promoting Open Systems', he said, 'and the better use of IT in British industry'.

Patrick McLoughlin MP

COMPUTERS IN BUSINESS – HELP OR HINDRANCE?

If you manage a small or medium sized business, you may have a significant investment in computer systems. You probably know all about the costs, but are the benefits equally evident? Regrettably, the answer is often "No".

Well, there are no easy or instant solutions. But there are some things going on which can help those who are prepared to help themselves.

Under the banner of Open-Exchange, there is a programme of assistance for users who feel they should be getting more value for money from their investment. It includes access to factual information and impartial advice at low cost; it involves problem-and experience-sharing; and it opens a vast network of personal contacts for mutual help.

Read all about it in the flyer enclosed with this edition of Open Systems Bulletin.

EⁱⁱR

*The Lord Chamberlain is
commanded by Her Majesty to invite*

Mr. and Mrs. M. R. Hamlin

to a Garden Party at Buckingham Palace

on Tuesday 19th July 1994 from 4 to 6 pm

Morning Dress, Uniform or Lounge Suit

We received the Lord Chamberlain's invitation to the Queen's Garden Party

However, I am sure that the invitation was purely a sop for my wasted research and financial effort. Nevertheless, we had always been great admirers of the Queen, Prince Philip and the Royal Family. It was a lovely day; everyone dressed up to the nines and Jaye looked beautiful in spite of being in great pain due to her spinal injury.

There were two military bands in the grounds of Buckingham Palace; the Army played a stirring selection from the shows and the RAF gave an exhilarating performance of Glen Miller music. We met some young chaps from the Queen's Flight and had a good chat but I was amazed that these young RAF flyers had not heard of the ACA (the Air Crew Association) and I did my best to enthuse them as we badly needed new blood.

The Queen and Prince Philip were there, also the Princesses Margaret and Anne. I have always had a soft spot for Princess Margaret and was sorry she could not marry Group Captain Townsend. I am also a great admirer of both Prince Charles and Princess Anne: they are stalwarts of the Royal Family, always putting so much effort into carrying out their many duties without the acclaim they deserve.

In fact, the Royal Family do a wonderful job and bring to Britain far more prestige and tourism income than many people realise.

The refreshments were excellent – superb cream cakes, ice cream and dainty sandwiches like those my Mother used to make. Yes, it was an honour to attend the Garden Party.

Heseltine gives IT high priority

The Government has upgraded the importance it attaches to the IT industry by switching responsibility to a senior minister.

In his first move as Secretary of State for Trade & Industry, Michael Heseltine has made Tim Sainsbury, one of his three most senior ministers, responsible for sponsoring all industry issues, including IT.

Since May 1991 responsibility for IT has been in the hands of Lord Reay, an under-secretary of state, the lowest level of government minister. Reay left the Government last week as part of the post-election reshuffle.

A DTI spokesman said the move promoted IT up the list of government priorities.

'It is an upgraded rank for

Sainsbury: IT will be high on his list of priorities

IT and IT is also high up Sainsbury's list of responsibilities,' he said.

The DTI already had a division dedicated to IT, but it was concerned primarily with marketing. Last week Heseltine said he would return marketing functions to the sponsorship divisions, abolished by DTI boss Lord Young in 1987.

Heseltine is also expected to drop the enterprise tag.

I saw the above Press statement on how Michael Heseltine, President of the Board of Trade, was going to make IT development a matter of major importance.

I decided to test its credibility by offering the Government full rights to the SystemSearch library for a peppercorn fee when it was worth millions. I received the following negative letter.

Maurice R Hamlin
Maurice Hamlin Associates
Winchester House
Winchester Avenue
Cjorley
Lancs, PR7 4AQ

Department of
Trade and Industry

151 Buckingham Palace Road
London SW1W 9SS

Enquiries
071-215 5000

Telex 881 3148 DHHQ G
Fax 071-215 2909

071 215 1208

11 July 1994

Dear Maurice

Thank you for your letter to the President of the Board of Trade, Michael Heseltine, dated 24 June. I have been asked to reply on his behalf.

As I am sure you appreciate, the Department is well aware of SystemSearch and its excellent capabilities. Unfortunately, I am afraid that it cannot accept your offer of donating the system to the nation in return for a modest annual lifetime income, or even as a one-off payment. The sale and acquisition of your service is a matter for you and the market to decide. DTI does not normally wish to be involved in such cases.

I will consult with colleagues to see what alternative action, if any, might be taken, but I am not optimistic. However, I will write to you again in due course, although this will almost certainly be after the holiday period.

On the question of OSiS, I think your perception is not quite right. The service was developed and launched as planned - as a signposting facility to other credible sources of Open Systems information, including facilities such as SystemsSearch. As I am sure you know from your own experience, it takes time to build up a sustainable product and OSiS is no exception, subject as it now is to the vagaries of the marketplace. I am confident that OSiS will prove to be successful in the long run.

I am delighted to learn that you have received an invitation to attend the Royal Garden Party. I hope you enjoy the occasion and that the weather is kind to you.

Yours sincerely,

Darren Greaves

dti
the department for Enterprise

This was a pathetic response from someone, allegedly of high responsibility and intelligence, who had personally seen the capabilities of SystemSearch and was aware of the limitations of the NCC and Level 7 Systems and it proved to me that they were used to playing with numbers, not realities.

October 1994 OSIS ceased trading. What a con!

Below you see what the UK press thought: -
October 1994 – the following is an assessment in the Press of the DTI's handling of the OSIS project when this costly scheme collapsed only nine months after its launch.
What was the DTI's inducement to refuse MHA's system?

"Today, October 1994, nine months after the official launch of OSIS, the DTI service has 40 Subscribing Suppliers, 100 Registered Users and 12 Areas of Software.

By comparison, SystemSearch covers -

5,000+ UK Suppliers
340 Different Industry areas
1,500 Different Application areas
30,000+ Application Software Products.

SystemSearch was not taken up by OSIS because some of the Consortium considered there were too many legal problems to setting up the managing company which would have included all the OSIS original members with MHA as the main information provider. OSIS is now managed solely by the NCC and Level 7 with three of the original Consortium- ICL, IBM and Bull lending token support.

The new concept was that OSIS will hold product and supplier information only from suppliers who take advertising space at £350 per page to a maximum of 10 pages. At the OSIS launch, the target was 1,000 users in the first year As stated in all literature appertaining to the OSIS service and even within its Launch brochure, the DTI's own market research showed that the prime need of industry was to have unbiased and informative product detail on what application software was available in each specific market area.

The DTI ended up with just 12 market areas out of 340 and 40 suppliers out of 5000 which gives OSIS less than 1X of suppliers and, at the most generous estimate, no more than 5X of available products.

This indicates the total failure of OSIS and proves how much a service Such as SystemSearch is needed."

The following press statements are confirmation of the DTI's attitude to ethics and to whom they really support in business.

1994 Management Consultants' News

"Department of Trade & Industry Gaff, DTI backs a book on How to Cheat.

They were promoting a booklet advising small businesses how to cheat and spy on their competitors.

Sheffield-based Strategic Consultants are at the heart of an embarrassing gaffe by the Department of Trade & Industry which has been caught promoting a booklet telling small businesses how to cheat and spy on their competitors.

Alan Stopford, co director of Strategic Consultants, wrote the publication 'Your Own Business'.

The firm is a £1 million plus turnover management consultancy. The booklet was hastily withdrawn after Board of Trade President Michael Heseltine discovered the contents earlier this month.

However, it has been in circulation for several years and was first commissioned by the Department of Employment, then taken up by the DTI when it assumed responsibility for small business advice under schemes like the Enterprise Initiative."

The Independent News   *Thursday, 16 February 1995*

Government IT Advisors are subject to vociferous lobbying and coercion temptation by high flying IT firms.

When new government technology proposals are in their infancy, particularly where new large scale previously untried projects offering huge financial gain for IT firms such as SchlumbergerSema, Applied Card Technologies, Sun Microsystems, Oracle, SodexhoPass UK, Northop Grumman and EDS. Etc etc; it is no wonder that Government IT procurement officers and project managers are open to vociferous lobbying and even coercion temptation from high flying IT firms.

Decisions often taken without sufficient practicality research and the prospective suppliers capabilities in respect of actual expertise and experience in the required technology, or in placing major pay back clauses in cases of time schedules and performance monitoring. So very many government contract suffer from time delays and exceeding budgets, if their were heavy penalties much more caution would take place prior to closing contracts

---

It must be remembered that there is a belief amongst many major IT players that one must do anything to obtain a contract because once the project is under way, more money will always be found.

No Government likes to admit its failures.

1995 - A happy family occasion:

My daughter Susan and her fiancé Mick tie the knot.

In her earlier years Sue had been a midwife working with the World Health Organisation in Algeria where she had many adventures, sometimes travelling fifty or sixty miles to tend patients in remote hill villages. When she returned to England she became the Medical Underwriting Manager for a major health insurance company and now works for Age Concern as a Community Services Manager. She has a deep knowledge of people and is an extremely kind and understanding person. Sue has four children from her previous marriage; Nadia, Karim, Gwenda and Ben. Her first husband and daughter, Toma, died in a tragic accident.

Mick Grimer is Vice Chairman of the Eastbourne Borough Football Club (formerly the Langney Football Club formed in 1964), an organisation which is a good example of true sportsmanship. The Club was started by Mick and Len Smith (Chairman) and a dedicated group of local lads. Today they have an impressive club house, a football stadium with a capacity of 4,500, a six lane indoor bowling hall, archery, youth section and many other activities for both young and old. All created and built with voluntary labour. The Club plays in the Conference League and today it is still run as a Community

Interest Club. An example of supporters being more important than money.

Another ACA Reunion:

In September we attended a three-day Air Crew Association Annual reunion in Brighton together with our friends Pete and Audrey Perry, Dudley and Beatie Pope and many others from the Blackpool ACA branch. As usual the ACA had booked the Hotel and a draw took place to designate democratically each Member's room number. We had been delayed and arrived last to find that we had won the Crown Suite which included a separate dining room, lounge, Jacuzzi bathroom and four-poster bed. Such luxury! We were delighted. The Saturday night banquet and ball were fantastic with the String of Pearls Orchestra playing for dancing. We all had a most memorable night.

Chapter 20 - Millennium and Yet More Corruption

Early in 1996 I read an article written by IT Specialist, Robin Guenier, Executive Director of Taskforce 2000, an organisation set up to assess the Year 2000 computer reliability problem.

It gave an early warning of pending IT disasters which would be caused by computers not recognising the change of year from midnight on the 31st December 1999 to 0001 on 1st January of 2000.

It was from his enlightened opinion that I set my Research Team to monitor and record which of the thousands of computer suppliers held on the SystemSearch database actually had application software products with the ability to cope with the century's date change. I wrote to Guenier offering our full co-operation and we agreed to keep in touch.

Due to the seeming lack of Government awareness and support for Taskforce 2000, I wrote to the Labour Party in an attempt to find out whether or not the Opposition understood the importance that senior Government Ministers should give to the massive loss to GDP by inefficient computer selection by Purchasing Officers and also to the possible disasters from the encroaching Millennium software failures if action was not taken to combat the problem immediately.
Mr O'Brien, the Shadow Minister for European Monetary issues, replied on behalf of Mr Brown:

His letter stated that he was fully aware of the problems *after* the Millennium and read "*Dear Mr. Hamlin, Thankyou for you recent letter to Gordon Brown which I am dealing with as the Shadow Minister responsible for European Monetary issues. I have indeed been aware of the difficulties with computers in after the Millennium. I asked a number of Parliamentary questions about it recently. I am grateful to you for you contribution in relation to the matter. Mike O'Brien.*"

Which proved he totally misunderstood that the problem was to correct computer software before the date change occurred.

On the 31st December the world had its first wake up alarm signal.

> The New Zealand Aluminium Smelter plant at Tiwai Point on South Island, New Zealand suffered a catastrophic failure on the 31st December 1996 when production in all the smelting pot lines ground to a halt. The plant's computer system made up of six hundred and sixty microcomputers had failed without warning at midnight. The problem was traced to a faulty computer software program which had failed to account that 1996 was a leap year and it did not recognise the 366th day. The shut down cost in excess of one million New Zealand dollars.

> Two hours later at Comalco's Bell Bay Smelter in Tasmania, a similar failure occurred; both systems had used the same software. The computer regulated temperatures in the smelters' pot-cells and when the computers failed, five of the pot-cells overheated and destroyed themselves.

At MHA we immediately increased our activity and started identifying software suppliers who had the specialist tools to detect and correct applications with a Y2K (Year 2000) problem.

> In the USA Peter de Jager, a company consultant with a Volatile Gas Manufacturing corporation disclosed, during an interview with the St. Louis Post, that he had carried out safety checks at his company's manufacturing plant which had exposed a chilling danger. He told the reporter that when the date in the company's

computers was experimentally moved forward to make 00 represent the millennium, an embedded chip failed, shutting down the plant's cooling system.

Without the cooling system, the plant would explode. De Jager said that the company which he did not identify, is now replacing its chips. He said one of his main worries was the mass of companies who weren't checking their factories. Imagine the financial crisis if computers had failed worldwide!

Some software was impossible to fix and there was much research and development taking place to evaluate and seek solutions to the problem. One bright area was Retail Services because companies using software from such firms as Microsoft were issued upgrades well before the Millennium.

The greatest problems were expected amongst large companies with custom built programs written years before, many in the COBOL programming language which was considered to be obsolete; pay rates for COBOL programmers doubled. Firms such as Micro Focus, whose share price halved after COBOL fell from favour, saw their share price soar as they offered Year 2000 repair kits.

I wrote to the Government offering our help and the services of our database and received the following response from Paddy Ashdown:

"Dear Mr. Hamlin,

Thank you for your letter. I am very grateful to you for taking the time to write to me. You make some very interesting points and I wish that I could reply to your letter at greater length. Nevertheless, I am most grateful to you for writing and putting your points across. I have thought it right to enclose a copy of my speech that I made to the House of Commons on the subject of Europe and a Referendum, which I hope you will find of interest.

Paddy Ashdown."

Mr M Hamlin
Maurice Hamlin Associates
Winchester House
Winchester Avenue
Chorley
Lancashire
PR7 4AQ

16th January 1997

Our ref.: RCC/refer

Dear Mr Hamlin

Thank you for your letter. I am very grateful to you for taking the trouble to write to me.

You make some very interesting points, and I wish that I could reply to your letter at greater length. Nevertheless, I am most grateful to you for writing and putting your points across. I have thought it right to enclose a copy of a speech I made to the House of Commons on the subject of Europe and a Referendum, which I hope you will find of interest.

Thank you once again for writing.

Yours sincerely

Rt. Hon. Paddy Ashdown MP
(Dictated by Mr Ashdown and signed in his absence)

This response from Paddy Ashdown bears absolutely no reference to the Millennium problem or the recurring computer purchase failures. How on earth did mention of a Referendum relate to the Y2K problem?

February – At last someone woke up. The UK Conservative Government's Department of Trade and Industry officially backed 'Taskforce 2000' to highlight the problem within industry, commerce and the defence structure but they did so with a laid back attitude.

Fortunately it was controlled by IT Guru, Robin Guenier, who as mentioned earlier, was fully aware of the likely worldwide catastrophic affects of computer meltdown in year 2000 but his capabilities were restricted by minimum funding.

I immediately got in touch again and agreed to expand SystemSearch in any way he thought practical.

In May 1997 Tony Blair led Labour to a landslide victory in the General Election. As a confirmed Tory, I had been greatly impressed by Tony Blair's new approach to politics, his planning and refreshing ideas appeared to offer a new and promising way ahead and for the first time in my life I voted for Labour.

Tony Blair had been the Leader of the Labour party since 1994 and under his leadership the Party adopted the term "New Labour" and abandoned the policies it had held for decades by moving towards the centre ground. In the first years of the New Labour Government, Blair handed over control of UK interest rates to the Bank of England, introduced the minimum wage, signed the Good Friday Agreement, introduced University tuition fees and established the Scottish Parliament, Welsh Assembly and the Northern Ireland Assembly, much of which was seen by the British public as highly commendable.

I wrote to Mr Blair to try to gain the Government's interest and enthusiasm for tackling both the atrocious loss of GDP by the continued purchase of incorrect computer systems and software and their pathetically casual attitude towards the approaching Millennium crisis.

No response was received. It appeared that Governments might change but they use the same blinkers.

According to Whitaker's Almanac - The number of a leap year must be divisible by four without remainder, unless it is the last year of the century, which can only be a leap year if its number is divisible by 400 without remainder.

23rd May 1997 - IT Minister John Battle issues a promise.

See below: -

COMPUTERWEEKLY
http://www.computerweekly.co.uk   Working for IT Professionals   Thursday 29 May 1997 (15)

Battle is on to beat bug

Update 2000

IT MINISTER John Battle has promised to make the millennium bug problem a top priority.

His promise follows a call for government money to create a millennium information resource which would provide UK users with a comprehensive list of products and their year 2000 status.

The call, by Tim Johnson, founder of industry analyst Ovum, has been backed by the chairman of the British Computer Society's year 2000 working party, John Ivinson, and Conservative MP David Atkinson, who is championing the millennium issue.

"I've raised this as an issue with government since last summer," said Ivinson, who

Johnson... call for funding

suggested the National Computing Centre, Taskforce 2000 or its year 2000 interest group as suitable homes for the information centre.

"This is one of the many initiatives Taskforce 2000 could do if it had the resources," said a spokesman for Atkinson.

Leader, p31

230

The following article highlights the fact that the new Labour Government showed no interest in the massive problem of computer system failures.

http://www.computerweekly.co.uk Thursday 12 June 1997

Millions lost as DSS ends legal battle

Tony Collins

THE DEPARTMENT of Social Security (DSS) has failed to win millions in compensation or recover legal costs over the abandonment of the £25m welfare benefits statistical system Assist.

Computer Weekly understands the DSS and its main contractor ICL have agreed a settlement which leaves the department without a new system or compensation for the benefits and savings it was to deliver.

Suppliers had expected these to amount to several million pounds.

The department also faces a bill for almost three years of legal costs amounting to at least £1m.

However, it will receive a repayment of £3.6m plus interest. This comprises instalments that the department's IT Services Agency

Disaster site... Assist started its ill-fated journey at Longbenton

had paid to ICL before work was halted in 1994.

The settlement comes in advance of a decision by the department on the final shortlist for the £1bn Accord project to integrate various welfare benefit systems. ICL and its bidding partner Andersen Consulting are in the running for the contract.

The DSS would not say how much the affair had cost the taxpayer.

The reason the project failed was the subject of the dispute. The suppliers said end-users had not been consulted adequately at the planning stage and later made many requests for changes.

This added to the system's complexity and pushed back deadlines. Even so the suppliers insist that the system was working at the time the DSS cancelled the project.

But the department blamed ICL for not meeting deadlines and said the system was rejected twice by end-users during two trial periods.

It also emerged this week that ICL had alleged it had evidence that the system was cancelled by the DSS to ease an internal cash shortage.

A spokesman for the DSS said the allegation had been dropped at an early stage.

In August 1997 Robin Guenier threatened to quit Taskforce 2000 because it was so grossly under funded. He said "I'm not doing this for my health. The Millennium is a major concern but there is no official funding, no real Government understanding or commitment. We have been granted a few miserly thousands, poor office facilities and no support. To continue raising industry awareness I have to get cash from somewhere. If I don't, I will leave."

Guenier was one of the most knowledgeable and capable IT professionals with a true understanding of the Y2K problem.

In October the DTI Industry Quango 'Taskforce 2000' once again reported it was suffering from a financial headache; the previous July the DTI donated a mere £170,000 to Guenier to get the Taskforce Awareness Programme off the ground but he had run out of funds and was relying on the private sector to meet its estimated annual costs of £500,000. Government Ministers appeared to have little comprehension of the likely disastrous effects on the world and, in particular, the UK economy. Ministers believed industry and commerce should deal with the issue themselves.

Blair Sacks Taskforce 2000 and launches Action 2000:

Tony Blair obviously did not understand the Y2K problem and took this opportunity to sack the efficient and knowledgeable Quango largely because Guenier gave him the unpalatable truth and he didn't take kindly to constructive criticism or being advised what was needed to fund a Millennium awareness program.

Robin Guenier commented on the newly set up 'Action 2000'

"It would be a good idea if it was properly funded, however, they had appointed Don Cruickshank to head the project and he could dedicate only one day a week to the job. MHA contacted 'Action 2000' to offer support but no glimmer of interest was shown.

A survey published at this time by PA Consulting found just over half of all British IT businesses believed their senior managers were aware of the Y2K problem".

On the 30th November the Sunday Times said "Tony Blair attempted to ease nervousness over fears that the Government was not taking the Y2K problem seriously enough; he insisted that they were on course to tackle the Millennium problem in the public sector computers with an anticipated programme that would cost about one £Billion."

Yet he had given Robin Guenier's 'Taskforce' only a few thousand pounds. This new about turn was admittance that Robin Guernier's voice had been the only one acknowledging the enormity of the problem.

My opinion of Blair as an honest politician plummeted.

Worries regarding the Y2K Millennium problem continued and the British Government backed the world's first "National Year of 2000 Awareness Week" which began on Monday the 10th December 1997.

I was invited to attend the Consortium headed by Mr Don Cruickshank and where Robin Guenier was one of the main speakers on non-compliant Y2K computers.

I spoke to Mr.Cruickshank and made him aware of SystemSearch's depth of knowledge of software in the UK. I told him that we were researching and adding to the database all Y2K tools that would help businesses check and, if necessary, correct their current software. Also, that we were searching for all possible correction programmes for machine tools with embedded software chips. I added that this information would be freely available to all. He asked me to write to him giving full details of SystemSearch.

I did so the following day but heard nothing.

A startling warning from the USA:

In March 1998 United States Officials responsible for Y2K conversion efforts estimated it would cost $2.3 billion just to fix the Federal Government's computer systems. The General Motor Corporation said it expected to spend up to $500 million and the Chase Manhattan Bank up to $300 million.

-0-0-0-0-

At long last, after many calls, I was asked by a Mr Coffin of Action 2000 to visit London and demonstrate the abilities of SystemSearch to their Managing Director, Mr Eddison, and his colleagues.

Following the on-line demonstration (as with other demonstrations to Government Officers) they exclaimed their amazement of the wide scope of SystemSearch's abilities and its speed and accuracy of information.

Mr Eddison asked me to send a report to them showing how MHA could help Action 2000 and the thousands of companies in need of Y2K assistance.

Within a few days I sent a report to Mr Eddison which set out how SystemSearch could help to negate the Millennium bug for many businesses.

Unfortunately, within the week, Ms Gwyneth Flower (an ex ATS army Lieutenant who seemed to have no understanding of the civilian computer market place) replaced Mr Eddison as Managing Director and when I contacted her she said that neither she nor her staff had any knowledge of either my visit to their offices or the report I had sent to them.

I was then asked to send a copy of the report and to give another demonstration on the 19th May, which was almost two months away.

234

I felt this showed how little urgency she felt for the pending Millennium problem.

-0-0-0-0-

The first Y2K disaster in the U.K. was at the London warehouse of Marks & Spencer when tons of food was destroyed. Their computer had read 2002 as 1902 so, instead of the food having a shelf life of four years, the computer calculated it was ninety-six years old and ordered it to be thrown out.

In the United States a similar problem happened in the warehouse of a freeze-dried food manufacturer.

A British Drug Manufacturing Company asked MHA for help after thousands of pounds worth of drugs had been thrown away because the sell-by date was past the year 2000 and the computer had assumed they were out of date.

David Bailey, Commercial Director of London Transport, delivered a positive message. He told the media that they were confident their transport system would run smoothly, however, he added "We are constantly asking ourselves, how shall we know what we do not know? It is important that we also have contingency plans in the case of the Underground not working." He added "London Underground is an on-line user of the MHA SystemSearch Y2K information database."

Early in May 1998 Action 2000 advertised for websites that could aid in solving the Y2K information problem. I immediately wrote to Don Cruickshank, Chairman of Action 2000, and reminded him of my meeting with him at the Consortium almost six months earlier and of my meeting and demonstrations to his previous directors, Mr Eddison and my arrangement to demonstrate my Y2K system to Ms Flower on the 19th May.

Again, as with the DTI and his earlier directors, he proved reluctant to talk to me or confirm Ms Flower's agreement to see a demonstration of SystemSearch's Y2K abilities.

Despite Action 2000's advertisements, I had to make several further approaches, both in writing and by telephone, before they finally and reluctantly agreed that I could demonstrate SystemSearch's abilities on the 19th May as previously agreed.

Ms Flower and Mr Tony Stock, the new Operations Director, attended the second demonstration at their premises. They showed no great interest in the system but asked how our database could assist Action 2000. I pointed out that for a very small investment they could have an on-line terminal installed at their Help Desk which would be in direct contact with the SystemSearch computer at our office and this would give them immediate access to every single software product available on the UK market and the ability to check whether or not that particular product was Y2K compliant. I added that they would also have access to all Y2K correction tools and suppliers' details. They sent the following email note to me –

"Dear Mr Hamlin,
Our main worry is not the cost of being connected to your service, or how business is crying out for guidance but how Action 2000 could avoid possible legal repercussions by assisting on-line publishing of information which might be incorrect.

SystemSearch would not be considered eligible to be included in Action 2000's list of companies offering advice on Year 2000 until we have found the time to vet a number of reference sites."

G Flower

I was dumfounded. Why was everyone I dealt with who was involved with the Government so determined not to be interested in SystemSearch, despite MHA having been an instrumental part of assisting Robin Guenier of the original Taskforce, and whose software had been proven to the DTI and was guaranteed by Lloyds of London.

We immediately sent the names and contacts of twenty-six companies (for reference purposes) many of whom were within the 'Top 500' list. David Cosgrove, NW Regional IT Consultancy Manager of BDO Binder Hamlyn, confirmed that their Consultants who used SystemSearch had almost instant access to information on 7,500 companies, their products, specialist areas, Y2K suitability, turnover, locations and so on, giving tremendous time saving and efficiency.

Ms Flower launched a useless and incorrect Y2K brochure:

It was only after I was shown a copy of this brochure devised by Data Dimension and distributed by Action 2000 to 60,000 businesses Nationwide that I learned that Ms Flower, almost immediately after she had been appointed, had awarded the contract to assist British business to Data Dimensions of the USA.

I immediately had my team match the Y2K advice given in Ms Flower's brochure against the SystemSearch database to analyse the quality of the information.

It showed that more than 50% was incorrect - totally out of date or irrelevant to the UK software market.

What happened to Ms Flower's earlier insistence to me that she could not accept advice from suppliers until they and their information had been carefully vetted?

July 1998

Year 2000 information packs sent out with incorrect data

Bill Goodwin

ACTION 2000, the Government-sponsored millennium bug awareness group, has sent out more than 60,000 information packs containing incorrect and out-of-date information.

The packs are a key part of Action 2000's campaign to raise awareness of the year 2000 problem and to put companies in touch with suppliers and consultants that can help them solve their millennium computer problems.

An information pack delivered to *Computer Weekly* this week contained a list of suppliers that included invalid

No warning... Flower failed to amend inaccuracies in packs

phone numbers, addresses that were up to two years out-of-date, and names of companies that did not exist.

Action 2000's director Gwynneth Flower has been aware of errors in its information pack since at least March this year, but has failed to take steps to warn people applying for its information packs of the mistakes, Lanacashire-based software consultant Maurice Hamlin said.

Hamlin also claimed that Action 2000's list of millennium-compliant products is misleading and out of date.

"The listing of 86 products – half of which are differing versions of the same generic product – out of 50,000 is of little practical use to any end-user," he said.

What on earth was Action 2000 spending its funding on? Funding which at that time stood at £1,700,000.

I thought that the farce must stop so, as seen above, I sent copies of the brochure and our corrective analysis to the computer magazines 'Computer Weekly' and 'Computing' to highlight the fact that Action 2000 had contracted Data Dimensions of USA to assist them with the Millennium problem and that Action 2000 had sent out 60,000 Millennium brochures containing information which was largely out of date, incorrect or relevant only to American businesses.

At last Action 2000 accepted that MHA had the most relevant and up to date information on the UK's Millennium problem, however, it was only sight of the above publication showing how badly they had handled the situation that made Ms Flower accept our services. What is it that the Government and its departments have against small but forward thinking UK companies? See contract letter below: -

They finally, if reluctantly, commissioned MHA. Our remit was to continue to extend and enhance the SystemSearch database which already identified Y2K compliance status of the most commonly, used software products.

MHA's Y2K website was officially launched on Thursday the 26th November 1998 and could be found and interrogated by anyone at http://www.systemsearch.co.uk - **Free of Charge.**

Maurice Hamlin Associates
YEAR 2000 IT EVALUATION

Winchester House, Winchester Avenue
Chorley, Lancs, PR7 4AQ
Tel: 01257 262776 Fax: 01257 264688
E-Mail: mha@systemsearch.co.uk
Web Site: www.systemsearch.co.uk

17th November 1998

The Editor
Aberdeen Independant

Fax: 01224 648642
Tel: 01224 618300

PRESS RELEASE

FACTUAL YEAR 2000 ASSISTANCE for companies trying to find out whether or not their software is Year 2000 Compliant.

TOTALLY FREE TO ALL INDUSTRY AND COMMERCE

Maurice Hamlin Associates was commissioned by Action 2000 to develope a database which identifies the Year 2000 compliance status of the most commonly used desktop software products. This listing also gives each product's technical statement issued by the supplier. Also, where available a link to download the supplier's correction patch to make the product compliant.

MHA intends to expand the product range, suggestions are welcome.

MHA is a company with 20 years experience in software research.

The quality of the information has already been acclaimed by Business Links

The free database can be seen at Web Address:
http://www.systemsearch.co.uk

The official launch is Thursday 26th November 1998. This is a new site that has not been registered with any search engines with the intention to enable journalists to preview the site before launch.

Maurice Hamlin
Managing Director

Note: SystemSearch's listings also gave each product's technical statement which had been issued by the supplier, and where available, a link to download the official correction patches. General information issued by suppliers was also freely included.

The following major companies relied on SystemSearch: -

BDO, BP, British Tourist Board Burroughs, Christian Aid, Coca Cola, Electricity Council, Fina, Glaxo, ICL, Informix, KPMG, London Underground, Maltese Government, Nationwide TV, NCM (Holland), NCR, Oracle, Price Waterhouse. Reed International, Reuters, Sears Plc, Smithkline Beecham, Swift of Belgium, Tradecraftraft, Zurich Insurance.

Here lies another tale of woe. Again I ask "When are we going to appoint an IT Minister who really understands IT and the market and who has the power to identify the causes of failures and recoup the wasted funding?"

By March 1999 MHA had found that most businesses likely to be affected by the Millennium were working hard to ensure their computer systems were ready for the Y2K date change over but, irrespective of all the Y2K discussions, analysis and reports, they were still worried.

Gwyneth Flower in her 'State of the Nation' update, pointed to her current research which showed only two out of every five UK businesses were on course for Y2K.

Action 2000 said four-fifths of firms claimed to be Millennium compliant but according to the Organisation's research, only fifty per cent had set up a proper bug evaluation program.

Flower criticised those firms of "an amateurish and unhealthy reliance on their own judgement".

In an attempt to convince companies of the need for action, Flower warned that the Health and Safety Executive (HSE) would be giving a higher profile to bug issues over the coming months and said "If the HSE is unhappy about a business's compliance to the bug, it will close the company down. Any firm using embedded chips in fire alarms, lifts and even lighting systems were potential targets for the HSE."

Despite Action 2000's threats, a Health and Safety spokesman said, "Closing firms down is not a very likely move. Certainly within the first and second quarter, we would be more likely to issue improvement notices whilst not ruling out the possibility of issuing prohibition notices later in the year."

Prime Minister, Tony Blair, commenting on Flower's 'State of the Nation' report said, "Time has very nearly run out for the firms that are behind. With less than ten months to go, they have two clear choices; use the time to beat the bug, or risk being beaten by it."

Action 2000's attempts to get the Y2K ball rolling appeared to be dogged by red tape and Gwyneth Flower admitted there was a limit to what Action 2000 could do to persuade companies to comply. She said "We have led the business horse to water but very few are taking an adequately long drink."

In April I told the media "In my opinion Gwyneth Flower's 'State of the Nation' address was merely a way of avoiding criticism should the Millennium prove to be a disaster. She had wasted so much of Action 2000's finances by initially appointing the less than knowledgeable American Data Dimensions information company without carrying out her own stated reliability checks, followed by issuing expensive, inappropriate and misleading mail shots and advertising to the general public telling the man in the street that he didn't need to worry about personal in-house appliances such as his television, fridge, iron, etc.

December: The Millennium was nigh. I forecast that there would be the odd blip but most major organisations, commerce, Government and the Military were ready. There were some people who thought 'planes might fall out of the sky but to the average person it was just the dawn of a new era.

Jaye had already booked our flights and accommodation to spend Christmas and New Year at the Don Pancho Hotel in Benidorm so that we could celebrate the Millennium in style. It was a Wow!

Year 2000 - by the end of January many people were asking if the fuss over the Millennium had been a damp squib.

On return from our holiday in Spain, accounts for the completion of our Y2K contract with Action 2000 were finalised and posted.

Imagine our amazement when we received a letter from Gwyneth Flower stating that she had not authorized my Company's involvement and that our invoice was not valid and she would not pay.

I just could not understand her weird and unethical attitude to business. Apart from having signed our original contract, Flower had appointed a member of her staff, a Mr Baker, to work in our office.

I was not going to suffer another Government con trick so I sued Gwyneth Flower and Action 2000; she paid up out of Court to avoid embarrassment but with poor grace.

The light fantastic:

We were looking forward to our retirement and as we so enjoyed our dancing, Jaye said she would like me to learn the correct Latin steps. Jaye was a trained gold medallist dancer but for years had had to adapt to my untutored intuitive dancing. We arranged lessons with an internationally known dancer and teacher, Albert Entwistle.

All went well until we concentrated on the Tango; after a few lessons Albert said, "Right Maurice, that's fine, let us now go through the whole dance to music." Off we went with what I thought was great style but half way through he stopped the music and said "Maurice, Maurice. You have seen too many George Raft films. A gentleman never dances the Tango with his hand on the lady's bottom." We laughed a lot and have very good memories of that time.

Millennium bug New Year hangover:

On New Year's Eve of December 2000/1st January 2001 the Millennium bug once again reared its ugly head. The problem was created because many IT programmers did not realise that year 2000 was a leap year. As a result, 2001 appeared to arrive a day early for many computers and they crashed in reaction to the anomaly.

In the USA, Convenience Chain Store 7-Eleven, was hit by this problem and many of the cash registers in its 19,600 stores, or affiliates around the world, lost the ability to process credit cards. They crashed out thinking it was 1901. Tills rejected credit cards because they looked as though they had been issued one hundred years into the future.

A spokeswoman for 7-Eleven said they had spent $M8.8 (£M6.2) on their bug prevention program which had left it largely free of problems until reaching the un-thought of Leap Year.

Chapter 21 – Millionaire to Pauper Overnight

Following our high exposure to the computer consultancy market during the Millennium campaign, MHA's SystemSearch (dubbed SearchandMatch by Barber's) was now recognized as the most advanced Search Engine on the international market and we were advised to prepare to launch the Company on the Stock Market.
I was told that a seventy five year old Managing Director in a developing IT Company would not be acceptable to investors as a good risk and that the Company needed a younger team to carry it forward.

I had to agree, so as a long standing Fellow of the Institute of Directors, I asked their advice on suitable candidates to take over as Chairman. We were offered two possibilities and as events unfolded it proved I chose badly.

The new Board consisted of John Knowles as Chairman, Nicola Jeffery Sykes as Sales Director, Richard Grenfell (our Research Manager of many years standing) as Research Director, Peter Hardcastle (our ex Bank Manager who took early retirement) as Company Secretary and Steven Hamlin as Systems and Development Director. I was to act solely in an advisory capacity.

After discussions with British entrepreneur, Bob Morton, who was Chairman of the Harrier Group plc. it was agreed that that I should resign from the Board but that Jaye and I would retain a 40% holding in the company and I was to receive an annual pension of £50,000. All rights to the software, hardware, etc. were to be taken over by the new company when launched. I accepted their terms.

Due to our unique position in the marketplace, there was talk of us becoming a multi million company within a very short period of time.

Appended are copies of Press editorials expounding the value and anticipated future of SystemSearch/SearchandMatch.

www.sourcewire.com/index.php
Monday, 02 October 2000 The independent resource for hi-tech and
business journalists
SEARCHANDMATCH.COM LAUNCHED!

The SearchandMatch product is the world's first software search
engine providing a definitive IT information and procurement portal.
The portal allows the instantaneous appraisal and matching of
customers' IT requirements against the SearchandMatch database
which covers over 100,000 software application products and 7,600
suppliers who market and support them. The database also holds
details on over 1,500 different software application areas within the
340 recognised Business/Industry sectors.

(*The original conception of SearchandMatch was pioneered by
Maurice Hamlin in 1978 when he was appalled at the tremendous
losses suffered by Government, Industry and Commercial company's
who bought totally inappropriate computer systems, often due to the
poor sales ethics of computer Company salesmen or the inability of
even the major computer departments and computer consultants to
evaluate a clients needs against the ever expanding plethora of
software available on the world market.*
*He stated that the only way to match industries application needs
against the market was to computerise computer consultancy; he was
laughed at, no one believed it possible, there was no such software
with the capability. He spent 4 years developing the very first 4GL
information retrieval software system and had 22 consultants
researching application products to build his computerised
information library.*
*Today's SearchandMatch is the ongoing derivative of his
Computerscan & SystemSearch Website (launched in 1980), which
he continued to develop and improve over the past 20 years.*
At 76 he retired selling all rights to the new consortium).

City e-Entrepreneur Invests a Million in SearchandMatch:

Wednesday, 22 November 2000
City entrepreneur Bob Morton has made a million pound cash investment in new search and procurement portal engine SearchandMatch launched just 6 weeks ago by MHA.

Total investment in the project is now £5 million and ensures further development of the portal and the software behind it, already being hailed as a revolution in search & select technology.

Bob Morton said: "The SearchandMatch tool will revolutionise information retrieved on the Internet as we know it, being highly flexible and relevant to all market sectors".

The SearchandMatch portal currently allows the instantaneous appraisal and matching of software needs on over 100,000 software application products and from 7,600 suppliers. The database also holds details on over 1,500 different software application areas within the 340 recognised business and industry sectors. Time spent on research and appraisal by users of SearchandMatch can be cut from 3 weeks to 5 minutes! Full searching and cross matching capabilities of any number of criteria is available, together with daily updates and other value added services.

Clients already include Centrica PLC, DHL, the European Patent Office, ICI, Lloyds TSB, Development Capital and Unicorn Systems. Strategic 'data feed' agreements are in negotiation with a number of leading information technology publishers. Plans for the portal are to expand the software database over the next 6 months into Europe and the US, holding data on 300,000 products from 45,000 suppliers.

The technology and software will also be applied to other business sectors where web site developers need 'content rich' data feeds to enhance their web presence. SearchandMatch also allows 'intelligent' web site advertising which can be dynamically targeted, offering new revenue streams for any web site."

-0-0-0-0-

However, within three months a cold relationship had developed between the new Board and me. I was refused entry to Board meetings and virtually excluded from all that was being planned. I only heard news of what was happening in the Company from my son, Steven (who had been retained as their Systems Development Director) and from the considerable media interest.

They first raised the new Company Secretary to Financial Director giving them control of the Board. They bought and encompassed a failing medical information company into the Group and then leased a large warehouse in Manchester which was converted into excellent offices and the new main computer centre.

In the autumn when the new offices were ready, the new self appointed Managing Director, Nicola Jeffery Sykes, advised me that they were ready to transfer the total computer installation from our property to the new premises.

I reminded her that I had still not received confirmation of my share issue for the new company or my £50,000 per year pension. She said that it was not possible at the present time so I replied "In that case, we go no further; you cannot expect me to let the heart of the system go without first confirming the agreed terms in writing."

She gave in and the appropriate document was signed.

The following editorials show how highly the IT industry considered the future prospects of SearchandMatch (SystemSearch) and also Morton's own statements.

PRESSWIRE – 14th November 2000
SearchandMatch gets another Million Pounds London, ENGLAND]
It is only 6 weeks old and it has already had investment of nearly US $6 million, but search and procurement portal engine SearchandMatch has just received another million pounds (US $1.42 million) from British entrepreneur Bob Morton.

Morton, who is chairman of Harrier Group plc, (and, for that matter, also of Baron Corporation plc, Vislink plc, Incepta Group plc, Planit Holdings plc, Systems Union Group plc, Clarity Group plc, BsoftB plc and InterClubNet plc) has great faith in the new product.

"The SearchandMatch tool will revolutionize information retrieved on the Internet as we know it, being highly flexible and relevant to all market sectors," said Morton.

Among early adopters of SearchandMatch are Centrica plc, DHL, the European Patent Office, ICI, Lloyds TSB Development Capital and Unicorn Systems.

Morton's investment decision is supported by recent findings of the Aberdeen Group, which predicts that 90 per cent of purchasing professionals will be conducting transactions over the Internet by 2002.

INDUSTRIAL FOCUS - February 2001
SearchandMatch and Mediapps provide IT intelligent source.
    SearchandMatch Limited announced a partnership with Mediapps, the SearchandMatch database is now integrated into Net.Portal a Web supersite that provides a variety of services including Web-Search, news, free e-mail, discussion groups, shopping and links to other sites. The major general-purpose Web portals are Yahoo! MSN and AOL. Many portals allow the home page to be personalized.

MEDIAPPS PRODUCT.
Net.Portal can now it is claimed, deliver to its users "Real-Time" Describes an application, which requires a program to respond to stimuli within typically milli or microseconds. Market knowledge of the latest technology solutions, cutting their research time by up to 95% and all major purchasing administration costs by up to 75% The SearchandMatch database contains over 100,000 software application products from over 7,600 suppliers.

COPYRIGHT 2001 A.P. Publications Ltd.
Potential customers include every company and organisation that has anything but the most simple software requirement.
    Customer time spent on research and appraisal will be cut by up to 95%, with huge cost savings.

HOSKINS GROUP plc -
One consultancy officer of Hoskins stated that the service reduced typical research times from 3 weeks to 5 minutes! The high human

and financial costs associated with research and appraisal during software purchasing decisions has all been eliminated, dramatically reducing the waste of valuable resources and project risks. The cost saving implications is enormous.

PROBLEM AND ANSWER -

At present, IT managers waste hundreds of hours every year searching magazines, trade shows and browsing the Net to find useful product information. By inputting requirements on-line through SearchandMatch, appraisal now becomes instantaneous. Full searching and cross matching capabilities of any number of criteria together with daily updating with other value added services.

Within 6 months of its re-launch the database will hold some 300,000 products from 45,000 suppliers with full coverage of the UK, EU, and US.

IDC reports worldwide e-commerce revenues are expected to grow from $111 billion in 1999 to $1.3 trillion in 2003. Supply chain transactions will reach $100 billion by the end of this year.

FORRESTER'S RESEARCH report entitled "Europe: The Sleeping Giant Awakes" shows that annual European on-line trade will reach 1.6 trillion Euros by 2004. Trials have indicated that e-procurement could slash purchasing costs by over 85%! (Source)

What followed was a disaster:

In May 2001 Jaye and I had been confidently planning a very comfortable retirement, even viewing an open touring car and planning to realise some of the dream holiday locations we had put aside whilst building up the business.

One day we were told that the Board had placed the Company into voluntary liquidation. We had had no prior warning.

In utter confusion we telephoned our solicitor who passed us on to the Official Liquidator who confirmed that nothing could be done about it. The action was legal and there was no redress.

I had received no notification from the new Board of any problem and my son advised me that he had been outvoted on all Board decisions before he resigned.

I was told that some of the previous Board Directors had obtained further funds from an investor to purchase the assets from the Liquidator.

It was just one blow after another. Jaye felt extremely ill and it later transpired that this theft had caused her to suffer a thrombosis of the brain.

I shall never forgive those ingrates who robbed us of everything we had worked for twenty-five years to achieve.

Jaye and I lost everything - our pension and our shares.

Why? How can it be legal? It was pure and simple theft!

PART 3

Journey into the Third Age

Chapter 22 – Disasters of Another Ilk

Jaye has such a strong character, she was able to fight back and recover but it was to be a hard battle for me over many years.

We found that when the company was taken over we had overlooked a personal guarantee we had made on behalf of MHA so we would have to repay £92,000 when we sold our house.

Jaye had been advised that living in a desert, or at least in a warmer, dryer climate would help her spinal problems so we agreed to immigrate to Spain and build a new life for ourselves.

We put an advertisement in the paper and the house sold immediately giving us only six weeks to vacate the premises. Whilst Jaye started packing, I took the dogs for a walk into Chorley to take my mind off our problems and saw an advertisement in the local Travel Agent's for a cheap seven-day break in a small town some thirty miles from Gandia. The holiday started in three days' time so I booked it thinking it would give us a chance to view property and arrange somewhere to rent after we left England.

Jaye thought I was joking when I told her about the holiday and although she had such a short time to pack, agreed it would be a good idea to look at Gandia and find a flat to rent.

She printed out two lists to use when looking for a new home -

1. Things we must have i.e. South facing, large kitchen, telephone line with ADSL, utility services and with easy access to medical services and essential food supplies without having to use a car.
2. Things we definitely did not want i.e. built on a hill, shaded by hills or buildings from the sun in winter, steep access to property, deep in the country, etc.

When we arrived in Gandia we were met by a helpful Spanish estate agent who, together with an interpreter, showed us fifteen small properties in one day, all deep in the countryside. We viewed only a few of them and although we wanted to live well away from the tourist track, nothing he showed us met our requirements.

Perhaps looking for a small property after our beautiful five bedroomed house with snooker room and huge garden was a bit of a let down.

Our Agent had done his best and we were running out of time so we told him we would not look at any more houses that day but instead would arrange to rent a flat. He said that, within our budget, he had just one more property on his books but he was sure it wouldn't be right for us as it was at the end of the road where his office was situated.

He drove round a large roundabout on which there were trees, shrubs and seats. To the left was a beautiful old convent with twin towers and to the right a South-facing block of flats in shady private gardens with many tall palm trees and a huge swimming pool. He pointed to a fourth floor flat at the end of the building. Seated in the back of the car, Jaye and I looked at each other, and I said, "We'll have it."

We arranged to view the property the following day and found it had everything we wanted and none of our dislikes. The block of fifty flats was four years old and had been built on land previously owned by the Convent. The flat had been bought for investment so was literally new. We had only one day of our holiday left so we gave an old established solicitor our Power of Attorney to buy the flat, opened a Spanish bank account and returned to England wondering if we had been rash.

When the day came to move out of our old house, we bade an emotional farewell to our friends and about twenty neighbouring children lined up along the drive to say goodbye to the dogs who were everyone's friends. The removal men said they had never seen anything like it.

We had paid a deposit on the flat and arranged for the bank to pay the remainder of the purchase price in due time to fulfil the terms of the Contract. We had arranged to spend a few weeks with each of our three children before leaving England – probably forever.

Four weeks later whilst we were staying with our youngest son and his wife, and just two days before the balance of the money was due to be paid for the flat, we had an urgent call from our Spanish Solicitor enquiring if we had already arranged to send the money to Spain as we were in danger of losing both the flat and our deposit.

We contacted our Bank who said they had no knowledge of either our money or our instructions. You can imagine our thoughts.

In my most positive manner I told the Bank I possessed a signed receipt for the money I had deposited after the sale of our house and that they must find it now or I would sue them not only for the loss of the money but for the deposit I had paid on the flat and also restitution for losing the property of my choice.

The following day we were asked to visit the Bank again and, with many apologies they told us the problem had been solved. Apparently whilst the clerk had been in the process of transmitting our funds to Spain, she had been interrupted, her screen had cleared and she had forgotten about the transaction.

The money was sent to Spain just in time and another headache was averted.

We spent our last weeks in England with our daughter and her husband in Eastbourne as it was an easy journey from there to the Channel Tunnel.

Passports had been arranged for the dogs: Tonto, a massive, beautiful, black standard poodle and Montie, a gentle Airedale. The day before we began our journey, the dogs had to have their final check at the Veterinary Clinic. Both passed their medicals with flying colours and the young Veterinary Surgeon said that Tonto, who was already eleven years old, would live for many years to come.

The next morning we woke up to whimpers of pain from Tonto and rushed him to the  Clinic where they tried for hours to save his life but he had twisted his gut whilst playing on the beach with the children the previous evening. It was hopeless. The lovely young Vet cried as she told us that even with major surgery, the dog would live in pain for the rest of his life. We all agreed it was kinder to put him to sleep.

We started the journey into our new life with tears in our hearts.

Chapter 23 – Our Angel Follows Us to Spain   (Angel 12)

As we drove over the Spanish boarder, I said to Jaye "Well Darling, this is the start of our new life". We had travelled only a few miles further when, round a curve in the motorway, we saw a pile of scrap metal scattered in front of us. With fast cars behind and to the left of us and lorries to the right, I had no possibility of swerving into another lane so I gripped the steering wheel more firmly and struck the metal squarely. There was an Almighty bang.

I slowed down as soon as possible but the engine sounded good and the instruments were normal. I thought I had got away with it but continued to reduce speed so I could move into the slow lane. I glanced into my mirror and to my horror, saw only a thick black cloud behind me.

It was a strange thing but the tyres, engine and bodywork of the car were untouched but the scrap metal had scythed off the underneath of the vehicle causing over two thousand pounds worth of damage, even so, I believe we began our life in Spain with good fortune. If the tyres had blown, the high speed and volume of traffic all around us could have caused a very nasty pile up.
This was the 12th visit of my Angel.

We were also fortunate with our insurance company because, as well as sending a pick up truck to tow us away to a nearby garage, they arranged to transport the damaged car three hundred and fifty miles to a main Ford dealer near our new home. They also supplied a taxi to take us to a nearby town where we transferred to a large rental car to get my wife and I, the dog and a heap of luggage to Gandia. Later, the Company wrote to say that we would not be charged for the transport or services and although no other vehicle had been involved in the accident, they were satisfied there was no fault on my part and consequently there would be no increase in the insurance premium or loss of 'no claims' bonus. Yes, I believe coming to Spain was a lucky break.

We arrived at our new home in Gandia on the 19th September 2001 and realised the flat was in an excellent situation; only five minutes walk from the centre of town yet the view from the ceiling to floor windows showed the beautiful convent, a Paseo (tree lined walkway with seats) which actually crossed the roundabout and an area of parkland. The whole surrounded by mountains but, most importantly, the flat came together with perfect neighbours.

During our first week in Gandia whilst we were waiting for our removal van to arrive, we stayed at the Borgia Hotel which was less than a kilometre away from the flat. We had a lot of work to do because although the flats were four years old, ours had not been lived in and we had bought it complete with the builder's rubbish. We also had to apply and wait for electricity and telephone to be connected.

On our second day in Gandia, whilst we were busy trying to clean the flat with cold water, we heard a knock on the door. There stood a smartly dressed young businessman who smiled and said, "I am Jesus. I understand you have no electricity. You must go to your galleria (laundry room)." I did as he said and he threw wires across the space from his window to ours, put temporary wires for lights throughout the main rooms, wired up the hot water boiler and then connected our flat to his own electricity supply. He then invited us to go into his home for a hot shower.

What a wonderful and unexpected reception!

Jesus was a communications expert and his wife, Chelo, a very attractive multi lingual career girl. They had a delightful and happy little girl who was almost four years old.

Jesus immediately arranged for an early connection of our telephones and ADSL and saw to the formalities of getting the electricity connected. We had undoubtedly landed on our feet.

Jesus, Chelo and Patricia became our Spanish family; always there but never intrusive. Truly delightful and caring people.

The reason we chose Gandia:

Over the years we had visited many beautiful places in Spain, ideal for a holiday, but not where we would choose to live the whole year round. A friend in Chorley had frequently told us that Gandia was "Just your sort of place" so one cold and rainy day during our Millennium holiday in Benidorm, we decided to take a coach trip there. It was raining when we arrived so we first called into a café to ask where the 'bus stop for Benidorm was located. The owner insisted on leaving the café and taking us to the ticket office because in those days you could not board a long distance 'bus without first obtaining a ticket. By this time the rain had eased off so we started looking around the City but by midday found we had run out of pesetas. One bank refused to change our English money as our passports were in Benidorm so we called into the offices of Gandia Travel who were very helpful and one of their Directors arranged for a different bank to change our money.

We were impressed with both the City and the friendliness of the people who appeared to be pleased to help a couple of aged foreigners who were rather lost so we decided we would like to stay there for another day. We asked the proprietors' of another café if they could recommend a hotel but no one understood what we said because their main language was Valenciano, however, a young lady said in English "I will take you." And she did; to an ancient hotel situated in the narrow streets of the old town. It was immaculately clean but furnished with dark wood and dark brown leather and was without heating. Later that evening when we returned from dinner, the proprietor had disappeared leaving all the room keys laid out in a neat row on the highly polished counter so we could help ourselves. We found the honesty amazing.

We learned that Gandia was the second city of the Comunidad de Valencia and the Administrative Capital of the La Safor Region and had first entered into history in 1094 when it was a Moslem farmstead.

The infrastructure and services of 20th century Gandia have been developed as the City evolved over the last thousand years. The surrounding mountains are covered in greenery and we were told that there is an enormous underground lake beneath the city so there is never a shortage of water. Gandia is unspoilt, yet a sophisticated working Spanish City of much style. It is well policed with a very low crime rate.

A mosaic marble paseo, the Avenida de las Germanias, has shady trees, fountains, flowers and ample seating on which to rest or just enjoy the passing scene. The avenue runs from one side of the City to the other and is almost a mile long.

Gandia has a luxurious and modern theatre, El Teatro Serrano, with ultra comfortable seating, state of the art electronics and a stage capable of accommodating any opera, ballet or concert. There is also a small cinema on the premises. The entire theatre was rebuilt on the site of an ancient playhouse taking care not to spoil the original facade. Some shows are expensive but most are very reasonably priced and many are free.

Along the Paseo can be found a magnificent building which was originally the home of Marquesos de González de Quirós and which is now the Casa de Cultura (the House of Culture) which hosts exhibitions of many forms of art and also concerts of classical music, jazz, pop, dancing, etc. which are frequently held in the garden during the summer months.

The Borgia Palace dating from the thirteenth century (once home of the Francesc de Borgia of the Borgia family) is also an interesting place and although it is open to visitors, it is still in use today as a Jesuit College. An Anglican Church service is held in the chapel each Sunday.

Gandia is a café culture with four wide pedestrian walkways, the best known of which is the Calle Major, which is renowned for its wealth of designer and modern shops. The City is completely flat and most pavements have been made wheelchair friendly and because most Gandians live in flats, the town is always alive. For instance, my wife's friends feel relaxed and safe when walking home after midnight.

The city has three very large underground car parks and an enormous square, the Plaza Prado, which hosts an amazing amount of events from ice-skating at Christmas to car and motorcycle shows.

Civic pride is much in evidence in the City's cleanliness and I take my hat off to the hard working street cleaning and parks maintenance staff. They deserve to be proud of their work.

Here there is no restriction on the amount of rubbish you can put out and it is collected in the early hours of every day of the year including Christmas day and Fiestas.

Four kilometres from the City is Gandia Grau, the port and yacht basin and the start of Gandia Playa (beach), which has twelve kilometres of golden sands. They are safe and cleaned every day. The beach is fronted by a very wide promenade with palm trees and delightful gardens. An underground car park runs almost the length of the promenade.

Gandia Playa is a favourite holiday playground for international visitors but especially those from Madrid and Valencia who own many of the apartments there.

Dating from the 1700s, the most important fiesta in the Valencian Region is the Fallas. It honours the memory of St. Joseph, Patron Saint of Carpenters and celebrates the first day of Spring. Each area of the City has a Fallas Society and in Gandia there are twenty-three, each of which is responsible for raising funds to build the huge and spectacular sculptings which are created out of paper mache, wood and plaster. It is an industry in itself. The Fallas are of ingenious design, sometimes beautiful, sometimes grotesque but always  full of fun and colour. They usually take the rise out of local political figures or poor services. For example, some years ago the Fire Brigade was late arriving at an incident and the following spring the Fallas in that area was a huge snail driven by the Fire Chief holding reins wrapped around the snail's horns.

The Fallas are burned on the 19th March and always with the Fire Brigade in attendance, frequently hosing down nearby buildings and trees. Some of the Fallas are taller than the trees and almost as tall as the surrounding multi story buildings. They are usually assembled at cross roads so that during the few days leading up the burning, the City is partially gridlocked.

There is a constant stream of parades, the participants wearing the beautiful Valencian national costumes and always accompanied by a band. It is an extremely noisy, happy and unforgettable event.

My wife became an avid student of the Spanish language whilst I started to design a web site to help people who wanted to immigrate to Spain. 2002 was the height of an ever-expanding community of con men involving Property Agents, Developers and Solicitors, many in the guise of friendly, helpful British. There was also much confusion over the payment of 'black money' as part of the property purchase price (illegal but universally accepted).

I decided it was time someone fought back so I developed and published www.practicalspain.com, which offered completely free, independent and unbiased advice in co-operation with the Alicante Consul General, Russell Thompson, a very forward thinking diplomat. The site had over one million hits in its first year.

My first real success was to force a crooked English Property Agent and his Spanish partner, a Solicitor in Oliva, to repay £70,000 to a lady they had duped into buying a condemned wreck. Their victim came over to Spain for a week's holiday to obtain a run down property and although she was aware the building was in a poor state she thought it could be made into her own 'place in the sun' by the time she retired.

The Estate Agent had assured her everything was legal and that she would receive her Escritura (papers of ownership) within a month. She contacted me nearly a year after she had paid for the property and made exhaustive attempts to obtain a response from the Agent and the Solicitor.

When I tried to talk to them, they were less than helpful so I asked for assistance from a dear friend, Adela, a multi lingual ex-Spanish Head Mistress who accompanied me to the Planning Office where, with the gentle persuasion of an Official (an ex-pupil), we were able to study the town's plans and found that not only had the English lady been sold a derelict property but it had been built in an unlawful place and was subject to a demolition order.

I wrote to both the Agent and the Solicitor stating that if the money was not returned within seven days, the tale of their duplicity would be broadcast on my web site for all to see.

This particular lady was fortunate and received £67,000 immediately. I didn't receive a thank you letter - perhaps it was lost in the post.

Many other unwary expats were not so lucky.

Prime Minister Blair's NHS disaster story:

On the 10th February 2002, I read of a massive change in the development and control of the UK's National Health Services - a £2.3 Billion reform.

Sir John Pattison, Headquarters Director of IT Research for the Department of Health, confirmed that he and his colleagues were given just ten minutes to make the case to the Prime Minister over what became the world's biggest civil IT-based modernisation programme.

On the 12th June the Health Minister, Lord Hunt, announced the redesign of the NHS IT control of its 1.3 million employees and the Nation's more than fifty million potential patients. The project was entirely supported by the Prime Minister Tony Blair, Chancellor Gordon Brown and Alan Milburn the Health Secretary.

It appears that this massive project was launched almost entirely without consultation or expert analysis by NHS grass roots IT specialists but was inspired by supplier briefings, the support of some NHS Chief Executives and Officials but particularly by Tony Bair who wished to impress the Nation prior to the forthcoming General Elections by launching a spectacular NHS IT programme.

After this announcement there was an outpouring of warnings from the NHS Consultants and the British Medical Association GP IT Committee's Spokesman, Paul Cundy, who said in the summer of 2002 that he could see little evidence of NHS staff expertise being used to design the National system. There was also a warning in Robin Guenier's article printed in Computer Weekly.

This programme appeared to be yet another ill conceived Government IT initiative launched without a proper evaluation or understanding of the enormity of the task. The massive expenditure was not sanctioned by Parliament.

Apparently enquirers to the Cabinet Office were told -

"There is no requirement for Parliament to ratify investment decisions, however large they are, because whatever we do, we do with the best of intentions. On this basis you must trust us. If we want to spend Billions on an IT project that, it turns out, we haven't thought through properly, we can. The Freedom of

Information Act cannot be used to discover how we make our IT-related decisions. We cannot be compelled to tell Parliament, or anyone else, how things are really going on any large Government IT project. The Public Accounts Committee and MPs have no right to query any item of expenditure."

Even when the Information Commissioner ruled that the Cabinet Office should publish most of the information requested by Computer Weekly on the NHS NPfIT system. The Cabinet Office still refused.

So much for Open Government!

My objection to the Health Service project is based simply on my experience with hospital departmental management staff such as those in the Isle of White Health Authority.

The new project was based on developing a massive central computer system with the ability to control and evaluate all specialisations, all hospitals, all patients and all doctors and services. Total integration was the eventual goal.

What they once again failed to consider was that any central system would only be as good as the information collected and transferred to them by the multitude of hospitals and centres which dealt with the patients. There are more than 350 NHS hospitals in England alone, none of which appear to have a common policy.

From my experience there were no Government directives to hospitals about the collection of information for Master Patient Records. Unless hospitals kept integrated records of patients' visits and treatments by various departments, related to Doctors and Specialists, and had the ability to communicate with each other and also with the central system in a fully pre planned and agreed method, the result could only end in utter confusion. Without information gathering starting in this way, the system was doomed to fail.

Blair followed the same path as all previous Technology Ministers and the DTI which was to take any path offering immediate political advantage.

Gandia, a caring City:

One day we left our car in the centre of Gandia and paid for an hour's parking. When we returned, well within time, we found the car had disappeared. We thought it had been stolen until we noticed a yellow Police sticker with a telephone number on it stuck on the kerbstone. When Jaye rang them she was told that cladding had been falling from a nearby building and the car had been towed away to safety.
They said it had been parked outside the vehicle pound where it could be collected and there would be no charge. What an incredible service!

-0-0-0-0-

Later that year our beloved Airedale Montie died. He had been a dear and faithful companion and was the first dog our neighbours' daughter had really known. Montie was Patricia's special friend and she was so upset when he died that Jaye wrote a superb little book for her which described how happy the dog's life had been. It helped her to come to terms with the loss of her first doggy friend.
    One of our friends, the ex senior psychologist of Greater Manchester, was so impressed with the book she said a copy of it would be a tremendous help to children suffering from trauma.
It will be Jaye's next project.

-0-0-0-0-

In April 2003 British Airways and Air France announced that Concorde would be retired due to falling passenger revenue and rising maintenance costs. This was a tremendous blow to the reputation of British manufacturing and not deserved. The crash at Charles de Gaulle Airport had been caused by runway debris, not aircraft failure. Concorde made its final commercial flight on the 23rd October and now stands on display at Filton; a fitting tribute to British/French co-operation and ingenuity.

Toledo and a tornado:

In June 2004 our friends, Jesus and Chelo together with Patricia, took us to Toledo for a long weekend. It was a magical place and a must for anyone who wants to see the old Spain. Originally it was the Capital of the country, a fortress built on a hill that had withstood many invaders.

The Cathedral is outstanding and the whole town is full of ancient multi cultural architecture and treasures including most of El Greco's masterpieces.

On the way home we called at Cuenca and had lunch in a restaurant, which overhung the ravine. Awesome!

A happy band, we were driving back to Gandia in perfect weather on a quiet Sunday afternoon when Chelo remarked, "Look at the sky. If I didn't know better, I would think that was a tornado." It was a light brown cloud with a tail and appeared to be many miles away but at that moment, it struck the ground to our right, and threw the car to the far side of the motorway. Jesus is a superb driver and kept control of the car whilst we were buffeted about by a fierce wind, and then pelted with hailstones the size of golf balls. The windscreen smashed and suddenly, it was over. The entire car had been pitted with hundreds of dents.

Chelo and Jaye were sitting in the back of the car with five-year-old Patricia between them and this amazing young girl just sat there, without a murmur, and watched the spectacle unfold even through the howling wind and the hailstones.

Two motorcyclists in front of us took shelter under an overpass and as soon as we could we followed them. They were exceedingly lucky to have been wearing helmets and heavy clothing, otherwise I do not think they would have survived.

What an experience! When the danger had passed, we knocked out the windscreen and continued a draughty but very lucky journey home.

The Spanish insurance company repaired all the damage to the car as they do not hide behind an Act of God clause.

Travelling in an emergency:

One evening in August we had arranged to go to a dinner dance with our good friends Gillian and David to celebrate Gillian's birthday. It was dark when we arrived at the restaurant and whilst I parked the car, the girls walked along a narrow unlit path which lead to the restaurant. Suddenly Jaye tripped; the builders had left one side of the path unfinished and she had broken her ankle. We could not get an ambulance and she was unable to get into the car so four big Rugby players lifted her gently into the boot of the estate.

I put the headlights on full beam, switched on the emergency indicators and hung a white pinafore out of the offside window before I started to drive the twelve kilometres to the nearest hospital.

We were stopped at the first roundabout by Police in a car who told us to keep going and said they would advise the Emergency Department that we were on our way. During the careful drive to the hospital, vehicles took notice, slowing down and giving way at roundabouts to help our cautious progress.

Note: The use of the white cloth, headlights and flashers is not legal but it is recognised by the Police and most other vehicles as the sign of an emergency.

Jaye was transferred to Gandia Hospital for the operation. She had a very bad luxation fracture and had also broken the ligaments. The Doctor told me there was a distinct possibility she would lose her foot. It was a very worrying time but on the way to the operating theatre all she said in Spanish in her semi drugged state was "I must rumba for Christmas." She spent six weeks in hospital but she did rumba again at the end of the year.

Chapter 24 - 80th Birthday

Many of our family came over to Spain for the weekend of the 4th February 2005 and together with ninety-eight of our English and Spanish friends and neighbours we celebrated my eightieth birthday with a luncheon and dance at the Moli Canya Restaurant.

Later that year Jaye was in the wars again. She was inclined to lose consciousness when looking up or walking quickly. The hospital found that she was suffering from spondylitis and that her neck bones were occasionally trapping the blood supply to her brain. It had probably been caused by an old car accident and she had to remember not to tilt her head backwards when looking up. We continued to dance, but not the tango.

The NHS Disaster saga continues:

The 2002 NHS IT Health programme named NpfIT and which was to have been completed by 2005 mushroomed in cost from £2 Billion to £20 Billion and its completion date was extended to 2014/15. There was no acceptable audit of the cost.

The Prime Minister should have been asked -
a) Why were MPs not allowed to ask question about the NHS system, its costings or its future viability?
b) Why the Commons Audit office was querying the cost?
c) Why the House of Commons Public Accounts Committee Chairman, Edward Leigh, claimed that it seemed to be turning into a massive white elephant?
   http://en.wikipedia.org/wiki/British_House_of_Commons
d) Why the main supplier for the system "iSOFT" was under investigation by the Financial Services Authority for irregular accounting?
e) From feasibility surveys carried out on doctors' practices, why did over 60% say they would not allow their patients' records to be transferred to the system?
f) And particularly why, when 'Accenture' (a major software provider for the system) withdrew in September 2006 did the Director General of the project, Richard Granger, charge the company only £63 millions when, under their 'Broken Contract' conditions, he was authorised to retrieve £1Billion. This saved Accenture (the Company by which Richard Granger was previously employed) £930 millions and left that amount to be recovered from UK taxpayers.

How long is this drain on the country's financial stability going to be allowed to continue?

The questionable use of National Security 'D' Notices:

On the 20th March we turned on the TV for the morning news and heard that British, American, and Coalition troops had invaded Iraq.

President Bush and our PM, Tony Blair, stated war was essential because Iraq's leader, Saddam Hussein, had weapons of mass destruction and missiles that he threatened could be released on the UK within 45 minutes.

This was despite the fact that Dr David Kelly, a top employee of the MOD, an expert in biological warfare and a former United Nations weapons inspector, did not believe it to be so.

Within days there were anti war demonstrations in many parts of the globe which were particularly relevant as the war was not sanctioned by the UN Security Council or in accordance with the UN's founding charter.

© Channel Five

On the 5 June, Kelly was sent back to Iraq, and again it was reported that he disagreed with statements put out by the Government who said the photographs of two mobile weapons laboratories (quoted as being for biological weapons production) were not mobile germ warfare laboratories and that they could not be used for making biological weapons. They were exactly what the Iraqis said they were - facilities for the production of hydrogen gas to fill balloons.

There followed a political storm. Kelly was called before a Parliamentary Committee where he confirmed that no trace of weapons of mass destructions had been found.

To my limited understanding, it appears he was used as a scapegoat.

On July the 18th the morning news declared Dr David Kelly has been found dead on moorland and that suicide was suspected. The following days brought many reports - some said he had been murdered to stop the truth being revealed whilst others explained that he had taken a mass of sleeping pills and had also cut both of his wrists with a blunt bladed pocket knife. Some reports also stated that the knife was clean of finger prints and without any trace of blood.

With no water available, how was that possible?

Regardless of the many variances over the reported cause of death, many people including medical experts, still believe he was murdered.

I must ask why Blair refused to allow a full coroner's enquiry and then issued a seventy year 'D' Notice disallowing all future forensic, medical or criminal investigation.

In other words, regardless of the truth, actual facts of the matter cannot be released until 2083 which means anyone guilty of wrong doing, or any adult who could even vaguely remember the facts of the case, will be almost 90 years old when the 'D' notice is lifted. Surely they are relying on longevity to wipe out any retribution against the guilty or their descendants.

One of the clauses in the Rights of Issuing a 'D' Notice states that - personal benefit, political and official embarrassment are not reasons for excluding material from public disclosure.

This reminds me of the 'D' notices issued on the two air crashes covered in the first part of this book.

It seems to me that the authority for issuing of 'D' Notices can be corrupted for reasons other than a need for national security.

Highway to Tango:

By 2006 we realised that life was not complete without a doggy companion so with our good friends Janet and Keith sharing the driving, we drove to a village North West of Madrid and approximately four hundred and fifty kilometres from Gandia, to one of the only two standard poodle breeding kennels in Spain. We stayed overnight in the village, which was in the throes of a fiesta, and a superb Latin band provided the dance music.

When the music is really good, it doesn't matter where you dance

- the best sprung wooden floor, the pavement or the road.

The hotel restaurant told us the speciality for the fiesta was lamb so we all ordered it but about an hour later when the food arrived, a small whole lamb was placed in the middle of the table.

The following morning they apologised to us because they could only serve steak for breakfast, as it was fiesta. We then collected our beautiful cream Caniche Gigante and named him Tango.

Remembering a very special person:

When our good friend, the Very Reverend Bruce Addison, retired to Spain he started the Anglican Church here in Gandia. He was one of the most devout, yet open-minded churchmen I have met and although he knew I did not believe in the Church of England's version of Jesus, he respected my views.

Bruce was an Oxford graduate who became an internationally renowned ballroom dancer and then an actor before he was called to the Church. He was ordained in Cambridge and from that time he was regularly head hunted so that during a long career working in Australia, Africa, Cologne Cathedral, the Embassy in New York, etc. and he didn't have to apply for a living.

When he was seventy years old, the Bishop of Uruguay asked him to take on the difficult job of Dean of the Cathedral in Montevideo. He was there only nine months but during that time he unified the congregation and tripled the attendance. He also made a point, as he had in Gandia, of visiting the sick and infirm who were unable to attend services.

He returned to Gandia for a short time to decide whether or not he would move to Montevideo on a permanent basis. He was under constant pressure from the Bishop because his work had been so successful and the congregation loved him.

The Bishop assured him that if he returned, he would have a flat close to the Cathedral and also a car at his disposal so he would no longer have to take long bus rides when he visited his flock.

One day Bruce left a message on our answerphone saying he was going to the hospital for a check up and that he would see us soon, however, two days later we found our friend had cancer of the spine and on our first visit to the hospital he only just recognised my wife and squeezed her hand. After that nothing. He was in such agony he was unable to recognise anyone and there was no possible hope of recovery yet all we could do was watch whilst he writhed in unspeakable agony for a further eight days.

Bruce was the personification of a good man so how could anyone believe this was God's chosen path for him. It should have been legal to help him find a quiet and dignified release.

Chapter 25 – The First Glider Pilot Flew in 1793

On 26th March 2007 Jaye and I, in company with thirty-four members and wives of the Costa Blanca Air Crew Association, took a five-day visit to Madrid.

It is a beautiful city with many fine buildings. We particularly enjoyed the Prado Museum, the Royal Palace, the Almuden Cathedral, Hippocrates institute and the massive Park del Retiro.

The highlight of our visit was the day we spent as guests of the Spanish Air Force at the Museo de Aeronautica y Astronautica at the invitation of Colonel Marco Angel Negron followed by lunch at the Club Barberam, adjacent to the Museum, where our host was Capitan Gutierrez.

Beer and wine were served before the meal and I remarked that I hadn't had beer for a very long time. When I was asked how long it had been, I replied "1943".

It was an extremely interesting and joyful visit.

Controversial historic note:

Many records state that Sir George Cayley invented and flew the first successful glider in 1804. This was an over statement because it was his footman who flew the glider, however, there is evidence that he was superseded eleven years earlier on the 11th May 1793 by a Spaniard.

El 11 de Mayo de 1793 en la localidad burgalesa de Coruña del Conde Diego Marín Aguilera, consiguió volar por primera vez conocida en la Historia de la Humanidad.

In Spain, Diego Marin Aguilera is called 'The Father of Flying' and the Spanish Air Force have dedicated a monument to him which can be found next to the castle from which he took flight. Diego was the eldest son of a large family of farmers and ranchers and lived from 1757 to 1799.

He was endowed with a great natural intelligence and devised many labour saving devices including a gadget to improve the functionality of a watermill on the river Arandilla, one which improved a Fulling mill (water mill for working cloth) and yet another to improve the cutting of marble in the quarries of Espejon.

Whilst he studied the mechanics of windmills, Diego Marin

278

conceived the idea of being able to fly like a bird and spent many hours in the fields studying the flight of eagles darting above the battlements of the castle tower. He trapped eagles and vultures and carefully studied the movement of their wings and tails, also body

weight relating to their length. This research nurtured the idea of building a 'heavier than air' machine to transport a man. He saved the birds' feathers, which he used later when he built his machine.

With the help of the village blacksmith, he built a frame, which included iron joints in the wings to allow them a range of movement and a pad to support his feet; the experiments and building of the large bird like machine took six years of intense work.

On the night of the 15th May 1793, accompanied by his confidant, blacksmith Joaquin Barber and his sister, they put the big befeathered glider on top of the castle rock. His flight began from there and he said "I will go to Burgo de Osma and

then to Soria." The machine flew from the starting point in the direction of Burgo de Osma in an attempt to fly across the river, however, after flying about three hundred and sixty metres he was forced to land due to a break in one of the bolts that moved the wings. He was not hurt so his landing was obviously controlled.

The following morning when his neighbours in Corunna found

out what he had accomplished, they mocked Diego and his machine, believed he was mad and burned the glider and its feathered hide. Six years later, this ingenious inventor died in his home town at the age of forty- two.

He was mistakenly thought to be crazy but in reality he was a man who should have been renowned as an open minded inventor and who had been born much before his time.

Due to the modern economic climate, the castle itself was on sale for one Euro in 2002 on the condition the purchaser would restore the crumbling building.

-0-0-0-0-

The first aeroplane to stay still and stable whilst in the air was called an Autogyro and was invented by Spanish pilot and aeronautical engineer, Juan de la Cierva y Codorniu, First Count de La Cierva.

Its first successful flight was recorded in 1923 and it is thought to be the forerunner of today's helicopter and Harrier jump jet. The Count moved to England in 1925 where, with the support of Scottish industrialist James G.Weir, they established the Cierva Autogiro Company. If you are interested in Spanish aero history, visit www.aviationmuseum.eu/madrid

Chapter 26 - The Adventure Goes On

One Saturday morning we left our car in the supermarket car park whilst we shopped but when we returned we found that another vehicle had damaged the off side of the car and partly torn off the rear bumper. No one came forward to accept responsibility but when we arrived home and parked in the underground garage, I noticed a tatty piece of cardboard tucked underneath one of the windscreen wipers.

A Spanish lady who had witnessed the accident had written a note giving the make, colour and registration number of the offending vehicle, also her name and telephone number. When Jaye rang to thank her, she said she hated vandalism and was willing to be a witness if necessary. What a lovely lady.

I called the insurers who provided us with a temporary car and traced the other vehicle. There was no charge and no increase in our renewal premium.

The death of a legend

Feb 1st 2010 - A sad day for all who were privileged to call John and Des Partridge friends. Wing Commander John Partridge DSO, DFC & Bar, also given the distinction to wear the official Pathfinders Badge, died at age 95. He will always be remembered for his tremendous spirit - even in his 90s, he and Des were always the life and soul of the party. Like Jaye and I, always first up to dance.

A truly British gentleman, a hero in both war and peace. Read his obituary, it is both dramatic and inspirational to anyone regardless of age. Connect to –

http://acacb.blogspot.com.es/2007/04/wg-cdr-john-desi-partridge-

-0-0-0-0-

We joined a Spanish class to learn to dance the Sevilliana and although Jaye didn't find it hard to learn, she kept falling over. Some of the other pupils looked at her in surprise but she just grinned and told them "Bebo demasiado vino." (I drink too much wine).

In March 2010 Jaye's mobility decreased rapidly, although the doctor assured her it was arthritis.

I arranged for her to have a private scan and was told that her spine had thirteen herniated (broken) discs and the condition will only progress. The stenosis is inoperable.

When Jaye received her Spanish Disability Certificate, we bought an electric four-wheeled scooter with the help of the Air Crew Association and it changed her life by allowing her to regain much of her independence.

The next visit to the Orthopaedic Specialist proved that Jaye was also in urgent need of a hip replacement. As we had already arranged to go to England for the summer and Susan had told us how good the Horder Centre was for hip replacements, we asked her if she would go ahead and make arrangements for Jaye's operation.

At 8.30 a.m. on the 30th June 2011, Jaye and I waved goodbye to Jesus, Chelo and some of our neighbours who had gone down into the garage to wish us well on our journey. Someone said, "You know, Spanish people of eighty six do not drive across Europe." Their concern was very touching and every night during our journey our special Spanish family would telephone us to make sure we were safe.

Our first problem occurred about twenty kilometres from home when our TOM TOM (sat/nav) tried to misdirect us and then stopped working altogether so Jaye took on the job of navigating the old way by using maps. We had four overnight stops and a wonderful journey through outstandingly beautiful countryside.

The dog took to travelling and hotel life but was in his element when he first found real grass, woods and meadows - in Spain, orange groves, mountains and city streets are his world. We avoided using motorways and paid only seventeen Euros in tolls.

We travelled through Spain to France via the Somport tunnel which is eight kilometres long and runs underneath the Pyrenees. As we exited the tunnel the scenery was breath taking. We felt on top of the world and then I noticed the fuel gauge light blinking. It was thirty kilometres to the next garage but all of it was downhill. I kept flipping the car out of gear to get as much freewheeling as possible and just as I was beginning to feel really worried, we arrived at a small filling station.

During our journey we had only one adventure. I had my wallet stolen whilst I was refuelling at an unattended petrol station in Poitiers so we called into the Police Station. We were getting nowhere with an off-hand young policeman when a bi-lingual officer arrived at the Station, took us to her office and spent considerable time with us making sure my cards were cancelled and she 'phoned Spain to assure Jesus that we were all right.

It was a Sunday morning and we learned that this attractive officer was a serious crime Detective Inspector who had two children. She was a credit to the Police Force and certainly promoted Anglo French relations.

We arrived in Eastbourne to a wonderful welcome from Sue and Mick and found my daughter had arranged for Jaye to have a hip replacement at the Horder Centre about twenty miles away.

The operation was totally successful and although the doctors and staff were extremely kind, they were professional in every respect and took considerable trouble over her spinal problems.

We stayed with Sue and Mick for eight weeks. Sue took great care of Jaye and Mick took us on delightful tours of the countryside – to ancient Alfriston, to Battle village which is the site of the Battle of Hastings in 1066 and to the magnificent Eastbourne Air Show, to name but a few. The whole episode was littered with laughter, a bottle or two of wine and many a good game of cards.

We also spent some time with our sons and Tango learned to retrieve golf balls. As we live in the orange growing region of Spain, the dog had been brought up to chase and eat oranges but in England he found apples were just as good.

After a memorable visit, we drove home without mishap by a different and slightly longer route.

European Union

On the 10th November 2011 it was confirmed that for the past seventeen years the European Union's accounts had failed to be passed as acceptable by the auditors:

It is no secret that I have little faith in the integrity of many public servants and this opinion is not confined to the UK. I am sure that unless there is a major change in EU Government Policy it will continue to be the same for years to come.

I have fought corruption by politicians and civil servants and their underhand dealings with big business for thirty years. To place our country before personal gain has always been promised by people elected to power but as revealed by the UK MPs' expenses scandal, many fall by the wayside. It is no wonder that all failed or rejected UK politicians seek election to the European Union.

2013 November – from MailOnline By Emma Thomas and Tim Shipman:

"Auditors again refused to sign off the EU accounts for the 19th year in succession. They revealed that the spending errors are up 23 per cent on year 2012".

Now, in May 2014, just as my book goes off to the Publishers for printing, we see the following headline – "European Union spent nearly £6illion in 'error' last year".

Elections for our MEPs are about to take place again and everyone should be asking how is it possible for the EU to continue ignoring the fact that their books don't add up. To lose almost £6Billions must mean massive corruption. Why can no one get an honest answer?

I would also suggest that they look into MEPs extravagant pay and allowances. Media research tells us that MEPs now have incomes up to 20 times higher than the people they represent. Whilst everyone else is asked to economize, most MEPs have enjoyed large increases in their salaries – even so far as including free hair cuts, etc.

-0-0-0-0-

In 2012 Simon Burns, The Coalition Health Minister in charge of the NHS, stated he was cancelling Blair's trail blazing NHS Master Patient Records IT programme which to date has wasted almost £12 Billion. He said it was years of scandalous waste of taxpayers' money on a system that never worked. However, I would like to ask what advice is to be given to hospitals to make sure they have a sensible on going purchasing policy and that all hospital record systems are gathering uniform patient information with a view to providing national medical statistics?

Hospitals need guidance as I advocated to the Isle of White Health Authority in 1983. They took no notice – why will it be different today?

-0-0-0-0-

On a brighter note, we are shown that the UK is recovering faster than most of Europe, having reduced its monetary deficit by one third. This is amazing considering the battering the weather gave to our shores and countryside. I trust that the assistance the Government promised for those most affected has been put in place.

-0-0-0-0-

Looking back over the last Millennium one has to be somewhat sad. Whilst so much has been achieved in the quality of life and healthcare, so little has gone forward in humanity and trust between nations and beliefs. In fact the attitude between Jews, Muslims and Christians has worsened, as for example in Israel and Gaza. Yet they all began from a belief in Abraham. Now they have ISIS who seem to believe in only their version of Sharia Law.

We hear that hundreds of Western youths are joining their forces but how can anyone brought up in a normal civilised family society be brainwashed into believing their edicts.

How can these young people believe that a woman (their mothers or sisters) has no rights to be educated or take up a job or profession? Or that if their fathers, brothers or uncles, etc. don't convert, they should be killed.

Anyone who does not believe that all governments (of whatever religious belief) should support those who are attacked have themselves to blame if this terrorism reaches their own doorstep.

-0-0-0-0-

2014 has been a strange year in Gandia with hardly a drop of rain between February and October.

I realise that some people grumble about us receiving the Winter Fuel Allowance but with temperatures between 30 and 40 degrees and incredible high humidity, we need air conditioning. Even so, we consider ourselves very fortunate to live in this place.

Jazie has been told she must have an urgent operation to put a titanium plate in her neck. She still smiles and jokes about how high her scrap value will be with titanium in her ankle, hip and soon to be in her neck.

There will be no way to avoid ringing the security bell at airports. I wonder if she will be allowed through to attend the happy occasion of our son's wedding in October?

We may be somewhat battered, but we are as close and as happy together as the day we met during my unexpected flying visit to RAF Scampton in1961.

Who could ask for more?

Epilogue – My beliefs.

Looking back, I believe those of my generation who survived the War were lucky to be born in the early part of the 20th Century. Life was simpler but there were many avenues of discovery for those with an adventurous spirit. Times were hard. Many people were poor but even so, it was considered a pleasure to dress smartly and act the gentleman; girls took pleasure in being feminine and dressing to the best their budgets allowed, regardless of social background. Romance and sex were something special.

When I was born the world population was estimated at two billion but in just 90 years it has exploded to over seven billion.

In today's open society, modern technology has taken away almost every sense of privacy, personal and diplomatic whereas past generations of government could discuss problems and hopefully reach a compromise. Today everyone is informed instantly of world events. They take sides immediately, often violently, before discussing the 'whys and wherefores'.

Greed is so often prominent in our thoughts and far too many strive for immediate gain giving little thought to the problem future governments will have paying worthwhile pensions to the ever growing millions of dependants.

My conscience is my faith. If there is a God then I think conscience is the greatest gift he gave us. It is the one thing all people have, regardless of colour or creed. We all have a natural inbred knowledge of what is right or wrong, good or evil. It is we who choose our path and the extremists who twist the minds of the young. If people in general were able to live and abide by what their conscience tells them is right, I believe it would be a better world.

World strife is caused largely by religious fanatics within all faiths; my view of religion is somewhat sceptical as I believe Jesus was a prophet as was Mohammed. Both created forces for great goodness yet many factions decry each other and commit atrocities.

All religious records were written by man and we only have vaguely remembered ancient stories of early history. Personally I think Abraham is closest to my beliefs; he is the basis of the Christian,

Jewish and Islamic religions but since that time much has been distorted by the tellers or writers of fabled stories, or for personal ambition.

Many of the written edicts are ridiculous e.g. 'Love thy neighbour as thyself.'

It is quoted by so many but it is an impossible belief to follow. How can you forgive the unforgiveable? It is like saying the Holocaust was a mistake or that those who commit heinous crimes do not know what they are doing.

I have family members who originate from various countries and religions. We all speak English but my son speaks Greek, my daughter French and Arabic whilst my great grandson speak fluent French, Arabic and Russian. My eldest grandson is a committed Moslem and we are a very happy and integrated family with no internicene strife.

Historians and archaeologists are constantly finding new wonders of ancient people whilst science, through the exploration of space, is discovering more and more of the millennia before Christ.

What are we to believe?

Lightning Source UK Ltd.
Milton Keynes UK
UKHW010642150619
344463UK00001B/38/P